Praise for *Volunteers*

"Riveting and morally complex, *Volunteers* is not only an insider's account of war, but it takes you inside the increasingly closed culture that creates our warriors. In the case of Jerad Alexander, that culture has also created a writer of remarkable talent."

—Elliot Ackerman, author of the National Book Award finalist *Dark at the Crossing*

"A beautiful and powerfully affecting portrait of a boyhood in a military family, in which contrasting and ever more complex views of America, war, and what it means to be a soldier lead to the decision to join the military and serve in Iraq. In that way, it's also a portrait of the stories we tell ourselves, and how those stories fare when our children grow up and try to live them."

—Phil Klay, author of *Missionaries* and
the National Book Award–winning *Redeployment*

"Alexander offers a well-attuned perspective of the military world and how its expansive influence not only motivates, but also arouses a justification for war itself . . . Alexander's insights into the myth-building ethos of the military . . . are well articulated, and he ably explores ideals of masculinity, heroism, and camaraderie within the military establishment . . . Alexander vividly captures the foreboding atmosphere of a country under siege and recounts the disturbing incidents he witnessed during his seven-month deployment . . . An absorbing memoir reflecting the realities of serving in the modern-day military."
—*Kirkus Reviews*

"Immersive . . . Alexander incisively captures his growing disillusionment with the military . . . Earnest."
—*Publishers Weekly*

"With this work, Alexander has staked his claim as one of the most necessary voices while contributing to a necessary and overdue examination of our military culture and what it means to be an American. An absolute triumph."
—Jared Yates Sexton, author of *American Rule:*
How a Nation Conquered the World but Failed Its People

"[*Volunteers*] will receive high praise for its literary quality, and deservedly so. [Alexander] writes with ease about the adrenaline-filled battle scenes one expects of a military memoir . . . Capture[s] the inexplicable mystique that war carries in our imagination and the dangers that mystique presents to those sucked into its orbit. Aspiring future Marines will no doubt stay up late reading *Volunteers*."
—*The American Conservative*

"Alexander's expertly crafted prose keeps the reader immersed and invested . . . A complete portrait of a life lived under the looming shadow of the American military empire and one of its eager participants. This intellectually and emotionally honest book will be a linchpin in understanding veterans of the Global War on Terror and the society for which they volunteered." —*The Wrath-Bearing Tree*

"What sets apart *Volunteers* from other literary treatments of modern conflict is that it understands war is not a destination but a state of being. 'The war is everywhere,' Jerad Alexander writes in this beautiful, dark chronicle of an American life and lineage shaped by empire, and this testament to moral and physical courage deserves all the accolades about to come its way and more. *Volunteers* is exceptional." —Matt Gallagher, author of *Youngblood* and *Empire City*

"*Volunteers* is a compelling twofer. In it, Jerad Alexander recounts his coming of age in an environment that glamorized war and his own subsequent encounter with the singularly unglamorous reality of combat. Vivid, intimate, and moving, *Volunteers* belongs on the very top shelf of 'forever war' memoirs." —Andrew Bacevich, author of *After the Apocalypse: America's Role in a World Transformed*

"The author writes particularly evocatively of the fantasies of heroism and patriotism that exist in American culture and the mainstream reverence for the military. An absorbing if dreamlike apologia for the way Alexander grew up, and a firsthand look at a closed culture that some Americans never get to see. Especially recommended for libraries with a significant military clientele." —*Library Journal*

"A reckoning of American identity, masculinity, and exceptionalism that dissects the U.S. military ethos, while capturing the popular culture that shaped a generation of service members. An eloquent and compelling memoir, written in the language of candor, humor, and grim realism." —Dewaine Farria, author of *Revolutions of All Colors*

VOLUNTEERS

GROWING UP IN THE FOREVER WAR

Jerad W. Alexander

Algonquin Books of Chapel Hill 2022

Published by
Algonquin Books of Chapel Hill
an imprint of Workman Publishing Co., Inc.
a subsidiary of
Hachette Book Group, Inc.
1290 Avenue of the Americas
New York, New York 10104

Excerpt from "The Lost Empire" by Derek Walcott used by permission
of the Derek Walcott Estate.

Library of Congress Cataloging-in-Publication Data
Names: Alexander, Jerad W., [date]– author.
Title: Volunteers : growing up in the forever war / Jerad W. Alexander.
Other titles: Growing up in the forever war
Description: First edition. | Chapel Hill : Algonquin Books of Chapel Hill, [2021] |
Summary: "The memoir of a young man from a long line of enlisted men and
    women, raised on military bases and shaped from a young age to idolize
    and glorify war and the people who fight it. After he joins the Marines and
    serves in Iraq, he must begin to reckon with the troubled and complicated
    truths of the American war machine"— Provided by publisher.
Identifiers: LCCN 2021016053 | ISBN 9781616209964 (hardcover) |
    ISBN 9781643752181 (ebook)
Subjects: LCSH: Alexander, Jerad W., [date]– | Iraq War, 2003–2011—Personal
    narratives. | Children of military personnel—United States—Biography. |
    United States. Marine Corps—Biography. | Military life—United States. |
    Military socialization—United States. | Militarism—United States. |
    Coming of age.
Classification: LCC DS79.766.A535 A3 2021 | DDC 956.7044/34092 [B]—dc23
LC record available at https://lccn.loc.gov/2021016053

ISBN 978-1-64375-325-6 (PB)

10 9 8 7 6 5 4 3 2 1
First Paperback Edition

Many names have been changed.
Memory is fickle and sometimes cruel;
events are as I remember them.

For the staff of the Overstreet Memorial Library,
Misawa Air Base, Japan. Thank you for the books,
and the refuge.

And for my family.

And then there was no more Empire all of a sudden.
Its victories were air, its dominions dirt:
Burma, China, Egypt, Africa, India, the Sudan.
The map that had seeped its stain on a schoolboy's shirt
like red ink on a blotter, battles, long sieges.
Dhows and feluccas, hill stations, outposts, flags
fluttering down in the dusk, their golden aegis
went out with the sun, the last gleam on a great crag,
with tiger-eyed turbaned Sikhs, pennons of the Raj
to a sobbing bugle.

—Derek Walcott, "The Lost Empire"

PROLOGUE

I ran down the trail like I thought a soldier would.

I was fifteen then, only smaller, but my camouflage uniform fit and the toes of my paratrooper boots chewed the earth. I smelled like moss and loam and dashed between gray trunks wrapped with vines and green roundleaf. The enemy flag was in my pocket now. I had stolen it for my team. I had won. Now I was running and felt like I thought a soldier should feel. I felt big. I wished only that I had a rifle in my hands.

I had been playing Capture the Flag in a field tucked in a corner of an American air base in Japan, but it might as well have been the Vietnam of war movies. I was a Civil Air Patrol cadet, the US Air Force's co-ed answer to the Boy Scouts, but in my fantasy I was with the First Air Cav or the Big Red One or the Fifth Marines. Ten of us had divided into two teams. We were all American kids, but to me the other team could have been the Viet Cong or North Vietnamese army. And I had won.

I had worked out a strategy with a friend before we started. I knew all the trails through the woods that surrounded the playing field. After jockeying around the field for a while, Tony gave me the signal and I ran as if to get a drink of water. Once I was out of sight, I slipped into the woods and found the trail that ran down the length of the tree line, where I felt hidden by the thick broadleaves and the wartime fantasies behind my eyes.

The opposing team was on the far side of the large field. I could see them through the leaves, but they could not see me. I heard someone from their team call, "Where's Alexander?"

I had made it down the trail and stalked back through the woods toward the end of the field behind the cluster of trees that protected the enemy flag. My insides rattled. I didn't want to be caught. I didn't want to fail. Just steal their flag and slip back into the woods like a ghost, then reappear with it among my teammates, victorious.

When I had reached their flag, I carefully pulled it from the notch of the tree it hung from and tucked it deep into the cargo pocket of my camouflage pants, then turned and shuffled away on my elbows and knees, with my chest on the earth, like a soldier crawling beneath machine-gun fire. I refused to look back at the guard, but I listened for sounds of his approach. I heard nothing. The two teams continued running and rushing around each other, angling, trying to get an edge. As I crawled, I waited for the enemy to grab me, to expose and capture me as a failure, or just chase me off like some street urchin. The darkness of the woods loomed closer, closer still, even closer, my heart in my throat, my skin tingling, a thin glaze of sweat on my body, senses acute and aware. Adrenaline ran through me like the snap of a high-voltage line.

Once I had crawled beyond the first trees, I stood to a crouch and continued toward the trail. I moved quietly at first, just as I had done at the beginning. But I was eager. I was the victor. My eyes were wide. Now my uniform smelled like the moss and the loam and the decay of the wet leaves. My fingers were dark from sinking them into the soil.

I began to run like I thought a soldier should.

The woods were dark from vines and thick canopy leaves, and for a moment maybe I was in an action movie. Maybe I ran like Elias in *Platoon* or Arnold in *Predator*. Maybe I ran through the A Shau Valley like Franz in *Hamburger Hill* or through the streets of Hue like

Joker in *Full Metal Jacket*. Maybe I was a character in a paperback war novel filled with scenes of tough vocabulary, fodder for the boyhood imagination of American war. Or perhaps I charged through the battles I would learn about later, when I was older and closer to the goal I could feel just out of reach. Maybe I sprinted from the Normandy coast toward the Rhine, marching with the GIs toward the final righteous destruction of the Nazi death machine—the pure epic fantasy of the American soldier. What if I ran across bizarre little islands my life would be soaked with at Marine boot camp a few years later—islands with strange names like Guadalcanal, Saipan, Peleliu, and Iwo Jima, all aiming at the end of the Japanese empire passing beneath my feet and buried in the fallout of the new nuclear era? But maybe I'm only insane in this moment, running down a trail in an outpost of America's own empire, dressed in camouflage. Another kid playing war.

My legs burned as I ran, but I did not notice. Instead, I felt pride and love and victory. My body screamed. I don't know how or when, but out there somewhere forward of me, along this trail, *yes!* There is a war and I'm going be a part of it, even if the war is wrong or flawed, baked with imperial hubris and patriotic filigree, I will go and shoot and fight and see the expanse of the next American war story. I ran hard, howling toward a glorified American machine-gun future. It was a future I was fine with.

ALPHA

Little I'd ever teach a son, but hitting,
Shooting, war, hunting, all the arts of hurting.
Well, that's what I learnt,—that, and making money.

—Wilfred Owen, "A Terre"

*OSCAR MIKE! The Marines are on the move! We are the Devil Dogs, the
Leathernecks, the Shock Troops, and the Hard Chargers—all born-to-kill
members of the Suck, the Green Weenie, the Rod & Gun Club, the Hard
Corps, Our Corps, the United States Marine Corps. We are modern-era
Visigoths with a bigger budget and better armor—Vikings of the Western
world complete with healthcare and heavy artillery. The Marine Corps is
like a high school gym class, with guns, and we flash down the highway in
western Iraq like a full-court press, rumbling with the menace of our V8
diesels in a long, roaring column of dusty armor spiked with machine guns
and automatic grenade launchers, littered with radios, hunting knives,
and cans of high-octane energy drinks. Crosses dangle from our necks
and the nylon bands that wrap our helmets have been marked with our
blood types—A+, O+, AB+—in permanent black ink, like sigils for the
apothecaries. Snuff and cigarettes sit in our pockets like manna.*

    *We can run a hard line back to Seattle and San Diego, the Bronx, the
Upper Peninsula of Michigan, all the rotting hamlets in central Oklahoma
and Nebraska and the Deep South. We've earned GEDs and public school
diplomas; we've pulled prison time in underfed community colleges and
worked off lazy academic hangovers in bloated party schools. We went to
class and sat bored through canned lessons on the Monroe Doctrine and
Manifest Destiny. We waved the flag. We pledged our allegiance and so here
we are. Maybe we loved you once. We are your friends, your brothers, and*

your sons. We are your fathers and your uncles. We are your husbands and ex-lovers and cheap one-night stands. We hate the Marine Corps, though sometimes we love it too. Oorah!

A large water tower dominates the wasteland like the fat king of a trash-hewn kingdom. It is the last day of summer and the lieutenant orders the column of seven Humvees into a laager behind a long berm south of a dusty town tucked into a bend of the Euphrates. We stop and open the Humvee doors. Flies emerge from the dirt beneath us and weave through our cigarette smoke. Rumors breathe into our binoculars and into our thoughts from beyond the berm—tales of fundamentalism, of stonings and beatings and martyrdom, the fodder of cable news, everything that has become the image of our enemy. I know as I sit here that soon we will have to go into all the towns and cities that carpet the banks of the river like moss and fight and kill all the things that scare us and anger us to make it safe for you thousands of miles away. Better over there than on Main Street, someone has said, and so here we are. And I am here, too, in 2005, a US Marine. I have come to Iraq like we all have come: on the back of a million war stories of the past American century, carried forward on the promise of vengeance and the belief in our own exceptionalism. We are Marines and we are Americans and our mythology is the sun we orbit. Oorah!

I sit and wait in the heat of the afternoon and listen to the radio pop with interrogatives and updates and situation reports from other units waiting for the war. Our objective is to fight. The lieutenant has been ordered by Rebel Six, our leader, to bring his platoon of Humvees and machine guns, and men with dreams of sex and college and home, to this berm and wait for the enemy to shoot at us so we can shoot back.

Big trucks loaded with furniture flee south down the nearby highway and east toward the big urban areas of Fallujah and Ramadi and Baghdad and Beyond. Orange-and-white taxis and crumbling import sedans course away steadily, helmed by nervous drivers with graven faces. Their wives ignore us; children fog the windows as they press their noses to the glass.

The driver of our Humvee, a corporal from Florida named Taylor, counts the dead on the fly strip he has hung from the turret. He taunts them like an avatar of middle school posturing—"No, you're dead. It's over." The machine-gun turret clicks as the gunner, an ex–college football player named Kozlowski, shifts his weight from one boot to the next and back again. His big black machine gun is clean and ready with a long belt of brass shells and bullets tipped with green paint and joined together with black links. The radioman, a new guy named Watson, ruminates with a wad of Copenhagen behind his lip. He listens to the handsets and stares into a daydream, with his helmet propping the door and his boot dangling from the cabin. After a while, the lieutenant, a big man with a red face wrapped with sunglasses like a state policeman, saunters off across the wasteland to another vehicle like a jolly hulk of government-sanctioned malevolence. The radioman sits in the lieutenant's seat and I sit in the radioman's seat to get out of the sun that beams into my side of the truck.

The presence of American military power around me is indomitable and impressive. I can feel it shouldering itself with the heavy weight of its own history, showcasing its muscularity. There are two and a half centuries of war-fighting experience packed into the space between the satellites in orbit and the soles of my boots as they cushion my feet against the hard floor of the truck. My armored vest is the most recent iteration of the flak jacket that saw its first American use in the skies above Japan and Germany and then while fighting communists in Korea. The Kevlar helmet that mashes the hair on my head and keeps shrapnel and even small-caliber bullets from puncturing my skull is the modern progression of the Stahlhelm worn by German stormtroopers during World War I and the M1 helmet worn by GIs during World War II. The Humvee is an extension of the World War II Willys MB, which once ferried commanders and troops in small numbers. The amphibious assault vehicles that will transport us into cities are the great-grandchild of the amphibious tractors that landed Marines on the black beaches of Iwo Jima. Every Marine helicopter that flits overhead is the direct descendant of the birds that choppered troops into and ferried mangled casualties away from the jungles and rice paddies throughout South Vietnam. There are even obscure apocrypha that suggest some of the older transport helicopters still have patches covering forty-year-old bullet holes left by the Viet Cong. Everywhere I look there are artifacts of the vast American empire generating its own hubris. "We're the best gunslingers on the planet," goes the general vibe. "Look how big we are. Look how strong we are. Look at alllll this firepower. Shoot at it, shoot at us. We dare you."

And so they do. It has never ceased.

The speakers in the minarets deep inside the town begin to crackle. A muezzin breathes through the static the first ghostly hums of the adhan with a soulful "allahu akbar." He transitions into the late-afternoon salat while other muezzins in the small villages across the river pick up their own calls to prayer. Soon the length of the Euphrates is full of haunting echoes, from here to the Syrian border and certainly beyond. The calls to prayer last a few minutes. Then they finish and leave us with the flies and the hard clicks of the turret and the fleeing caravan. The radios chirp with quiet missives back to Headquarters. I sit in the Humvee and feel alone, the unwanted guest from a crumbling empire.

A hollow metallic thunk sounds out in the distance. Did I hear it? Maybe not. But Taylor and Kozlowski stiffen, tense, as if plugged into a low-grade current.

"You hear that?" Taylor asks.

The air flutters.

The first mortar round strikes with a roar. The wasteland becomes a kaleidoscope of milliseconds that shoves the outside world into the periphery. Everything is now. Kozlowski drops into the turret and sits on the gunner's strap. Taylor curses. Watson simply shuts his door, as if closing it against some unneighborly annoyance. Another round strikes, its sound erupting from beneath the ground in a flash of thick smoke and dust. Its concussion rolls through my chest, a sensation that is both remarkable and terrifying. How long have I wondered what that feels like? As I begin to close the door, I notice the lieutenant sprinting across the dirt.

"Get to the other side!"

I clamber out of the Humvee as the lieutenant reaches the door. I sprint around the tailgate. My armored vest flops wide open. WHOOOOM—another round roars and rattles my teeth. I begin to giggle. I climb into the

Humvee and slam the door. Over the radio, the lieutenant orders his platoon to move out.

A wretched feeling passes through me. What if a shell lands on us? Right through the turret? A single mortar round that flies from the tube with a hard metallic pop, one that arcs high and fast and lucky? What if it comes down like a hole-in-one shot? All that rubber and plastic and bulletproof glass and electronics, all that flesh and blood, my flesh and blood and dreams, eviscerated and plastered across the inside of the Humvee like a wartime Jackson Pollock horror. I want to scream, "Move this thing!" But I don't. I am a US Marine. I am too scared.

The platoon folds into a column as the sun drops to the western hills. The dirt takes on an ashen quality, but the sky ignites with fiery orange hues.

The mortar rounds drift away as we trundle toward the shadow of the big water tower, but they are replaced with something else. I hear it over the rumbling engine—a crackling menace, a string of fast pops. Someone is shooting at us. Their bullets pass overhead. Now I know what that feels like too.

"That came from the water tower," the lieutenant says. He orders the column to circle. He orders us to fire with a tuned rage.

"Pepper the shit out of it."

The platoon hesitates at first. The gunners have done this before, but not at people. The first shot gives permission for a second, then a third, fourth, a fifth, all rolling and growing until booms and bangs rattle over the top of one another. There is no lull in the firing and each gun sounds out with its own unique pitch. The SAWs clatter like drum rolls. The M240s thump like Toms. The big .50-calibers hammer out thumb-sized nightmares with hearty bass drum crashes. Each trigger pull is timed to a silent terrible phrase taught to prevent the barrels from overheating: "Die, motherfucker. Die!" The bursts are synchronized with the gun next to it so that there are no gaps between them. Together they roar with an orchestral harmony.

Kozlowski fires long, fine strings. The bursts rip down the barrel and into the smoke and dust that has erupted around the base of the water tower. Brass casings and black links rain down from the guts of the machine gun, *clattering onto the metal floor around the gunner's feet. The smoke from burnt propellant drifts into the cabin. The deep red of the sun's last light glows through the smudged windshield. It mixes with the smoke and turns the inside of our Humvee into a death-metal tomb. The little demons on our shoulder whisper to us through the clatter of the machine gun and we bellow our love of death and battle, the chemicals running through us, the hell of this place, and the culmination of our collective want, our desire, to be here, to see this, to stamp this inside us: this moment we see battle for the first time on the last day of summer. So go back to your classrooms and your shit jobs. Go pick up the mouth breathers from day care. Go back to your squabbles and bickering and petty tantrums. Go pick up your fast-food dinners and watch your reality TV. We'll be here, doing this, doing this weird little savagery called war. We are no longer a part of your world. Perhaps we never were. Listen to the machine guns. Listen to them kill. Listen to the howls of our battlefield climax as we scream "Get some!" like every war-movie cliché we've ever heard.*

I light a cigarette and pass up cans of ammunition. With the smoke and the cigarette and the red haze and the harsh noise of the machine guns, I am the picture of every GI my childhood eyes have ever seen.

The lieutenant orders all the guns to cease. Maybe we have won. Maybe not. We have no tally. Nevertheless, the party ends and the mood inside the Humvee deflates. Most of the guns stop within seconds, but like the last kid out of the pool, one petulant gunner rattles off an extra burst.

After a moment, the lieutenant orders the column to circle back onto the road and head south a few hundred meters before turning off onto a small piece of high ground and circling into another laager. Night comes. He calls the battalion mortars to drop flares, and within a few minutes great balls of magnesium fire drift above the water tower, casting it in sickly orange light. He learns from headquarters that a big flying gunship is on its way to pound the town with its cannons—the price for its sins. We stand in the darkness and retell the story of the battle like kids recounting the scenes from their favorite action movies, only today we are the stars. Someone says we've earned our Combat Action Ribbons today and we beam.

The lieutenant walks off by himself out on a knoll and watches the flares leave their long, wispy trails of smoke over the tower. I walk up beside him.

"I'll tell you something, Sergeant Alexander," he says softly, "but don't tell anyone." In the sky above, the first throb of the big gunships' four engines sound out over the wide desert. Soon high-explosive shells the size of footballs will fry the streets.

"I love this shit," he says. "I really do." We watch the flares.

That night, I stand guard in the turret of the Humvee. Taylor, Kozlowski, and Watson pull out poncho liners and tuck into a shallow depression next to the truck. The lieutenant dozes in his seat inside the cabin. I rest against the black machine gun with my face coated in dried sweat and smoke. The radio handsets hiss with soft static and quiet interrogatives. The gunship drones in the starlit sky above. It cracks off shells with deep thumps that erupt with showers of metal and sparks in broad arcs.

I light a cigarette and feel the dirt in my boots and under my fingernails. I exhale and watch the night and feel like the luckiest man on the planet and that nothing after can ever feel the same. The shells from American airpower, the kingbolt of my history, blast the earth behind the low hills. Their sparks and shrapnel glitter in a fine, wide plume. Just look at them. Ooo-fucking-rah!

I

I remember the sound of fighter jets idling in the cool Utah morning before sunrise. I was only six, but when I think about them now, a room filled with details of that era opens, which I can recall with a strange clarity—the echoing rattle of my stepdad's Harley Sportster coming down the hot street in the afternoon or Black Sabbath playing from the tall cabinet speakers in the living room on the Fourth of July. But there are gray areas at the edges, too, like old photos in last-century library books, the memories tied together by episodes and sidebars—all flawed and based on feeling. Love is a feeling I remember. Love and awe. A love of war stories and soldiers, of fighter jets and machine guns and uniforms, a love of history and fantasy. A love of America. A love and awe of flawed and dangerous things.

I remember that the whistling jet turbines on the far end of the flight line had awoken me again. I could hear them through the walls of our quadplex between Valiant and Magnolia Streets. The air force called our neighborhood Area C, but sometimes my mom and stepdad and all our neighbors would call it Afterburner Alley. They said it with mild pride. They also said it with an eye roll.

At idle, the F-16 Fighting Falcon blew a harsh, gassy note, a cross between a hiss and a sharp whistle. Its idle was so loud I could hear it while I played on the jungle gym during first-grade recess at the elementary school three miles away. Sometimes I could hear it even farther in the distance, as if it were propelled by some jet-fueled wind. After the Fighting Falcons took off, pictures on the walls needed to be straightened. The sound of fighter jets was the background racket in our house throughout nearly my entire childhood. There were many mornings, mornings like this one, when I was awakened by a dozen jets taking off, one after the next or in pairs, producing a roar so thick I buried my head under the pillow and cursed the stupid US Air Force and its stupid fighter jets.

This morning, I decided to try to watch them.

I had tried before and failed. The apartment in the quadplex where we lived was built sometime after World War II. I had moved carelessly before, and the tired planks of the hardwood floor had creaked under my feet. Then I'd heard the door to my parents' bedroom open and managed to dart under the covers just in time for my door to open with the hazy visage of my mom's or stepdad's face aiming at me. They were light sleepers. "Get your butt back in bed," they'd say.

I learned the trouble spots in the floor after being discovered a time or two. The trick was to push against the floor just enough to make the wood bend without complaining and move to the next spot only once the wood beneath me felt comfortable. I slid from beneath the covers and sat up slowly. I pressed one bare foot onto the floor. Not a sound. I pressed the next foot.

After a few minutes, I reached my large bedroom window and stared between the slats of the white blinds. On the far side of the playground and beyond the double layer of chain-link fence, soft blue lights edged the concrete flight line like gemstones lit from the inside by ancient starlight. Aircraft hangars and maintenance buildings glowed with yellow bulbs on the far side. A work truck flitted between them on some lonely predawn business. I knew that soon the sun would crest the tall ridges behind me and cast the airfield in a cool, arid blue, but before that, the jet fighters would roar into the sky.

I couldn't see them when it began. Afterburner Alley sat on the south end of the two-and-a-half-mile-long runway, less than a thousand feet from where the jets took off and landed every day. I already knew they almost always taxied to the north end of the runway from their ramp positions near the center of the base.

After a moment, the first pilot pressed his throttle forward and the air roared as the turbine came to life with a rage of noise. The window glass began to rattle lightly.

The first Falcon didn't come into view until it was just lifting from the flight line, about midway. Its landing gear was retracting into its guts, the curved doors closing behind them. The long blue-and-white vortex of the afterburner flame marked its momentum as the floor quivered beneath my bare feet and the windowsill trembled under my fingers. The sound reverbed inside me. I jammed my fingers into my ears, but I watched anyway.

Look at it! Look at the way it knifes through the sky, the way it moves as if gravity means nothing, as if its power is bigger than Earth and the physics that bind us to it. The rising sunlight sparkled against the Falcon's polished canopy. Its satin gray two-tone paint punctuated the smooth, aggressive curves of its nose and upper fuselage. The hard angles of its wings and tail breathed the fine precision of its intractable mathematics. Watching it fly was the guitar solo of some rock-'n'-roll power ballad my stepdad blasted on his stereo—a flagrant totem of sex, youth, masculinity, and general righteous power, the hubris of a Cold War eighties America mixed with the tuned ghosts of old World War II glories. *Look at it! Look how grown up it is!*

My bedroom door opened behind me. It was too late to dart into bed. My stepdad stood in the doorway. I don't know if it was me or the fighter jets that had awoken him. It didn't matter.

"Get your butt back in bed," he said.

I was six years old. By the time the Falcons finished taking off, my ears rang. I didn't mind so much anymore.

• • •

The air base sat on a plateau wedged between Interstates 15 and 84, with the city of Ogden to the north and the communities of Clearfield, Riverdale, Roy, Sunset, and Layton lining its western border. Farther west, out past the Great Salt Lake and Antelope Island: a desert wasteland. The mountains of the Wasatch Range loomed to the east. When the new Fighting Falcons landed in the fall of 1980, the valley up to near the mountaintops was cascaded in brilliant golden hues of autumn and marked by the twin golf-ball-like radar domes perched on Francis Peak. Soon after, the mountains would be buried under blankets of thick snow that reached to the lake. While the main part of the base and the airfield were flat, much of the landscape around the military neighborhoods had been terraced out of the hillside. I always assumed the air base had been named for the mountains and the slopes instead of a long-dead test pilot. No one really called it by its official name: Hill Air Force Base. Everyone just called it Hill and we treated it like an American castle. Inside it, my stepdad fixed the Fighting Falcons when they were broken.

His name was Alan and he was tall and lean with a trim mustache. He wore jeans, sometimes with a big belt buckle and Harley-Davidson T-shirts. He owned a Harley Sportster and a long-barreled .44 Magnum revolver, similar to what Clint Eastwood had in the *Dirty Harry* films he loved, and he carried a folding knife in his pocket. He was from a mobile home up a dirt road in north Georgia and his dad was an air force veteran, first of the China-Burma-India Campaign of World War II and then Vietnam. Alan was in the air force, too, a noncommissioned officer, a career man. He rocked out to Ozzy and Boston and Van Halen and Hank Williams Jr. on the big Pioneer stereo he had bought while stationed in Okinawa. He drove a green-and-white Ford truck with a V8 motor. He was gruff but liked cats, kind and playful but hated lying and when people chewed with their mouths open.

Alan was capable of generating laughter so deep my face and stomach would be sore for hours. He was a prankster who would poke out a finger and say, "Pull it," and when I did, he'd fart. Sometimes on weekends, if he woke first, he'd move one of the large Pioneer cabinet speakers outside my bedroom. Then he would quietly open the door and press play on the stereo and ignite my Saturday morning with the hard reverb of Metallica's "Master of Puppets" at eighty decibels. One morning, I awoke to him vacuuming my room. After I refused to move, he lifted the big iron Kirby from the floor and held it a foot above my head until I was properly awake. During the snowy winters, he parked his cold-averse Harley in the back of the dining room and we'd wake up to the revving motor while he let the exhaust blow out of the sliding back door.

He loved that Harley and therefore so did I. It had chrome pipes and a black gas tank with SPORTSTER written in burgundy down the side. He'd tuck a wad of Copenhagen behind his lip before heading out to wash his bike; the back pocket of his jeans was worn out in a small circle where the can pressed against the denim. He snapped, "Why do you like candy?" when I asked him why he used it. One afternoon, I asked him about it again. Sick of my pestering, he pulled out the can, opened the shiny lid, and offered me a small pinch. "Put it behind your lip," he said. I did as he said, but the bitter tobacco exploded across my mouth, and instead of spitting it out, I swallowed. The nicotine roared through me and I was nauseated and dizzy for hours, lying on the cold edge of the curb of the nearby parking lot while he finished washing his motorcycle.

He loved my mother dearly too. Once, not long after I met him, my mother, who was also in the air force, deployed to Norway for a few weeks of training. One night, he stood in the living room and listened to his stereo with a Budweiser in hand. At one point, he howled with some inner torment and I ran into my bedroom to hide. He came in after me and hovered over me as I lay on my bed. I could see his red face above me and I could see he was in tears. He was young and in love and he missed his wife. The next morning, when it was time for him to go to work, he sat me on the backseat of his

Harley and told me to hold on tight. He cranked the loud, clattering motor, and with my small hands clinging to his olive-drab uniform, he roared down the dark road and delivered me the short distance to the day care center where I'd spend the day until he got off work and picked me up. I thought he was the coolest person in the world, and when he said, "I love you, son," I'd reply, "I love you, Dad," and when I did, I meant it.

Alan's Harley tolled the end of the workday. He'd pull into the carport and kill the motor and come into the house hero tall, dressed in camouflage utilities heavily starched, pressed, and preened with cuticle scissors until all the seams and buttons were free of any little threads that might have come loose. His boots were hard black with a semigloss shine, and if it was warm, his sleeves were precisely folded under his four dark blue staff sergeant stripes. After he kissed my mother, he hauled back to the bedroom and changed into a pair of jeans and a T-shirt, then lowered his frame into the brown La-Z-Boy in the living room. He let the leg rest jerk his bare feet into the air and he drank a beer while my younger sister played on the living room floor. I sat nearby, either on the couch or on the lounger across from the recliner and tried not to bother him. He wanted to unplug in front of the television for a while after a long workday. But it was tough sometimes for me. He worked around the thing I loved. He answered my silly questions as best as he could with the bored tenor of a worker who is too close to the thing that amazes outsiders, especially a boy.

Boys generally aspire to follow the men who fill the role of father, at least to a point. His job, and the job of most of his friends, was to repair and maintain the electronic heads-up display that allows pilots to track their altitude and speed, their heading, the angle of the aircraft, and other data while keeping their eyes on target. It was a job he performed with simple pragmatic professionalism, without passion or interest. Growing up, it seemed strange, sometimes unfathomable to me, that he never took an interest in these things.

Passion is often supplanted by the monotony of routine. Maintaining war machines is typically a nine-to-five day job at its core. But like firetrucks and footballs for other kids, and aside from my *Star Trek* and *Star Wars* toys, fighter jets quickly became a supposed future that slow-burned in my imagination.

On rainy mornings, I'd sit in class with a No. 2 pencil sharpened to a fine point and begin to sketch side profiles of the Fighting Falcon with the letters *HL* on the tail—the tail marking for the 388th Fighter Wing, my stepdad's unit. The angle of the tail and the shape of the nose were particularly important. When drawing the Falcon from the front, the oval of the air intake had to be perfect, as did the viper-like slope of the fuselage as it blends into the wings. If I got it wrong, even a little bit, I'd ball it up and toss it into the trash and try again. In a closet at home, I found a technical manual that showed the layout of every instrument panel in the Falcon cockpit and I snuck away with it, my secret scroll. While I couldn't even begin to understand what an eighth of the dials and switches meant (and was equally amazed any pilot could), I drew replicas of the diagram on loose-leaf paper and memorized their names—the Electronic Warfare Prime Indicator, the Up-Front Integrated Control Panel, the Throttle Friction Control, and the Horizontal Situation Indicator.

Occasionally my stepdad would rent action movies from the nearby Blockbuster or the base movie-rental shop. He'd come home with the videotape hidden under his arm; he'd playfully goad me, refusing to reveal the title until we were settled in front of the television with our plates of fish sticks and mac and cheese. This time? *Iron Eagle*, and I hissed *yessssss!* until my stepdad looked over and said, "Don't talk with your mouth full, son." But it didn't matter. For the next two hours, I'd watch a teenage boy fly a Fighting Falcon with a Vietnam vet to save his fighter pilot father from the death grip of the terrorist nation of Bilya, a hackneyed obfuscation of Libya, while under the warm American blanket of eighties rock-'n'-roll riffs. And if not *Iron Eagle*, I'd jinx over the Nevada desert in my F-14 Tomcat with Goose in the backseat and that arrogant Iceman clogging my radio with his teachers'-pet smugness as we competed in *Top Gun*. Once the movie was over, I'd brush my teeth and fall asleep to the electric guitar still buzzing in my ears as the fuel of fighter pilot dreams and awaken to the real-life idle of the Fighting Falcons.

At school, it felt important to be cool. In every grade, a pecking order developed between last year's kids and the new kids who came to school after the air force had moved them to Hill from elsewhere in the empire. There were the cool kids and there were those in orbit of the cool kids. I tended to drift on the fringes—a nerd longing to be cool but without the ephemeral *something* that makes kids cool. Maybe it was the sneakers I wore, or the sneakers I didn't wear. Or maybe it was the cold sores I would occasionally get. Maybe it was because I was smaller than most of the other boys. Whatever the case, being cool felt like chasing a whimsy, something out of reach. I wasn't cool, and so I read and hung out with kids who were my friends and dreamed of an adulthood where I was heroic. And cool.

We took everything inside us and brought it to the playground— our comics, movies, and television shows. Boys played like action heroes at recess in the grass field near the blacktop where kids played tetherball. We put our arms out wide and pretended we were fighter jets. We pointed fingers at each other and said "bang!" We whispered the curse words we picked up from home. All the cool kids knew them in Spanish, and when they said *puto* and *puta madre*, we laughed. Words like *humping* signaled the hazy and cheap future of our manhood. We flexed with them like dubious totems of maturity and traded them like social currency, then pleaded with the teachers when they caught us and cried when they called our parents.

I built stories around the stories I was told and the movies Alan brought home. I wanted to be like Michael Jordan or Dan Marino or Arnold Schwarzenegger. I liked cops like John McClane in *Die Hard*, who killed bank robbers, who did it like a gunfighter from the Old West. I blasted around the front and backyard on imaginary adventures lifted out of *Rambo*, *Indiana Jones* or *Star Wars*, my fingers coated with Dorito dust and veins throttled with carbonated corn syrup and caffeine. I ran to school every day through streets with names like Liberty, Yorktown, and Minuteman, with the soundtrack of last night's movie playing on repeat behind my ears as I recited the Pledge of Allegiance with my small hand over my heart. My friends' parents bought them Starter jackets with the logos of sports teams emblazoned on them and posters of WWF wrestlers. I wanted an American military uniform. All around me were the uniforms of the people meant to protect us from fear—American Beowulfs battling the horror of un-American Grendels. Alan's uniform was a security blanket as much as it was something to aspire to. It represented a shield against whatever was waiting for us on the far side of the Berlin Wall or on the broad boulevards of Pyongyang and Beijing. But it wasn't him alone. It was our entire kingdom. His uniform was the same uniform everyone else wore, the same as all his friends.

There was Rye—the barrel-chested biker who was quick with a knife. He cursed incessantly and smoked Marlboro Reds. He wore a wallet with a chain attached to his belt. He was unsophisticated and raw, as if he were living in a world not bound by military rules and regulations, or even society—a Tough Guy. He possessed a hair-trigger temper and he could go off at any moment for any intrusion on what he deemed his. One warm afternoon, I played on the front lawn with his stepson, Josh. A motorcycle parked deep in the nearby carport suddenly roared to life. Rye had been watching the motorcycle for a friend who was deployed. When the bike started unannounced, Rye burst from the house with a pocketknife in his hand, ready to fight the thief—until he realized the friend had come home and pulled a joke on him. In another life, Rye might have made a great Hell's Angel. He probably knew a few.

Rye had given Josh an air force promotion exam study guide as a present. After we gorged on candy one Halloween, Josh pulled out the large book and flipped to a page with a breakdown of the medals and ribbons soldiers and airmen wore on their chest.

"If you could have any of them, which would you want?" he asked.

I scanned the colors and their names—the Distinguished Service Cross, the Air Medal, the Presidential Unit Citation, the Vietnam Service Medal. I didn't know where to start, so I pointed to a Silver Star Medal. I liked its red, white, and blue bands and the gold star that hung beneath it. It felt grand and honest. It looked like the kind of medal the hero gets at the end of the movie.

Josh looked at me quizzically, as if I had picked something simple, quaint. "Really?" he asked.

"Yeah. I like it. So?" I snapped. "Which one would *you* pick?"

He pointed to a medal. It was a gold heart with the profile of George Washington centered in a purple backdrop and it hung from a rich purple ribbon flanked with white stripes. It was the Purple Heart.

Josh regarded me with a strange wonder. "I read they give it to you if you're wounded in battle."

Then there was Fly. His name was George something-or-other, but everyone just called him Fly because of a large fly he had tattooed on his chest. He once told me his father had the same name and the same tattoo. He sometimes rolled his pack of cigarettes in his shirtsleeve like some fifties-era Greaser. His job was to work on the landing gear of the Fighting Falcons. One summer weekend, he threw a barbecue at the house he shared with his wife in nearby Ogden. That afternoon, before the party, my mother and I ran into him while she shopped at the Base Exchange. He offered to take me with him to his house to hang out while my mother ran errands before the party. She agreed. This was the military; its uniforms bestowed an inherent sense of trust and fealty.

He took me to the house and rocked Rush and AC/DC songs at peak volume on his Fender. After my mother showed up, he told me to hide behind him in the living room. I fit right behind his legs, out of sight. My mother posted in the kitchen, sorting through frozen hamburgers and hot dogs and potato chips. While they talked over the bar that separated the two rooms, Fly reached behind him and held his Budweiser in front of me and gave it a little shake. I took it from him and took a long pull and handed it back. I was about ten and the beer was cold and bitter and forbidden.

Then there was Killer. His name was Keith, but everybody just called him Killer, which I didn't understand because he was a genial, intelligent man with brown hair and friendly eyes. He reminded me of Brent Spiner, the actor who played Mr. Data on *Star Trek: The Next Generation*. He wasn't married and didn't have children. He goofed around, always wrestling and joshing. Killer worked with my stepdad fixing avionics gear in the Fighting Falcons, but he went to night school at the University of Utah, grinding away on a degree in computer science. As my stepdad grew older and began to settle, he sold the motorcycle and began dabbling in computers as a hobby. A few times Keith took my stepdad to a computer lab at the university and showed him things on the green screens of the proto–information age. But Keith wasn't stuffy. He was a drinker, a fun drunk, and there were plenty of mornings he awoke on our living room couch to a glass of water and an aspirin.

Every few weeks my mother would suggest, "Let's have some people over Saturday," and that weekend the house would come alive with the stereo playing fighter jet rock from KRSP, "The Arrow." As the sun set on Liberty Street, my stepdad's friends and their wives and girlfriends filled our house with the sound of opening beer tabs and the spark of cigarette lighters, backed by Bon Jovi and Cinderella.

These were the Americans that kept the Fighting Falcons flying against the communists, but they never boasted or bragged about it. Except for perhaps Rye. It was just a job; for many, a career, but still just a job. They talked about their motorcycles and the upcoming Metallica concert in Salt Lake City. They riffed about TV shows and MTV videos:

"Did you see that new video for Guns N' Rose—"

"I wanna see that!" my voice shot out from hip level between my stepdad and Killer.

"Don't interrupt, son," my stepdad said gently.

Sometimes my stepdad's squadron threw barbecues under a large pavilion, complete with a dunk tank and a bouncy castle. Kids lined up at the fountain drink stand and made Suicide Sodas—large cups of ice filled with 7-Up, Coke and Diet Coke, Dr Pepper and fruit punch and root beer, all in one dumb mixture. We guzzled them and filled our guts with charred hot dogs, then snagged grasshoppers in our palms. Around sunset, we went home and listened to hair metal on the stereo and played on the front lawn or in my bedroom until past midnight.

During summer, the base hosted a large air show where I waited in line to sit inside a Fighting Falcon. When my turn came, it felt like climbing into the cockpit of a dream. I frustrated the young hot-shot aviator with a blizzard of questions until he shooed me away. Then I headed over to the big hangar, where I touched the side of an attack helicopter and picked up different rifles and pistols displayed by the security police. A young airman let me put an M-16 rifle into my shoulder and aim down the sights at the big lights of the hangar bay. He showed me how the charging handle worked and how to clear a jam.

"All you have to do is slap the magazine with your hand, then grab the charging handle with two fingers, pull it back, and just let it go," he said. I tried to pull the black charging handle, but the rifle was too big in my hands, and for a moment I felt sheepish and guilty for being too little to do it.

Later, the Thunderbirds, the air force aerial aerobatics team, spooled the turbines of their red, white, and blue Fighting Falcons on the wings of the flight line, complete with the snap-and-pop ceremonial routine orchestrated by the crew chiefs, and lifted into the sky. I watched with wide-eyed wonder as they performed maneuvers and stunts in tight formations, the planes executing them through pure mathematics and a dash of patriotic magic. Sometimes a big lumbering bomber arrived, flying in loud and low on a pretend carpet-bombing mission, punctuated by pyrotechnics that torched the dead grass on the far end of the airfield with a chain of massive fireballs—the stand-ins for high-explosive munitions. I watched and cheered with Rye or Killer, my mom and stepdad, and all the other airmen who packed our house those nights, and then Josh or Chris, or maybe all of us, raced to the soda machines and made more Suicide Sodas and got back in line to bug the pilot with more questions.

American servicemembers had children with partners from the countries they were assigned—Filipino American children who had fled Luzon with their air force parents after Mount Pinatubo exploded, Korean American children born from the heavy American presence that stares down North Koreans across the Demilitarized Zone, Japanese American children, and children from across Latin America and from Spain and England and Germany, anywhere there might be Americans climbing into uniforms and sent across the ether of foreign policy. The military felt like a pure form of the American idea of a melting pot while also providing an instant beacon of American familiarity that partly transcended our origins. Every kid that came around, even if they were new to the base, was spiritually tethered to the community by virtue of their father or mother putting on the uniform every morning.

The military was our world; the outside world felt gray and chaotic, shapeless, less noble. There was a quiet, unexpressed notion that we were superior, standing on the ramparts looking down at all the peasants in the muddy, unkempt American ground beyond the moat. We wore the air force and the Fighting Falcon like a family crest; the military was our kingdom. With my stepdad and his friends, watching the Fighting Falcons as they darted and hummed overhead in the summer at the end of the Cold War, our castle felt impenetrable.

I could feel layers of purpose beneath the daily currents of my American world. Every morning, the airmen like my stepdad and Rye and the rest dressed in their uniforms, climbed into their cars and trucks or onto their motorcycles, and clattered to the offices and hangars and maintenance shops bordering the airfield, where they spent a workday before they turned around and clattered home in the afternoon to supper and beer and the television. But there was something deeper and broader in their energies, even as their workaday routine felt like the cells of a beast at rest, perpetuating itself in preparation for some far deadlier purpose. Perhaps it was duty or honor or sacrifice, or all the other words we associated then, and even now, with the act of serving in the military. Perhaps I just wanted it to be.

It was certainly woven into the flag we hung every morning in class and hummed somewhere between the words of the Pledge of Allegiance. Everything sparked with righteousness. There was a fantastic sense that we were plugged into the heart of what it meant to be American. These weapons belonged to us, and every time we touched them or listened to their roar in the sky as I played on the front lawn, it felt like touching our history and my future in the same instant. It felt happy and hopeful, warm, gleaming with the sun and the wide-open path of the American Dream. All I had to do was hold on. It was easy. And when I saw the bumper stickers that blotted the chrome on pickup trucks, a bumper sticker that read JET NOISE: THE SOUND OF FREEDOM, I laughed because I believed it was true.

II

Chris was a year younger than me. He had a waterbed and he wore black Air Jordan high-tops and a black Chicago Bulls pullover Starter jacket. Chris collected baseball and basketball cards and kept track of their worth in a Beckett price guide. He had a Michael Jordan card worth a hundred dollars. He showed it to me when we first met, but he didn't brag. Then we played *Teenage Mutant Ninja Turtles* and *Contra* on his Nintendo in the laundry room of his house. Chris usually played. Mostly I watched.

Chris had a BMX bike. It was black with red grips and he had the handlebars pushed slightly forward so that when he rode it his body leaned forward in a way that looked cool. It had pegs screwed onto the rear axle for friends to stand on and ride with him. I rode a colorful Huffy—red and purple with white handlebars. I got it for Christmas. I liked my bike, but I sometimes wished I had a BMX bike so I could look cool like Chris.

We liked to build jumps out of wooden planks at the bottom of a steep hill near our houses, then push our bikes to the top and zap back down with the handlebars tight in our small hands, launching from the rickety jump, floating forward soundlessly, then landing on the pavement of Freedom Circle with our chains flopping and tires straining. Or else we'd ride to the top of Liberty Street, at the top of the long hill into the base neighborhood, and blast down the sidewalk to the big field past my house, only to leap from our bikes like daredevils and tumble to the grass like stuntmen from action movies.

It was near the end of summer, just a few weeks before the beginning of fifth grade, those last days of freedom that carried a backbeat of urgency and pending schoolhouse doom as our moms threatened us with back-to-school shopping. On the other side of the world, far past our American childhood knowledge of geography, Saddam Hussein, the dictator of Iraq, stormed nearly ninety thousand troops across the Arabian Desert, invading Kuwait in a myopic burst of hubris, avarice, and indignation over outstanding national debts. Aside from a few holdout actions, the bulk of the Kuwaiti army, a speed bump compared to the invaders, fled south to Saudi Arabia to avoid annihilation. Kuwaiti emir Jaber Al-Sabah ran into the Saudi desert with the army, but his half brother was killed defending the Dasman Palace. Iraqi soldiers crushed his body under the treads of a tank. By the end of the day, Saddam's troops had sacked Kuwait City and much of the surrounding country. A few days later, the dictator declared Kuwait the nineteenth province of Iraq.

I knew nothing about Iraq or Saddam Hussein or his war with Iran that had racked up so much debt. I knew nothing about Kuwait. The Middle East was a sandstorm in the eyes of my worldly understanding. But I knew that if I clipped a playing card to the frame of my bike just the right way, the card would clatter like a cheap Harley when it flicked against the spokes.

The invasion of Kuwait built slowly in my consciousness, like the first whine of a Fighting Falcon turbine. It began with the nightly news. Dan Rather, Peter Jennings, and Tom Brokaw became the messengers of coming dread, delivering missives about UN resolutions and American and British edicts threatening war against the Iraqi despot. My awareness of it grew the day my stepdad used the kitchen table to lay out desert uniforms and boot socks and sundry items like shaving cream and sunscreen, all meant for a duffel bag to be packed and ready to grab at a moment's notice. The static began to swell when all the Saturday night partying ceased, when the barbecues stopped grilling hot dogs and hamburgers, when I stopped running between the feet of Alan's friends, zapped on Chips Ahoy! and Coke. The turbine began to roar when President George H. W. Bush said, "At my direction . . . key units of the United States Air Force are arriving today to take up defensive positions in Saudi Arabia," and pierced my ears when many of the Fighting Falcons took off from the airfield one day and never returned.

Then one predawn morning at the end of August, my stepdad opened my bedroom door. I was told it might happen, but I didn't want to believe it. He left the light off when he came in, expecting me to be asleep. But I sat up in bed and said, "Huh?"

"Shhhh, don't wake your sister," he hissed.

The roar of the invasion was deafening in that moment, but through it I could hear him speak when he softly said, "Bye, son." Its rage was so brutal and complete that I cried into my pillow after he turned and left, paralyzed as the front door opened and the screen door creaked closed, as my stepdad walked into the darkness with his duffel bag and vanished.

Our house had been broken into, a piece of our family stolen. We had been living in a haze of complacency, but now Alan was gone, sent to the Middle East for Operation Desert Shield—the big troop buildup and defensive operation meant to protect Saudi Arabia, specifically its northern oil fields that were within striking distance of Saddam's army. My mother understood these things, but I didn't and neither did my sister, who was old enough only to recognize his absence. Wars come and snatch people away, sometimes temporarily and other times permanently. We were a military family and we had no excuse for ignoring this probability, and yet for the first few weeks we walked around in a daze punctuated by flashes of raw nerves.

I was ten years old. Little things began to cause my eyes to flood with tears, nonsensical trivialities like a stubbed toe or dinnertime, and I would have to blink and wipe under my eyes and go play with my USS *Enterprise* toy and get mad at myself for not being a man about it like my stepdad. At night, I would lie in bed in the dark and listen to the television in the living room, where my mom sat on the recliner, or listen to the brief snatches of conversations she had with girlfriends and family on the phone at the far end of the kitchen. The rumors of war. Occasionally I could hear my sister in the next room openly sobbing with long, breathy moans. Sometimes I would too. Quietly. My mother was soft in these moments. She would come into my room and sit on the edge of my bed and tell me she understood and that it was okay. But when I asked if she knew when he was coming back, she'd say, "I don't know." Then she walked out.

It felt like a large cavity had been hollowed out inside my chest. I could feel its edges grating against my rib cage as I walked to school in the morning, my mood matching the coming sad beauty of autumn. I didn't have to look into the future before he left, at least not in any real way. I could wade in the imagination of childhood without commitment or concern. Now I had to think about when my stepdad, my *dad* for all day-to-day purposes, was going to come home, and I had no answer. I wasn't even sure where he was, only that he was somewhere in the Middle East. We all just assumed Saudi Arabia and wouldn't learn until later that he'd been deployed to the United Arab Emirates, a place I had never heard of, much less cared to know anything about. Instead, we all called it "the Desert" or "the Sandbox."

The news hissed at us with special reports on the efficacy of the Iraqi army, the fourth-largest army in the world, complete with videos of the feared Republican Guard, who were considered battle-hardened elite troops ready and willing to cut our throats. The nightmares of chemical and biological weapons were threatened as a real possibility. It was hard to picture my stepdad facing that, since his job would have kept him away from the front lines. But I was a kid, too, prone to fantasy, and sometimes I wondered.

"Mom?" I asked from the backseat of our car one afternoon. My sister sat next to me.

"Uh-huh . . ." my mom responded. Fleetwood Mac played on the radio.

"I was wondering . . . Could Dad die?" I asked.

My mom responded immediately, almost derisively. "No. He's a long way from anything. You don't have to worry." I wasn't sure if she said it because she knew something she couldn't share or if she didn't want my sister to begin crying. But my sister cried anyway.

I came home from school in late September to find a letter on my bed. I sat on the brown carpet with my back against the bed frame and gently opened the envelope, removing the neatly folded paper. Alan's handwriting was small, precise. I read it as carefully as my ten-year-old impatience allowed. I tried to read it with his voice, and while I could hear him, he sounded distant, as if down a long, dark hallway. The letter divulged little about his life in the Desert or what he was doing. Instead, he focused on details between us and pushed mild reminders to do well in school and stay out of trouble and help my mother and sister while he was away. I was the man of the house, he wrote, and my chest swelled. When I was done reading, I refolded the paper just as it was and slipped it back into the envelope and set it on my dresser. Perhaps I was the man of the house, but I also felt miserable and quietly maudlin for the rest of the evening. I wasn't miserable for receiving a letter. I was miserable because it was only a letter. He was still gone.

We received a small care package soon after. Alan had managed to find little gifts to ship back to us. I received a toothbrush that had the crude head of a teddy bear on the top of the handle. When I pressed the bear's nose the head played "Frère Jacques," the French nursery rhyme. It was a little too young for me, but whenever I played it, my eyes welled up and I felt like a "chicken." A videotape arrived in the mail not long after. The United Service Organizations had sent a team overseas and began to record messages for servicemembers to send home to their families. The tape arrived just as the leaves were beginning to fall from the trees and our front lawn was colored in gold. My mother put the tape into the player, and after the tracking settled, my stepdad appeared on our television. My sister squealed. The message was short—maybe five minutes. He told us he was fine and my mom said it looked like he had put on a little weight. His hair was shorter than usual and his face was tan. He told my sister he loved her and she began to cry. He told me to do well in school and to stay out of trouble. The mischief was still in his eyes, but there was a moment when he looked sad. The video cut abruptly and suddenly he was happy again. Then he signed off and the video went dark and he was gone. We rewound and watched it again. Then one more time. My sister and I wanted to watch it once more, but my mother said no. Three times was enough. She had to make dinner.

My mother attended nursing school at a nearby university and most of her classes were at night. Once school let out, I walked to a cul-de-sac near my house where Chris lived with his mother, his stepfather, who was an air force security policeman, and his young sisters.

His mother brought in extra money working as a babysitter for military kids around the base. With the war overseas, it was a seller's market. Their house was routinely filled with a bevy of neighborhood boys and girls, but most often my sister and me, until my mother came home from school late in the evening. When she would finally call, we walked alone across the long, dark field from Freedom Circle to our house on Liberty Street and went to bed.

It began to rain more often as fall deepened, drumming the threats of coming snow against the roads and sidewalks, filling the air with the smell of dust and old iron. At recess, Mr. Potter, my fifth-grade teacher, took the class to the library instead of turning us loose in the cold rain. Kids huddled around the broad, round tables and riffed

MC Hammer lyrics. I walked to the encyclopedias and pulled one out by the top of its spine. I sat on the squat step stool and flipped through it, passing pictures of history and art until I stumbled on an entry for the US Army. It was short, maybe a half page with a few pictures of soldiers in basic training or fighting a war somewhere. A long chart of ranks appeared alongside pictures of their chevrons, followed by the shiny insignias of officers' ranks. The chevrons of the enlisted always interested me more. They're what I saw on a regular basis. Officers were part of another world. The few I had met were usually kind but also reserved and studious, even boring, like principals or bank managers. They lived in bigger houses on other parts of the base and their kids were well dressed—the children of knights and lords. They had the quiet confidence that comes from the security of money and high status in the kingdom.

I pestered the librarian to photocopy the page of ranks and that afternoon I rushed through the rain to Chris's house. We sat in his bedroom that evening and I dug the rumpled photocopy from my book bag and showed it to him.

"Dude, let's start an army," I said.

"Heck, yes!" he said.

We picked ranks—sergeants, like our stepdads—and that weekend we recruited one or two neighborhood kids, like Donald, who did Daffy Duck impressions, and a couple of the kids who palled around Chris's house under his mother's watch. Then we sprinted to the nearby slope that terraced our level of the neighborhood below the next and made our fort in a clump of old trees. Armies have forts and ours was somewhere between Liberty Street and Freedom Circle, but we were only able to guard it until the streetlights came on. During those hours, it felt like filling the vacuum left by everyone who had been sent overseas. We were the men now.

A group of kids formed another army around a set of twin brothers from up the street. They came down the slope one Saturday afternoon and were met with a shower of dirt clods from our fort that erupted into dust around their feet. Chris and I charged from the fort screaming with our troops and chased them down the long, flat top of the slope, hurling dirt clods at their hips and arms and narrow chests. Hard but not *hard*. Never at the face or the eyes. Never in the nuts. Almost never. They retreated into the woods, fleeing back to wherever they had come from. I took one last shot and pegged a kid in the back with a dirt clod and yelled gibberish that felt adult-profane and action-hero mean. Then our army gathered and cheered and retold the story about how we defended our little hill until the streetlights came on and we all had to go home for dinner.

Most of the airmen who had hung around our house blasting heavy metal and grilling hot dogs in our backyard had been sent overseas. Killer came by once or twice, but he was muted and solemn. Some just vanished, like Rye and Fly. Mainly I just hung out with Chris.

Time clicked. The Desert and the absence of my stepdad wrapped us in a soiled blanket. We moved through the monotony of daily routines—homework littered with fractions and mixed numbers; incomplete sentences; fighter jet drawings balled up at the bottom of my book bag. Dirty laundry sat in a pile and blue globs of toothpaste stuck to the bathroom sink. We recorded episodes of *Star Trek: The Next Generation* so they'd be ready for Alan once he returned. My mom played *Tetris* on his computer. I snuck spoons of German chocolate frosting from a can in the back of the kitchen cabinet. My stepdad loved German chocolate.

Everything in our house became a patchwork of concessions and alterations to the schedule and life we had known. Sometimes dinner was pared down to Domino's pizza, ham and turkey sandwiches with chips, or cans of Chef Boyardee at the dining room table. There was an undeniable sense of just making do. Just getting done what we could while we searched for the Other Side, wherever and whenever it may be. Don't complain, don't fret, just do it—your laundry, your homework, brush your teeth without being told, help with the dishes. Transgressions felt more personal, carried more import; I was jostling the already precarious equilibrium of our house. Despite that, though, there was a strange sense of calm, a mutual empathy for the emotional exhaustion we all felt. We knew we were all confused and hurting. We tried to give one another a break.

Yellow ribbons began appearing on cars and tacked to bulletin boards at school. Lee Greenwood's country tune "God Bless the U.S.A." found new life on the radio. We hummed it in the halls like a gospel hymn while our insides rotted from the waiting, the waiting through Halloween, through Thanksgiving, and into the snowy-gray slush of December. I spent my nights at Chris's. His mother took us to see *Ghost* and suddenly "Unchained Melody" portended love and loss in a way that made my guts feel weird. Then *Memphis Belle* came along and suddenly I wanted to bomb Nazis to ashes with my B-17 Flying Fortress. But I can't. I'm stuck on this base, in the snow, and lonely, and my stepdad—my *dad*—is gone and there is nothing I can do about it. I'm just a dumb kid. And so on clear nights before my mother comes home, I sit on the snow-covered slope between my house and Chris's and look down at all the blinking Christmas lights and amber streetlights and wish I were something else—maybe a fighter pilot, maybe a starship captain, maybe a submarine commander, maybe married to a beautiful girl, maybe just *grown*. But I wasn't any of those things. There were so many years left and plenty of maybes and everything seemed so far away and there was nothing I could do.

Our information was a bad blend of circumspection and rumor, all unfounded and unverifiable. I knew nothing. I had barely heard of Dick Cheney or Hosni Mubarak, Margaret Thatcher or Colin Powell, Tariq Aziz or Yitzhak Shamir. Our military world orbited around General H. Norman Schwarzkopf, "Stormin' Norman" as he was called, and he became the Hero King, our Grant/Pershing/Patton reincarnate. He was Our General, the Atlas who carried the stone burden of all our hopes. He was the man who we hoped would grind his American 11½-inch regular boot into the back of the Iraqis who shattered our families. Out of that hope burst a strange, hot fuel that pushed me past the flat Christmas morning when we opened presents with perfunctory movements and cheap estimations of childhood glee and then slid quietly into the New Year. The news was alive with one deadline: January 15, 1991, the day established by the United Nations for Iraq to pull its troops out of Kuwait or face military action. What that meant wasn't entirely clear, but a dim realization began to form as I listened to the Fighting Falcons take off from the runway and watched them fly on the nightly news. There would be no escaping it, no turning back. The fear of a wounded national pride far too often trumps the preservation of human lives. The Iraqis were not going to leave Kuwait. Battle was coming.

I stopped looking at the curve of the fuselage and the glint of sunlight on the canopy of the few Fighting Falcons that had remained behind. Instead, I flipped through books in the school library that showed the dull green bombs and white missiles that hung from their wings—the Mark 80 series bombs and the GBU laser-guided bombs, the Maverick missiles, and the 20 mm Vulcan six-barreled cannon that shoots off six thousand bullets per minute, each bullet larger than an adult thumb. There was the BLU-109, a long bomb with a one-inch-thick steel casing designed to penetrate bunkers and concrete aircraft revetments and annihilate whatever lived inside. Then there was the AIM-9 Sidewinder, the missile perched on the Falcon's wingtips and used to shoot enemy planes from the sky. The Mark 82 Rockeye II bomb was my favorite. When a Fighting Falcon cut one loose, it dropped to a certain height and opened like a clamshell, releasing two dozen bomblets the size of McDonald's Big Macs that crackled directly above the ground and spread shrapnel into vehicles and people. Even the name sounded cool—Rockeye II—like the sequel to an action movie I had yet to see but wanted to. These were the weapons I knew that would be tossed at the Iraqi army in the Desert. I knew they would hit hard. I knew that they would aim for the eyes. I knew they would go for the nuts. Inside me, I knew I wanted them to.

We called their dictator "Sad-dum" and "Insane Hussein." We looked at him like he was everything America wasn't. He wore a dictator's uniform and America didn't have dictators. Maybe his people had been our friends once, perhaps that was true, but our wounds and patriotic filters of history failed to allow us to see it. He had ordered the invasion of another country and that was *casus belli* enough in the eye of the American sense of fair play, regardless of any complicated desires to protect oil or the Kuwaitis or the Saudi royal family. Those details did not matter. We hated him and his soldiers and wanted them dead so that our moms and dads could come home and our kingdom be made whole again.

The days clicked toward the fifteenth, the deadline. Then it passed and the world seemed to go *Oooooooooo!* like a classroom poking fun at the kid caught passing a love note. Maybe it was all just one big joke. Had Sad-dum made a deal? Had Bush? We knew nothing and so we went to school and work and watched the news and MTV and waited.

The next day, I walked to Chris's house from school in the late afternoon. It was cold. I turned into a shortcut in a space between two rows of houses and saw Chris hustling down the snow-filled alley in his Chicago Bulls jacket.

"Dude, *come on!* Something's going on," he said. He breathed fast gouts of steam in the white afternoon. "They're getting *bombed.*"

We ran up the alley and burst through the front door of his house as his mother snapped at us to shed our wet boots. We tossed our jackets and gloves and book bags into a pile and clustered in the living room. The television beamed a special news report with live video of green tracers arching over the minarets of Baghdad. Iraqi antiaircraft fire clattered through the static between the frantic voices of Peter Arnett and Gary Shepard and their anchors in New

York. Once again, as if we were watching the movies my stepdad had rented on rainy Sunday afternoons, the television was our conduit to this world. Only this time it was real. The screen dazzled with pure white light as two-thousand-pound Red, White & Blue bombs struck the earth and showered fire across the center of Saddam's dictatorship. My skin tingled. My hair felt electrified. The war had begun! Our moms and dads were fighting it!

It felt like a release, an end to the months of building tension that had pressed down on me through fall and into the holidays. I lay in bed that night and imagined I was in the cockpit of a fighter jet over Baghdad, the green glow of the heads-up display dazzling my eyes as I "pickled" bombs into their bunkers and headquarters, as *ack-ack* glittered and popped around me. The next day, I bounded to school and we talked about it, about how cool it was to watch all the tracers and bombs on TV. Mr. Potter wheeled in a television and tuned into the news about the air battle over the desert. Then he told us stories about Korea, his eyes alight with an old proud fire. During recess, we played in the snow and pretended we were fighter pilots lining up to bomb bridges and tanks and Iraqi soldiers, hooting when we scored a hit, bellowing like men when the *ack-ack* tore our planes to shreds.

Every night for the next month, the television blasted images of fiery jet launches from aircraft carriers and grainy night-vision footage of stealth fighters gliding through the sky like death shrouds. Fighting Falcons, weighed down with green bombs with EAT SHIT AND DIE, SADDAM written in chalk along their curved drab flanks, taxied along desert runways. Grainy thermal imaging and bomb-nose cameras sent back ghoulish videos of all those bombs striking bunkers and bridges with the white heat signatures of hapless Iraqis standing about shooting the breeze just moments before their molecules were scattered across the cold ether. The howl of air raid sirens became the new Iraqi national anthem. A few weeks after the first bombings, my mom, sister, and I went to a Chinese restaurant in Riverdale.

A firehouse down the street began blasting its own air raid siren. I laughed. "It sounds like Baghdad," I said. My mom laughed too.

There were never any notions of failure or defeat. We had jets like the Aardvark and the Eagle, the Tomcat and the Hornet, the Warthog, the Prowler, and the Fighting Falcon. Big, strong names. Mean and American, just like the streets of our castle. *They* had cheap tin-can names like Fitter, Frogfoot, Flogger, and Foxbat, names that we gave them, names that made them out to be cretins, trolls, and cowards, and no one was surprised when they fled helter-skelter into Iran.

The war was filtered through eighties action flicks and the Pledge of Allegiance and "The Star-Spangled Banner" and commercials hawking Air Jordans, Mitchum deodorant, and Diet Pepsi. When our bombs fell, I imagined the bad guys were tossed from their sandbag bunkers in front of a burst of stuntman pyrotechnics—their arms flailing, their rifles tossed entirely in slow motion. Their bodies did not come apart. They just flew like olive-drab rag dolls, and when they landed, they were dead as if asleep with their eyes open. They died like I died on the playground or in the neighborhood when we played war and pantomimed action-hero manhood. Someone would say "bang" or "pow" and I would spin, eyes clenched, face to the sky, mouth wide in a Wilhelm scream, and fall dramatically into the snow. At ten years old, the Persian Gulf War sounded like Guns N' Roses' "Welcome to the Jungle." It sounded like Bon Jovi's "Wanted Dead or Alive." It sounded like the Clash's "Rock the Casbah." I listened to AC/DC's "For Those about to Rock" and "Thunderstruck" on the radio in my bedroom, chanting along with the pictures of fighter jets screaming across my mind.

I collected Desert Storm trading cards and thumbed through the pictures of machine guns and fighter jets. I watched Patriot missiles arc into the televised night sky like shooting stars on Scud-busting missions to save the helpless from despotic Stone Age rage while I ate popcorn from a big Tupperware bowl on the living room floor and imagined I was the man who launched the missile.

In late February, during the last hours of the hundred-hour ground offensive to liberate Kuwait, Stormin' Norman gave "the Mother of All News Conferences" before a bubbly international media. I listened as he told the story of this war as if our armies were outmanned underdogs able to outsmart the enemy only through guile and professionalism and outfight them with a bravery and aggression tuned beyond all comprehension. We had stomped them into the earth, crushed them beneath a righteous boot painted with crude yellow ribbons and American flags, like a child's cheek painted at a fairground on Independence Day. Our troops had "closed the gate," Schwarzkopf said. Everything that remained was trapped amid the Euphrates and its bombed bridges, the Iranian border, and the sweeping formations of allied tanks and armored vehicles barreling eastward. The Iraq-Kuwait border had become the Kill Box and anything inside that was capable of shooting was doomed.

Until now, I had never fully comprehended how big the American military was in terms of its reach and power—that it was massive and sharp and fast and that I could be a part of it someday. I listened, knowing the history was already written. The Iraqis had no chance in my mind. How could they beat *us*? No one beat our dads and our Fighting Falcons. It was impossible. Schwarzkopf was only verifying what I had already accepted and filed away as a cheap memory. We had won. We had won before we had even started. That is what I learned.

The snow melted until Hill was the color of dead grass. The snow on the peaks remained, but the sun warmed and hung in the sky a little longer each day. The first hints of spring were always my favorite time of year. My birthday came and left and then the rumors began in the school playground: "I think they'll be home before . . ." slipped to "I heard they'll be home after . . ." and then inevitably turned into a morose "I have no idea when they'll be home." My mother didn't indulge or pass along these rumors. Her own experiences as an airman and a child of the military steered her away from speculation and hearsay. Her general attitude was that no one in our caste inside the castle really knew anything, and the ones who truly did weren't saying. Not yet.

But finally, in late April, when the new grass had finally grown, she explained she might, she may, it's likely, probably, could very well wake my sister and me early some morning should the phone ring and she get word to pick Him up from someplace but that we shouldn't bank on it. Not yet. Because it still might not happen. But it also could. Maybe. And so I slept, confused but ambivalent, until one April weekday morning before sunrise my bedroom light snapped on and I awoke to see my mother standing in the open door with an expressionless face that faintly hid a tense backbeat of excitement and anxiousness.

"Dad's home."

Twenty minutes later, I stood bleary eyed in a dim holding room near the tarmac with sleepy kids and mothers and wives with makeup smeared across their faces. At some point, fathers and husbands were going to emerge from the transport plane with Arabian sand still tucked into the crevices of their boots, but we had hurried and now we had to wait. And wait. And wait longer, until finally they began to appear one by one.

Alan strutted into the holding area with his lanky jaunt and beaming face. My mother spotted him first and said, "There's Dad," and my face broke into a hard, red grin. Then he was with us, in our proximity, physical and touchable. His smell had returned. His young, fatherly gravitas filled the air around us. It was hard not to stare at him, to pester him with questions, or to talk endlessly to fill the minutes and hours and days, weeks, months, all the way back to the previous August when he was stolen until my mom finally said, "Jerad . . . hush."

My sister latched on to him. Sometimes he'd carry her in his arms, then set her down and let her doddle around his legs, but she never traveled farther away than the length of her tiny arms. We returned home soon after sunrise and my mother decided I could miss school that day. How could I go to school with my stepdad home, here, right here in the house, *in our house*?

Alan remained somewhat aloof, impassive. He was certainly weary from the long trip, but there was also a distance to him. His voice and his mannerisms were the same as before, but he felt separate, as if a small part of him had never seen us before and he didn't know what to say. I continued to pester him in the way a fifth grader might. He looked at me with soft but slightly pleading eyes beyond some need for a local respite and said, "Son . . . give me a bit." Finally my mom sanctioned his request—"Jerad . . . hush"—and ordered me to take my sister out to the front yard to play. Then she locked the front door behind us for the afternoon.

A few weeks later, my fifth-grade class was tapped to participate in a massive recital. Normally these things happened over Christmastime, when various teachers ran us through "Silent Night" and "Jingle Bells," which made us all groan with malaise until Christmas break finally freed us from its dumb pageantry. But this time, we would sing in tribute of all the troops who went to the Desert. Our class learned "America (My Country, 'Tis of Thee)," "America the Beautiful," "God Bless America," and finally "God Bless the U.S.A." by the Marlboro Man of cheap patriotism, Lee Greenwood. Instead of belting out these jams to a small pond of foldout chairs in our own cheap gymnasium, however, we would perform this for a cross section of the air force community on the main stage of the big high school just outside the air base—a complete theater with plush foldout seating, stage lighting, and an audio system. We rehearsed furiously. We wanted to be good.

When the time came, we were bused to the high school and sent to our assigned seats in the audience. The auditorium was packed with airmen from the base, many in uniform. Fathers and mothers filled the seats while teenagers ditched class and snickered as they watched through the gaps and narrow windows of the main doors. Our class was called forward and we marched to the stage and carefully filed onto the narrow metal benches of the foldout bleachers. The stage lights were warm. The audience was a blur of dark shapes. My stepdad was out there, but I wasn't sure where. The rising sounds of the first song echoed across the theater. Our conductor marked the tempo with her baton and we began to sing.

Many in the audience sang along with us. We didn't sing for the relief of Ethiopian famines or for Israeli-Palestinian peace or for the end of Apartheid. We didn't sing for the end of poverty or racism or sexism. Instead, we sang old songs that carried flags across battlefields and graves and the thousands of old bones of the Red, White & Victorious. Our prepubescent voices harmonized the exultations that only those who believe they are the Best can truly manage. We sang praise for our superpower victory over the forces of a tin-pot dictator seven thousand miles away. By the time we got to Lee Greenwood, we were in a state of evangelical euphoria, shouting with a rage as hot as the afterburner of a Fighting Falcon and the shrapnel of its cluster bombs. We sang like a warning and our voices reverberated throughout the theater and down the halls of the high school, through the bathroom cigarette smoke and the geek whiff of science lab ozone, out the big main doors and into the American springtime air, announcing that Iraq was at the center of our ire now and that we'd be at war with the Desert in our hearts forever.

My stepdad and I spent the rest of the year silently reconnecting over all the *Star Trek* we had recorded while he was away. He called it "Taped Space." On Friday and Saturday nights, while my mother worked a shift at a nursing home, he would pull out a tape, press play, and we would watch a few episodes in the dark living room. I would sit on the couch with a stack of crackers and my USS *Enterprise* toy next to me. He'd sit in his La-Z-Boy with his feet up and a Budweiser on the end table. Sometimes he'd poured an inch of beer into a mason jar and I drank it like a man. Having no taste for it yet, I wondered if I could feel the alcohol working. I'm still not supposed to tell Mom. Then in the morning he'd awaken me with the vacuum cleaner or the dog or Metallica at eighty decibels to the static of the idling of the Fighting Falcons out on the runway and their roar as they blasted into high orbit with their afterburners. Maybe after, I'd head down Freedom Circle to Chris's with another list of chevrons. Maybe it was time to start another army.

III

I had lots of toys—Micro Machines and Hot Wheels, Transformers and G.I. Joes. The Transformers almost always broke within a month or two; Joe's plastic guns got lost down the floor vents and the front lawn. LEGOs were popular until my stepdad stepped on a rigid plastic piece with his bare foot on my bedroom floor. I didn't have to throw them away, but I didn't get many more of them either. I also had a castle from the *He-Man and the Masters of the Universe* cartoons. Castle Grayskull was big and green and plastic and had the face of a skull with dark gray eyes molded on the front. It closed like a case and inside were red plastic levels for different floors and a cheap ladder for Skeletor and his minions to climb up and down when executing their various bad-guy plans.

Scale model kits of fighter jets were a big deal too. I would meander through the toy section at the Base Exchange and look through all the boxes, weighing the merits of one jet over another. If I received money at Christmas or on my birthday, I'd buy one and take it home and within an hour I'd have the instructions splayed out across the dining room table or on the carpet next to my bed and a crumpled tube of model cement in my hand. I was never patient, so the models rarely lasted, but whenever I finished a kit, I'd lay in bed and imagine slashing across enemy territory on a bombing run or shooting down Soviet-era planes.

Sometimes I didn't think I had enough toys, or the right toys, but I did. My parents were wary of Nintendos and Segas and didn't buy one until much later. They said it was for our own good, which is probably partially true, but I think, too, they didn't like the idea of it clogging up the living room television. As a result, I was always behind in the culture of cool in video games. I liked them, but I also sucked at them.

But if I couldn't shoot 8-bit bad guys on television, I always had my toy guns. My first one was black with a collapsible stock and a plastic foregrip that was painted to look like wood. It resembled a cross between an Uzi and a Thompson submachine gun. The tip of the barrel had an orange plug inserted inside it so cops would know it wasn't real. My family has a picture of me with it. I lived in Afterburner Alley then, and I stood with my purple Utah Jazz jacket unbuttoned and a thick mop of light brown hair on my head. It was a cloudy day and the flight line far behind me was quiet. I held the toy gun level at my waist—one hand on the pistol grip, the other on the foregrip. My expression was mischievous and cheeky.

It was easy to wrap my fingers around the pistol grip. The gun was electric, and as long as there was a battery inside, a rattling mechanism made popping sounds whenever I pulled the trigger. Once the first battery was used up, however, I spent most of the time yelling the required "boom" and "pow" and "bang." Sometimes I yelled them before the battery ran out too. I played with that gun every time I saw one on television—whenever Arnold Schwarzenegger killed Latin American mercenaries in *Commando* or battled communists and a man-hunting alien in *Predator*. "Ol' Painless is waitin'," Jesse Ventura said as he stalked through the jungle with an absurd minigun in his hands.

Later, I got a blue-green pistol that looked like a German Luger. It was made from cheap molded plastic and when I pulled the trigger, a spring-loaded gear made clicking sounds based on how fast I pulled it. If I pulled it quickly, the clicking blurred into a whirring.

I didn't play with that pistol much; it was boring. I usually passed it off to another kid whenever we decided to "play guns" around the neighborhood. Eventually the rubber band inside broke and it wouldn't make noise anymore.

I had a submachine gun too. It was orange and black and clattered strongly. It was well made and lasted through a thousand deaths until finally, when bored one afternoon, I tore it apart so I could play with the noisemaker inside.

I also had a cap gun. It was black with fake-wood handgrips and shaped like a snub-nosed .38 caliber revolver. The pistol swung open at the top to load the cylinder. The cylinder was metal, and when I could get them, I placed red rings lined with tiny powder charges onto the cylinder, and when I pulled the trigger, it popped like a real pistol, complete with a spark and a small puff of smoke that smelled like we thought gunpowder should smell. It had an orange plug in the barrel, just like all the others. Sometimes it was fun to make the caps go off by striking rocks against them or just ignite them with a magnifying glass.

But my favorite was a plastic M-16 rifle. It was on sale at Walmart and I'd begged my stepdad to take me to buy it after I received Christmas money from a relative. It was blue and made a similar clicking sound to my cheap blue-green pistol. It seemed sturdier than the others, but I found out it wasn't. While charging through some fantasyland neighborhood battle, I tripped and the barrel jammed into the dirt, splitting the rifle right at the center. I tried to glue and tape it back together, but it never held for very long. Glumly, I tossed it into the aluminum trash cans in our carport.

I knew my parents had guns. The real kind. Alan had a long-nosed .44 caliber Ruger and a .357 Magnum. I had seen both whenever he cleaned them and in family pictures. In one picture he was dressed in a rock T-shirt and jeans, and he held the Ruger straight out with both arms, aiming at some imaginary villain. In another, he had his arms crossed in front of him, a pistol in each hand. I liked to look at the pictures because he had the guns and I thought he looked badass cool. I knew his guns were somewhere in my parents' bedroom tucked away in their nightstands and in the closet, but I was too terrified to seek them out. I wasn't terrified of the guns; I was terrified of what my parents would do if they caught me holding one of them.

One summer, before the war, when I was eight or nine, we took a family road trip across the country to Alan's father's home in northern Georgia. His dad set up a target in the pine trees near the house and handed me a .22 caliber rifle. The bullets had seemed small and unimpressive as he inserted them into the weapon. After he finished loading, I put the rifle to my shoulder. The wood stock felt warm in my hand. I fired shots at the target and it was fun to have the weapon buck lightly against my shoulder. Afterward, I was given a chance to shoot Alan's .357 Magnum. Those bullets were long and aggressive and slid into the cylinder in a way that suggested a certain deadly refinement. When I held it in my hand, its weight seemed like pure American authority. I fired all six shots, each drop of the Magnum's hammer causing the weapon to kick against the palm of my hand. It felt mean and manly; it felt grown up. I sensed something primal in it, a power at the end of my thin arms, and with it in my hands, I believed I was bigger—a vindicator, a protector, a soldier, a gunfighter, an action hero, the idea of an American. After I fired my six shots, my stepdad brought out his .44 caliber revolver. He stood tall and lean, the big cannon in both hands, and fired six controlled shots. Holes nearly the size of dimes appeared in the target tree each time. A slab of bark fell from its flanks. Each shot roared across the woods in a cacophony of aggression that was scary and visceral and wonderful. When we finished shooting, my ears rang.

In late spring, the year after Alan returned from the Middle East, a pair of air force security policemen parked a Humvee on the grass near a small convenience store on the base. A sleek black machine gun had been mounted to the Humvee turret and the airmen were letting children fire off blanks. I learned about it when a few neighborhood kids strutted past my house like afterschool *pistoleros*, flaunting belts of shell casings that drooped from their narrow bodies.

I begged my mother until she agreed to drive me to the Humvee. A thick energy built in my stomach and tightened my throat as we got closer and I began to hear the machine gun hammering off blanks with bursts of short, hard popping until *BOOM!* I saw the gun on the top of the Humvee, bucking against the shoulder of some kid. As soon as we parked, I bolted from the car and dashed across the parking lot to the Humvee, with my mother hollering to watch for traffic. I jumped over the curb onto the neatly manicured grass and stopped at the Humvee.

One bored airman smoked a cigarette in the driver's seat with the door open. The second airman stood in the turret helping children properly hold the machine gun and brush out the spent brass and black links that piled up inside the cabin below the gun to the grass. Kids who had already taken their turn sat in the grass reassembling the brass and links into belts as souvenirs.

The boy ahead of me was too small to stand on the large ammunition can and reach the buttstock and trigger, so his mother perched inside the Humvee and helped the airman hold her boy so he could shoot. After a moment of awkward wrangling—the airman inevitably had to hold the boy up by his armpits—the kid squeezed off a five- or six-round burst that hammered against my eardrums with an addictive reverb.

I vibrated as the kid was lowered into the cab and allowed to crawl out of the Humvee to the grass. His face was a punch-drunk mask of awe and bewilderment. I quickly stepped around him and climbed up, concerned about appearing like a pro at climbing into a Humvee and not some neophyte twelve-year-old. The airman in the turret was young. He spoke with a thin, practiced veneer of patience and good humor, like a threadbare checkout clerk at a grocery store.

Undoubtedly, he would have been happier back in the barracks cleaning up for a night in town or a drunken springtime barbecue than tending to a gaggle of children and their mothers.

I stepped onto the ammunition can, my right shoulder against the buttstock of the machine gun. The gun smelled like hot metal, gun oil, and the ozone fragrance of burnt propellant. A belt of blanks draped down from the left side of the gun to a second ammunition can that sat on a flat mount.

I wrapped my hand around the thick black pistol grip. The airman instructed me to place my left hand over the top of the buttstock, press my right cheek into the stock just behind my hand, and aim down the sights. I looked down the length of the weapon. The gun was locked into a fixed position. It was aimed at an arbitrary car in the parking lot across the street: a dusty white Honda.

"Whenever you're ready, dude," the airman said. I was nervous, but I rested my finger against the cool black trigger. I pulled it.

The gun chattered a half-dozen times—two, maybe three, seconds. It happened so quickly I barely registered it beating against my shoulder and cheekbone, or the subtle flames that burst from the end of the barrel, or the smoke that drifted from beneath the feed tray cover that held down the belt of brass blanks. It was like something had grabbed me by the shoulders and violently rattled the change from my pockets for one hard moment. Once it was over, I slowly peeled myself from the machine gun. My right shoulder throbbed slightly, but I felt no pain. My cheekbone tingled.

"*Cool*," was all I managed.

The airmen told me to climb down. A new kid waited below. My knees rattled from the thrill of shooting the big gun. As I lowered myself into the cabin, a spent cartridge rolled my foot underneath me, and before I could catch myself, I slammed my knee on the steel floor beneath the turret. I sucked wind between my teeth but refused to cry out or wince or show anything other than simple soldier-like toughness. I gnashed my teeth. There is no pain tolerated around machine guns.

I climbed out of the Humvee, hiding my limp as best as I could. I sat on the ground and began to press together my own belt of spent cartridges. The brass was tough and smooth and it took some effort to press the cartridges into the stiff black links. After I had assembled a belt around eighteen inches long, I climbed into the car with my cheek still tingling and the sound of the machine gun barking as more children arrived. Word had gotten around and they had begun to line up, all staring up at the big black machine gun with electric eyes.

Three months later, I left Utah and never returned.

BRAVO

A man becomes the creature of his uniform.

—Napoleon Bonaparte

Cory names the hooch "the Chateau" after a resort he'd visited in Pennsylvania. He says his father-in-law took him there once, where they gambled and got drunk. He tells me this as he smokes one of my cigarettes on a crumbling plastic lawn chair out in front of the Chateau under the remains of camouflage netting that has been tied to the roof and draped wide over the gravel porch.

The Chateau is a long, wooden hut at a forward-operating base built on top of an old train depot that once managed the logistics for the nearby fertilizer and cement factories. Links of freight cars rust in long lines in the center of the camp, the rotting detritus of Iraqi infrastructure. The navy chaplain holds services in an abandoned passenger car. Saddam's Scud missiles once launched near here at Israel during the last war. Now, Rebel Six and his staff commiserate over cigars on an officers-only slab of concrete next to the old administrators' building surrounded by barbed wire. Marine mechanics fix their trucks in the massive bay once used to repair rail cars and engines. Medevac helicopters sit in a hollow near the Chateau, and when they take off in the middle of the night to pick up casualties, their rotors shake loose the dust into a thin haze.

There are nine of us in the Chateau, but the three men from the intelligence section don't hang out with us much. Instead, it's just Cory and his team— the double-jointed sophisticate who wears a Scottish driving cap and smokes a big pipe; the former army airborne soldier turned Marine grunt *who laughs as if suffering through a seizure; the quiet older man who plays fantasy games on a laptop in his bunk at night, and the cherubic lance corporal who jokes of stabbing terrorists with his bayonet affixed to the barrel of his rifle. And me next to Cory, propelled to the war by my own history and its form of the American Dream.*

The Chateau is a refuge. After the firefight at the water tower, I find them holding court and bitching and talking shit and playing video games. It's night and early autumn and this far up the Euphrates River, near Syria, the stars band the sky in a cool smear. It's pleasant and after chow we cluster on the plastic chairs with mugs of powdered hot chocolate stolen from the mess hall. We pass rumors about the war, like the one about Rebel Six ordering airstrikes on the bridges over the river, and we don't know if it's to keep insurgents from flowing into the valley from the north or to keep them from fleeing so we can kill them. These are small rumors, relatively meaningless, but there are bigger ones, like the rumors of street battles that might be coming in a matter of weeks or days, and as we pass them around, they deaden the air.

The urban areas in the river valley are largely empty of Americans, a result of overtaxed resources in an underestimated war and reinforced by antioccupation violence. Before coming, I had heard stories of bomb factories, of houses where humans were tortured and eviscerated as heathens and apostates. The Marines conducted two large operations around Ubaydi and Karabilah the previous spring. Some were killed in heinous ways, like the men who died in a horrible fuel fire when their armored vehicle detonated a massive bomb beneath it. I know of a man from that blast; I know that he is alive in a hospital somewhere in America with most of his body torched to a blistered mass. I know a staff sergeant who was shot dead in a building not far from where I took mortar and rifle fire on the last day of summer. And the corporal who smothered an insurgent hand grenade with his helmet to save his friends just a few kilometers away? He survived, but the concussion destroyed his brain. He lived for eight more days, just long enough to get back to the States.

Years later, they'll hand the man's family a Medal of Honor and name a navy destroyer after him.

The valley feels like a blot of anger and death. A pair of American outposts, one directly on the border and one in the desert near a highway crossroads, are mortared and sniped at routinely. To say we are not welcome is an understatement. We are not wanted by the villains of our own war movie for reasons we can only assume conflict with our own storybook values. But these things matter little to us. We know we will go into the valley, and when we do, we will do so loudly and violently and with dumb mirth because we are Marines. But before we do, we'll make more hot cocoa and play Ghost Recon and Halo and watch Chappelle's Show and wait for our mail to catch up to us. We don't dare pine for home, not yet, but we'll trade emails with girlfriends and wives and imagine we can sustain these relationships in a vacuum for seven months. We watch the news as Hurricane Katrina destroys New Orleans. I know that Erin is there helping look for bodies in the wreckage of nature and neglect. I know that she would rather be in Iraq with the infantry. We are Marines.

While we wait, the cherubic lance corporal talks about killing hajjis and we laugh at his youth. Cory and I make Airborne-Marine double over with fits of boyish laughter so we can laugh, too, as the double-jointed Sophisticate smokes his gaudy pipe and affects a Sean Connery accent and the quiet old man inside loses himself in sorcery and spells. After a time, we stub out our cigarettes and dump our cocoa dregs to the gravel and climb into our dusty racks, and as I lie in my rack, I hope the Black Hawks don't get called out into the night and erupt the Chateau into a fog of wheezy dust as a nightmare reminder of the valley on the other side of the low hills.

This Chateau will not be our last. There will be another in a few weeks, maybe a month. Rebel Six will kick us out of this Chateau to make way for a tank platoon that arrives for the coming offensive. He'll do this across the camp. Some will say he's doing this to anger us before turning us loose on the insurgents in the valley, to keep us frustrated at the Marine Corps and its pettiness. We will build the new Chateau in a hidden space in the back of the massive supply warehouse from wood we pilfer around the base. It will sit on a concrete slab, and when the rains come, the mud-packed drainage system will overflow brown rainwater across the floor and it will be a wonder we aren't electrocuted by the strings of extension cords that run through it. The supply Marines will blast the Beach Boys at top volume throughout the day, to levels beyond absurdity. It will be a cold place, devoid of the coziness of the first Chateau, the cocoa and the stars. But we make it a home, or at least a shelter from the war, as best as we can. The cherubic lance corporal will spend the tour without firing a shot from his prized rifle and Airborne-Marine will be branded a coward. Sophisticate will pine for the end of his tour above everything else and the old man will remain static behind his computer. Somewhere in there, Cory will lose his wife and I will shoot at human beings, but in our own ways, in ways little and big, we asked for this.

IV

I was a kid raised by my mom and two dads. Stepdads and stepmoms were routine around the base. Officers' kids never seem to have these problems, but I never bothered to wonder why. Like Luke, a kid Chris sometimes hung around with, who lived in a large house with a basement where he used to watch laser discs on a massive television. Luke had brand new roller blades and Air Jordans. His father was an older man, lean and weathered, and he had LT. COL. in front of his name above his mailbox, the abbreviation for "lieutenant colonel." I knew that because my stepdad did not have LT. COL. on our mailbox, I had better tread lightly or else he might have to answer to Luke's dad, like kids answering to the principal. When he spoke to us, which was rare, it was with a quiet authority and breeding and inner dignity that suggested he knew his power and expected us to know it too. We didn't go to Luke's house often. I was never sure if that was his intention or ours.

A month before my stepdad came home from the Desert, in 1991, a neighborhood kid held a birthday party at a Chuck E. Cheese off the base. When we pulled into the parking lot, Chris and Luke and I and a few other kids dashed from the side door of his family's Chevy Astro in a tornado of screams and howls, barreling toward the glass front door of the restaurant like arcade Visigoths ready to lay waste to pepperoni pizzas and the current high scores on *After Burner* and *Galaga*.

We sang "Happy Birthday" and ate cake as the birthday girl, someone I didn't know well, opened presents at the far end of the table. Afterward, we pumped the adults for quarters and paddled the big buttons on the video games until they said "Game Over," and then we jammed our fingers into the returned change slots, hoping in vain to kill more bad guys with an Uzi in *Operation Wolf*. Broke, we glumly huddled around Chris as he battled his way, slack jawed, through a few levels of *Rush'n Attack*. Finally, with all the quarters spent and not a high score conquered, we piled back into the Astro and cruised home. But it was midafternoon and sunny, so we burned off the energy playing in the field between our houses.

After an hour or so, Chris's mother stepped outside. My mom had called her. I needed to head home.

I mumbled a quick goodbye and took off at a trot. Something must have gone wrong. I made a quick mental scan of my room—I had made the bed that morning, none of my toys were out, or at least on the floor where she could step on them. Or were they? I couldn't remember. I also wondered if Alan was okay. The Gulf War might have been over, but he was still in the Desert, waiting to come home.

The front door was open behind the screen door. I could hear the television in the living room. I opened the door carefully, cringing at the harsh creak of the hinges and the hiss of the hydraulic arm. I wiped my shoes on the welcome mat and stepped into the house.

"Jerad?" my mom called out. Her voice was calm.

"Yes?" I said softly.

She was in the La-Z-Boy in the living room, watching TV.

"Go pack a bag," she said. "Your dad's here."

My eyes widened. The sunlight that beamed through the sliding glass door of the dining room grew in warmth and brightness. The air took on a static charge and the tiny hairs on my arms stood. Blood rushed into my veins. My insides quaked. *My dad is in town! My real dad! He's here!*

I dumped the school-day nonsense from my book bag—balled-up fighter jet drawings and division homework—and crammed it with shirts and pants and socks.

"Don't forget your toothbrush," my mom called from the living room. I snatched my toothbrush and my comb and shoved them in the bag, too, then sat with my bag in the lounger and silently watched *The Phil Donahue Show* on the bulbous screen of our Zenith television. But not watching it, not really. My mind was far too frenetic, shoved with far too many endorphins of anticipation to focus on any one thing. Everything around me suddenly seemed too slow, too old, too worn, too exhausted. I struggled to sit still. Everything that was coming would be an endless barrage of high-octane adjectives—cool, incredible, dope, amazing—and at some point, in the next thirty minutes, maybe less, hopefully not more, it would begin. I waited to hear the sound of a car door on the street, to hear the doorbell. The minutes on the VCR ticked one by one, the colon blinking off and on between the digits. Somewhere out there in the next fifteen minutes or maybe forever was a world of excitement, of movement, of speed, of sitting in the front seat fast and free, blasting down the interstate with my dad, hustling, living, breathing some other life and maybe a future too. *How many more minutes? How much longer? It should be soon. It has to be! Where—*

BINGBONG.

Boom! I sprang from the lounger with my bag tossed over my shoulder and bolted for the front door. I could see him through the screen, in the shadow of the carport. My dad! Standing tall in jeans just on the other side of the threshold. I burst through the door and wrapped my arms around his legs and smelled his aftershave. My dad! He's a character who lives behind a fog far out west, in California, but he's also a hero who airlines into my life and whisks me away and now he is here and nothing else matters. *My dad!*

After some pleasant but stiff talk between my mom and him about when I'd be returned home, I sprinted across the front lawn to the curb where his rental car was parked. He had a different car every time. This time it was a Mitsubishi Montero, complete with a compass on the dashboard. He opened the door and I climbed into the front seat. My insides felt as if they were vibrating. He started the motor.

"You know what the fastest car in the world is?" my dad asked.

"A Lamborghini?"

"Nope," he said with a smile. He put on his shades and dropped the shifter into gear.

"A rental car."

Blast off!

My father spent a decade in the air force, first as a boom operator in an aerial refueling tanker, a big commercial airliner built to gas up fighter jets as they flew at twenty-five thousand feet. In the late seventies, before I was born, he refueled F-14 Tomcats, the kind of jets Maverick flew in *Top Gun*, that the United States had sold to Iran just before the Islamic Revolution sent the shah fleeing into exile. Soon after, my dad became an air traffic controller and was assigned, along with my mother and me, to Hill where he worked in the control tower that gave the Fighting Falcons permission to take off and land from the sprawling runway. But the air force sent my dad to an air base in Korea for a yearlong deployment, right at the beginning of my childhood. I was too young to have any memories of that time, but it wasn't long after he returned that my parents divorced. His absence might not have been the singular reason, but it undoubtedly contributed.

After they divorced, he was assigned to an air base outside Merced, in central California. I lived with him for nearly a year, but a pair of incidents ended our time together. First, I fell out of bed and fractured my collar bone and for a few weeks I struggled with an awkward brace around my upper body. The second incident came late one evening a few months later. My dad sent me to bed before sunset, but I awoke and quickly realized he was gone. I had no idea where he went, but I wasn't scared. I was, however, concerned about a missing *Star Wars* toy pistol I thought I had left somewhere outside. With no one to stop me, I went out the front door and spent some time walking around the apartment complex in search of my toy, until at some point in the night I was taken in by the folks in the leasing office and handed off to child protective services.

I spent the next few weeks in foster care at an old house somewhere outside Merced while my dad—and my mother, as she still retained legal custody of me—navigated the California judicial and child protective systems to free me. I remember it was a worn place with a dirt lawn, rough hewn and without warmth. There was a mechanical unfriendliness to the house, with my foster family pantomiming the motions of nurturing with all the skill of washed-up actors. It felt like they believed they were doing me a favor by boarding me at some great expense. Once I was released, my mother demanded that I be returned to her. Whatever plan she had for her own air force career was hiccupped, perhaps terminally, by my father's immaturity. I learned later he had gone to a party. I was somewhere between three and four years old.

My dad left the air force soon after. In 1981, air traffic controllers with the Federal Aviation Administration had gone on nationwide strike for better hours and wages, effectively disrupting US air travel. For their trouble, more than eleven thousand strikers were fired by the Reagan Administration, for life. My dad, once he left the air force a few years later, and thousands of others were hired by the FAA to fill the void and he was assigned to the large air traffic control center in Palmdale, California, in the desert north of Los Angeles.

In the years after he returned me to my mother, he came and went into my life like a spirit pushed forward on the breeze of a passing airliner. He would appear in town around my birthday or Christmas, stay for a few days, and then drift back to California again. My mother had full custody of me and visitations were entirely voluntary and dependent on her whims, which were forgiving. If he came into town and it didn't conflict with my schooling, he was allowed to take me for the weekend, sometimes longer. Once we spent more than a week together when he flew me to visit my grandmother and two uncles in the rural town in southwest Oklahoma where he was from. When we weren't together, he always made sure to send cards and presents. He called regularly.

He had dark brown eyes and hair, like me. He had thin wrists and large hands like me too. He was a bachelor. He rode motorcycles but not Harleys. He listened to rock but not hair metal—Rush and CSNY, mainly. America and Grand Funk Railroad. He wore a dark mustache, and whenever I saw *Magnum P.I.* on television, Tom Selleck reminded me of my dad. I pictured him in California living a sun-kissed life—lots of parties and concerts, cool evenings on the Ventura Freeway listening to Steely Dan, beautiful tan women with blonde hair, like in all the music videos I had seen. He seemed to carry a sense of quiet freedom shaped by the New Age wistfulness of the old California counterculture.

I called him my *real* dad. A way of separating them, drawing a needless line between biology and love.

After we blasted from my house on Hill, we sped south down Interstate 15. Once we rounded the curve of the highway past the ridges south of North Salt Lake, the glittering skyline of Salt Lake City came into view against the backdrop of the Wasatch Mountains. We checked into a hotel and he let me watch what I wanted on the television, even hold the remote. Everything with my dad was a novelty—a weekend of constant firsts, even if they truly weren't. He was in town for me and me alone. I didn't have to share him. I could talk about school and girls and bullies in ways I never could at home. I was the singular focus of his attention and I took advantage of it, speaking incessantly about *Star Trek* and fighter bombers, of music on the radio.

"Here," he said from his bed, handing me a set of headphones from his Walkman. "Listen to this. It just came out."

I put them on and he pressed play. The first chords of "Silent Lucidity" by Queensrÿche began to play. I listened through the song, amazed by it for its own merit and also because it was new and my dad had thought enough of me to let me hear it on his Walkman.

"I'm trying to learn to play it on guitar," he said. *My dad!*

Later, we went to the movies and he let me pick. We watched US Navy pilots go against regulations and bomb Hanoi in *Flight of the Intruder* and then he bought Wendy's and we sped up to the heights to the north and ate hamburgers and french fries while looking down at Capitol Hill, Greater Avenues, Downtown, and Central City, the shiny postmodern reaches of One Utah Center, and the bronze Eagle Gate Tower. The capitol sat directly below us, but its light was cowed by the opulence of the Mormon Tabernacle and the gleaming Salt Lake Temple. Afterward, we returned to the hotel and fell asleep to late-night TV and the hum of the air conditioner.

I awoke the next morning to the whine of a blow-dryer. The hotel room smelled like aftershave and aerosol deodorant. He clicked off the blow-dryer. "Ready to go, bud?"

I climbed out of bed and dressed and brushed my teeth and ran a wet comb through my hair. It was Saturday. There was no time for anything more, no tomorrow, not when you're eleven. We piled into his rental and sped to a nearby Denny's and I ate a big pile of pancakes soaked in syrup, flanked by scrambled eggs and bacon and washed down with orange juice, while my dad ate a Denver omelet and drank coffee. My dad asked me about school, if it was going well. I said it was. He paid for everything with a green Amex card with a Roman centurion in the center, just like I had seen on the commercials. I asked him if I could hold it and he said sure and handed it to me after the waitress returned it. I had never held one before. It was tough, official; it held the gravity of freedom in the raised silver numbers and I knew those numbers would get me something cool today.

We drove across town to the Children's Museum of Utah and we spent the morning brushing the sand from fake dinosaur bones and watching blue-and-purple lightning seek our skin as we pressed our fingertips onto the glass spheres of plasma lamps. The complete cockpit of a jetliner was housed in the far back of the museum and I climbed inside and sat in the pilot's seat while my dad took on the role of copilot. He pointed out switches and dials; showed me how the flaps worked and how the throttle quadrant moved. Then we pretended to go on a bombing mission over North Vietnam, just like Lieutenant Jake "Cool Hand" Grafton and Lieutenant Commander Virgil Cole in the movie we had seen the night before. Finally, we pretended to crash and bailed out when a new group of kids wanted a shot at the controls.

Time fired. Everything became too fast and breathless. I was running constantly. I felt every minute needed to be packed with something, anything: adventure, motion, speed—a desperate attempt to burn every minute into memories. My dad was here, now, and tomorrow we would drive back to the base and everything would end terribly.

We walked the five floors of the Crossroads Mall, sifting through the shelves at the bookstore and flipping through the tapes and CDs at the music shop. I aimed us toward the Toys "R" Us, pretending to stumble upon it as if by accident. I ran through the shelves and fell upon the model kits, quietly scanning the flanks of the boxes—past the Fighting Falcons and Tomcats, the Flying Fortress and Mitchell bombers, the Hind and Cobra helicopters, all the dumb Corvettes and Mustangs and trucks. My eyes ran wide, but I dulled them with a veneer of practiced calm over the spaceships—the USS *Enterprise*, the *Millennium Falcon*, the Star Destroyer, and all the sci-fi fantasies between them. If he understood this game, this transaction, he played his role with just as much practice as I played out my hidden desires. I settled on a large model of a Klingon battle cruiser and marveled over the box cover, careful to conceal my avarice.

"This one is pretty cool," I said.

My dad looked down at it. "Yeah, that's not bad."

The air hung silently between us.

"I wonder what this would look like on my dresser. It's probably pretty cool to build. I love the way it looked in the movie," I said, testing.

"It might be kinda big, don't you think?" my dad said.

"Naw. It'd fit just fine," I replied, trying to keep my voice even.

A mom walked past with her daughter. My dad's eyes followed the mom for a moment with a look I was only beginning to understand. Once she was gone, he turned back to me. I kept looking down at the box cover. I wanted the model and I was holding time hostage. It was a negotiation tactic I had learned through many of these visits. He did not want to disappoint. He was my dad.

"Want to go watch a movie?"

"That's cool," I said. I lifted the model a little higher. "Can I take this with me?"

Back at the hotel room that night, we sat on our beds with a Toys "R" Us bag between us and ate pizza. I mimicked the way he folded the slices of pizza in half with his fingers. He told me he knew a lot of the spots in Los Angeles where movies were shot. He told me of one or two celebrities he had seen while hanging out in Hollywood, but I didn't recognize their names. He told me there was great camping in the mountains and he told me he liked to ride his motorcycle around the desert and I pictured him taking the curves with the wind whipping around him, a hazy image built from Hollywood clichés.

I knew this man was my dad and that when he came into town he bought me things. I knew he didn't like it when he found out I also called Alan "Dad." But he wasn't in my house and I was a kid and didn't have any real choice. I also loved Alan and didn't want to hurt him. I knew my dad didn't like my mom much; I understood that in the way I understood I was a child with love split three ways by the chasm of divorce—a state I couldn't yet grasp as a concept any more than I could grasp the Bernoulli's principle that kept fighters jets in the sky.

Both my dads held equal fealty in my mind and heart. But I rarely spoke about one in the presence of another. To do so seemed like a betrayal. Alan had direct access to my upbringing, the formation of my values and beliefs and attitudes toward the world, but he did not have access to my past or my lineage or even the chemical makeup of my being. Those keys belonged to my father, regardless of how removed he might have been to the gristle of my daily life. Those keys are, in part, what started the ignition inside me once my mother looked at me and told me was coming to pick me up.

Sunday morning came just as Saturday had, but clouds covered the valley in a slate of gray doom. Somewhere out there was an airliner on its way to the airport and in a few hours it would lift off again with my dad inside it to take him back to California, to his life. But I would not be on it. I would be home, in my bedroom, with school waiting for me in the morning.

We ate breakfast quietly. We were in no rush, but the trip was expiring and soon he would have to aim the rental car north, back toward the apartment he once shared with my mother and me when I was little. Then he would make the turn into the base and navigate me past the flight line and the hangars, the control tower where he had once worked, then onto base housing and into the life he stole into on holidays and birthdays and the odd weekend. Every moment revealed a growing desperation within me as I clung to the remnants of energy that had coursed through us the past thirty-six hours. I felt smaller, more diminutive, my courage melting into my sneakers and soaking the heels of my socks. As we wove through the mountains, behind the big peaks that dominated the landscape of my home, an ugly tension built inside me that swelled in hard pulses and made me sag in the front passenger's seat. As we joined the interstate and began the final push toward Hill, all the landmarks that made up my life looked shoddy and used and I wanted all of them to blow into the Great Salt Lake and calcify like the bones of all the dinosaurs sure to be buried under the lakebed. By the time we reached the air base, the tension had become unbearable and I began to cry—simply, just quiet sniffles, and I felt guilty over it. I knew it wasn't fair to be sad. My dad was here, he had come to see me, had traveled all that way, had bought me things, but I was sad anyway and crying.

"You okay over there?" he asked.

"Yeah," I managed.

"What's wrong?"

I gave up my usual response to questions too hard for me to answer or rationalize or even accept. I gave him the child's answer: "I don't know."

V

The cells of the American military, the average servicemembers, are in a state of constant geographic flux, tethered to the country by their uniforms and the towns and counties that had raised them. No one place is permanent. From the moment an individual is sworn in, their home becomes the camps, forts, ports, and air bases scattered across the world. The stops in a military career are just waypoints across the expanse of the empire; its residents, the temporal characters riding the spearheads of foreign and national defense policies and the whims of generals and bureaucrats. On the edges of its empire, America becomes a separate entity, a physical and spiritual object regarded and revered, dubiously or otherwise, as a beacon of patriotic nouns—liberty, freedom, justice, democracy, and so on. Our homes abroad are the outposts of American exceptionalism.

Alan was due for an assignment to another base and suddenly everything we had built in Utah became meaningless. I had finished elementary school and would now walk into an unfamiliar middle school with an entirely new set of faces and personalities. Our time at Hill would soon be relegated to old stories and fading memories. Friends drifted into the background. Chris and his family moved away suddenly; I never learned why. My mom told me Chris had left a letter for me. I looked everywhere, but I never found it.

My family had no idea where we would be assigned. There was brief talk of Hawaii, but none of us believed it. Hawaii was far too coveted to be taken seriously. For a few months, we were slated for an air base in Germany, but the military machinery jerked that rug from beneath our feet, marking that air base for closure instead. Finally, the military settled on Japan.

We began to dismantle our house. We found a new home for Mitzy and Rotzy, the family dogs, and we sold the cars and the furniture. The bed frames went one day, the couch the next. The La-Z-Boy vanished, so did the lounger. I packed my things—my belt of spent machine-gun cartridges, my books of World War II aircraft, my *Star Trek* novels, my Gulf War trading cards and the *Time* magazine insert of the military defenses of Iraq that my granddad Don had sent me. My Klingon battle cruiser was boxed up with my fighter jets and a big, long submarine, then taped and marked with my name, all to be shipped overseas. Finally, we left our house on Liberty Street and vanished from Hill Air Force Base. But the air force filled the vacuum, as it always did—there were new families with new kids, new parties and hillside battles and trips to Chuck E. Cheese under the whine of the Fighting Falcons.

I saw my dad on a brief layover in Los Angeles. We ate hamburgers quietly on a stone table in Santa Monica. I was leaving the country for three years. He did not know when in those three years he would see me again, if at all. He told me he felt wronged by it. It seemed unfair for him to tell me that, to level that burden on me as if I had any agency in the decisions the US military issued for me by way of my stepdad. I also understood the injustice he must have felt, but there was nothing either of us could do. I wasn't even sure I wanted anything to be done. He took me back to LAX and I met my mother in the bright California terminal and boarded the plane and left the United States.

We landed in Japan twelve hours later, long after sundown, and made our way through the terminal at Narita International Airport, outside Tokyo. As much as I remember the terminal at LAX, I recall nothing of those first few minutes dashing through the Narita airport. The time it took to get us through customs and past the duty-free shops and kiosks and newsstands registered in my internal recorder as little more than static. The recorder didn't pick up until we boarded a shuttle bus to take us to Yokota Air Base, en route to our final destination. But even my memory here is hazy—just flashes of staring out the window into the darkness and seeing the glow of Tokyo on the far horizon. I remember we checked into the military hotel on the air base and had only a few hours to sleep.

The next morning, we boarded a large gray air force cargo plane with two big propeller engines on each wing. We climbed through the small side door onto the rough metal deck with two dozen other families and traveling airmen and sat down on the narrow seats surrounded by pipes and hydraulic lines and switchboxes that lined the bulkhead of the plane. "They're called jump seats," my mother said.

Our luggage was strapped tightly to the metal deck. A crew chief with a pockmarked face and dressed in a flight suit passed out foam earplugs and I wondered if this was what it was like to go to war—loaded onto a gray transport and shuttled like men to fight. The big engines cranked to life and moved the propellers until they roared in a piercing sustained throb. For the next hour or so, my mom tried to manage her airsickness as the transport bobbed through the clouds and we bounced on the red webbing of our jump seats. Eventually, the plane descended and gently touched down at Misawa Air Base near the far northeast corner of Honshu. When the narrow hatch opened on the flank of the plane, we stepped out single file into a cool afternoon sun, the clouds having broken after a late-summer rainstorm. We walked into the air terminal where Alan waited, and at that moment whoever we had been no longer mattered. The old reel was replaced with another.

Named after the town that surrounds it, Misawa Air Base could trace a hard line right to a brutal piece of history. In mid-1941,

Japanese engineers constructed earthen facsimiles of US cruisers and battleships along the banks of Lake Ogawara, at the northwest terminus of the air base. Japanese aviators used the setup to practice low-level torpedo runs, examining and refining their techniques until finally they had them down so cold that on a December Sunday that same year they sunk or damaged more than twenty American warships sleeping in the crystal waters of Pearl Harbor, killing and wounding nearly thirty-six hundred Americans.

American airpower eventually pounded the air base into dust once its strategic bombers were in range near the end of the war. In the years after Japan surrendered to the United States, the US military established more than fifty camps and bases across the Japanese homeland, defending the country and the far reaches of America's own empire from North Korea, China, and the Soviet Union. US engineers rebuilt Misawa Air Base in their own image after the war, planting a broad island of America in the modest green elegance of the Japanese countryside. Within a few years, the base hosted US airpower flying air defense missions and eventually supported war efforts in Korea and Vietnam, serving as a large signal intelligence hub for gathering information on American adversaries.

Alan had arrived a few months ahead of us. After we loaded our bags into his small white sedan, he took us on a tour of the base, pointing out its landmarks and cream-colored buildings from the car windows—the commissary, the Bank of America branch, and the Base Exchange, where we quickly stopped to buy a small television. We toured past the two elementary schools and the combined middle and high school where I would start seventh grade in a few days. At the center of the base, across from the headquarters, was an oval park. There, large American and Japanese flags fluttered and two vintage fighter jets sat like the final achievements of sepulchral taxidermists. Much like Hill, this new air base felt sterile and uniform, its rich green lawns and clean streets and sidewalks shaded by lush oak and beech trees, an overly manicured ideation of folksy hometown Americana. The streets had names like Gettysburg, Freedom, Yellowstone, Falcon, Rushmore, and Republic.

Due to a housing shortage on the base, my stepdad had rented a house in town near the rail station. We lived on a narrow dead-end street lined with eight identical two-story homes. There were three small bedrooms, a bathroom and a half, a living room, and a small kitchen. The walls were thin, and when the winter came and buried the street with snow, we relied on big space heaters in the living room and in each bedroom for warmth. On weekend mornings, I would turn on the heater in the living room and sit in front of the vents, shivering solely in a pair of shorts but knowing that once the coils glowed and the fans kicked on I'd be enveloped in a blanket of hot air as I watched sitcom reruns on the Armed Forces Network. We didn't have many movies. All the "Taped Space"—the *Star Trek: The Next Generation* we had recorded during the Persian Gulf War—had been shuttled off to a storage warehouse in the middle of America somewhere, so we watched *The Empire Strikes Back* and *The Terminator* and *Terminator II: Judgment Day* almost on repeat, and at night I imagined being a soldier in the Resistance, fighting alongside John Connor and Kyle Reese.

On weekday mornings, I waited outside a convenience store across from the rail station for the bus to take me to the American school on base. In the afternoons, after the bus dropped me off, I played with three stray dogs that lurked around the neighborhood or I walked down to the nearby field where Japanese boys played soccer. On Wednesday nights, American missionaries assigned to the Mormon church down the hill taught Japanese to anyone who cared to show up. I learned introductory words and phrases like *konnichiwa* (good afternoon), *konbanwa* (good evening), *ogenki desu ka* (how are you?), and *domo arigato gozaimasu* (thank you very much). It wasn't until I tried my thin tourist-like knowledge on rapid-fire native speakers that I was reduced to a vacuous shrug instead of the one word they failed to teach me: *wakarimasen* (I don't understand).

I stopped going to the Mormons after a few weeks. I'm not sure if it was a child's boredom, the proselytizing that began to creep from their pores, or because they simply refused to teach me any Japanese profanity.

My mom insisted we take in the culture as much as possible. We went to Japanese restaurants almost weekly, even if only to try out the Japanese menus at the local McDonald's. "It's *different*," she would say in each case, as if to emphasize their separateness from America and a conscious deviation from our usual Western themes. We traveled across the northeast side of Honshu Island, down to Hachinohe where there was a large mall with an amusement park in the center, then over to Aomori for the cherry blossom festival in Hirosaki Park, its trees bursting with pink pedals, as if sunrise clouds had settled and fixed to their branches. We tried to pack our Americanness into tightly confined balls to appear as inconspicuous as possible in front of the Japanese. We strove to avoid being the stereotype of the Ugly American. We bowed and said *domo* in thanks. We took off our shoes before entering homes and even a few businesses. We learned how not to use chopsticks: sticking them straight up in our rice would bring bad luck and laying them across our bowls was disrespectful to the chef. Our house routinely smelled like Japanese curry. We watched Sumo wrestling and raunchy Japanese game shows. We walked Green Pole Road—a long, narrow street near the main gate of the air base that was full of shops and marked by the green poles that held up the long awnings on each side—and marveled at the sunny advertisements for coffee and Coke. We window-shopped to the bouncy backbeat of the early J-Pop explosion and we traveled to festivals around the prefecture and to the nearby beaches. "You can't swim in the ocean," my mother warned. "The undertow will suck you out about twenty miles and drown you."

We wanted to be welcomed visitors in someone else's sacred home, to play the role of guest, to adopt the quiet grace and humility and remarkable warmth of the Japanese people we were surrounded by. The year we lived in Misawa City was a peaceful testimony to the effects of culture and art. The beat of *taiko* drums and the soulful whimsy of *shakuhachi* flutes dulled the nose-camera bomb footage and night-vision *ack-ack* blips that had fueled the wonder/angst of my Gulf War / *Nightly News* eyesight and the bomb and fighter jet lust that had grown from it. I was living in the center of a beautiful and self-assured world; it was impossible not to be absorbed by it.

But it was also a life of contrasts. The American military was a star we slowly orbited from our quaint Japanese home. The base was our benefactor. It was a warm presence, and though I had many schoolmates who had bounced with their parents from one foreign posting to the next, never living in the United States, the military nevertheless tethered us all to those united states half the planet away, reminding us that no matter where we were in the empire, no matter the culture we elected to experience, we were always Americans first. There was no escaping it, even if we wanted to.

The American military broadcasts its own television networks over the Japanese airwaves. Instead of typical advertisements for American products, the military aired commercials proselytizing all the American prides and honors of uniforms and duty with hearty stories of old battlefield heroics, PSAs about soldiers and Marines in World War II who died knocking out Nazi or Japanese pillboxes to save their buddies, or American POWs who held their tongues and sent secret messages of hope to their comrades while surviving in Vietnamese prison camps. Between *Seinfeld* and *Friends*, I listened to quick thirty-second stories of Bronze Star and Silver Star recipients, men who were handed Distinguished Service Crosses and Navy Crosses and even Medals of Honor for their at-all-costs bravery during various "times that try men's souls," all played against the cemetery sounds of military trumpets honoring the dead. Every night around eleven, after the American broadcasts closed the day with a quick nod to our hosts—a soft, humble rendition of the Japanese national anthem—our television speakers crackled with the bombast of the

"The Star-Spangled Banner," while on the screen blended images of American fighter jets carved through wide blue skies, king-like battleships belched fire from their sixteen-inch guns, tanks crushed across the desert like jet-fueled chariots of destruction, and the hard faces of young American infantrymen with strong chins stared steely eyed into the maw of some tyrannical hell.

I wonder now what it might have felt like for some Japanese channel surfer to flip through the television stations and stumble on the images of American war machines blowing across the screen accompanied by the reverb of the American national anthem. What would an American around Topeka or Bakersfield or Pittsburgh think if suddenly coming across a strange station between ABC and NBC and hearing the eleven measures of the Japanese national anthem while images of Japanese infantrymen stormed across the Pacific with the flag of the Rising Sun fluttering behind them?

A small group of Japanese teenagers clustered on the beach past the high-water mark and began shooting bottle rockets into the sky. At first, they jammed the stems of the rockets into the sand and let them sail into the air, but a boy with rust-colored hair held a bottle rocket in his hand by the tip of the stem, lit the fuse, and launched it into the sky from the tips of his fingers. After he did it a few more times, his arms dazzled with sparks, a few other boys began to emulate him.

The beach was two hours south of Misawa, at a place called Fudai in the Iwate Prefecture, situated between a number of large forested hills and a small cove flanked by jagged cliffs and rocky outcroppings that emptied into the Pacific Ocean. Directly south, out of sight of the campground snugged against the hills, was a small port for a fleet of Japanese fishing boats. Full of seagulls, Fudai was an idyllic and peaceful place where time was marked by waves that beat against the beach. The water was too cold to swim, however, even in summer. My family had set up camp with a few other sergeants from Alan's new squadron. The campground was filled with Japanese and a scattering of other Americans, whom my mom and stepdad regarded with mild disdain. When the Japanese walked by on their way to the beach or the communal bathrooms, they looked at us with thin, passive smiles and bowed. We would bow back and wave, sometimes trading food, always eager to please. We tried to communicate, but the language barrier was always too great.

The boys fired the rockets for a few minutes before one of them turned toward another group and launched a bottle rocket at them from his fingertips. The rocket zapped across the beach and detonated at the feet of a boy who cried out a litany of what seemed like Japanese profanity as he flicked the sparks from his foot. The others laughed. He quickly fired a bottle rocket back and it exploded in the pack. Some darted out of the way; others just turned their backs to absorb the shallow pop.

From there it became an exchange—two armies with bottle rockets streaming between them, firecrackers tossed like bomblets to snap at their feet. It seemed like madness, the defiance of every safety video ever produced on the dangers of fireworks.

I approached them with a combination of fascination and stupidity—or perhaps just youth. I was given a handful of bottle rockets and soon I was diving to the sand as sparks glittered in the space between the warring parties. We cheered the hits and cursed the misses of our little beach war. It was loud, dangerous, loaded with threats of injury, all staved off by the quick reflexes of young boys in a way that amplified our sense of invulnerability. I singed my fingertips with the lighter until they stung. I felt the charred paper casings on my bare toes and smelled the thick sulfur of burned propellant in the air. I was thirteen, and a boy, and our fireworks were loud and colorful and dangerous but only dangerous enough to make me shake away the sting of a hot lighter or the sparks of a fuse. But a primal rush followed those rockets as they zipped across the beach at the other team and popped among them. We did not want to hurt them, nothing like that, but it was a victory if we made them flinch. Buried in our cheap pyrotechnic pantomiming was the idea of enduring battle like men, a universal language that told us the pain in our fingers was somehow tethered to the idea of being tough, that surviving battle was the representation of strength, and as I walked back to my campsite with my clothes smelling like smoke, my fingertips throbbing, and my ears ringing, I felt happy.

VI

I walked through the aisles of the Base Exchange on a rainy autumn Saturday in 1992. The Exchange was a department store reserved for servicemembers and retirees and base employees. We leaned on these stores for a sense of American normalcy, racked as they were with name-brand clothes stamped with MADE IN CHINA and MADE IN TAIWAN and MADE IN SINGAPORE. I sagged as my mom flipped through blouses and rayon slacks and passed idly by the big Sony televisions and Pioneer stereo receivers and Hitachi VHS players. I went to the movie and music section and sifted through B-movie action flicks and Nirvana and Enya CDs bound with chunky plastic antitheft frames. Afterward, I walked toward the sprawling food court to buy pizza. Inside the small arcade, a pair of boys pumped quarters into *Terminator 2: Judgment Day.*

A gaggle of teenagers circled a large foldout table near the food court across from the bookstore. I vaguely recognized some of them from school, but they were dressed in sky-blue air force dress shirts with dark blue air force trousers, or in starched camouflage uniforms and shiny black boots, like what my stepdad wore to work every day. They had glossy ranks pinned to one collar and silver insignia that read CAP on the other. Their names were stitched above their pockets and a big patch on their shoulders bore the image of a red propeller tucked inside a white triangle surrounded by a large blue circle. A red-and-white banner above it read CIVIL AIR PATROL.

We're a civilian auxiliary of the US Air Force, they explained, formed just before Pearl Harbor. Back then, we patrolled the American shoreline in spotter planes, hunting for Nazi and Japanese submarines bent on attacking the coast. The kids told me they didn't hunt subs anymore, but they still marched and wore uniforms and learned how to function as a military unit. I knew about the Boy Scouts and had even gone to a few meetings in Utah, but I had never seen kids in military uniforms or even thought it was possible. And yet here they were, American subalterns in training, wrapped in the armor of the kingdom. After I collected their pamphlets and flyers, I lurked around the edges of their orbit until Alan chased me to the car. I had no chance. I was hooked.

The following Tuesday evening, Alan drove me to a crumbling two-story building near the youth center on base. Painted in two different shades of tan and peeling in flakes the size of maple leaves, the building seemed on the verge of being condemned. It smelled like old office furniture and insulation riddled with remnant asbestos. We walked into the CAP offices on the second floor. The woman in charge was a studious air force captain. She sat behind an old pistachio green tanker desk. Over Cokes, she explained the fees and the requirements and sent us on our way with membership forms and prices for all the badges and pins I would need. There was no decision to make, at least not by me. I wanted to join instantly. At home that evening, my mother agreed, and I went to bed that night with my imagination wrapped in camouflage.

My mom took me to the uniform shop a few days later and bought the smallest sets of uniforms they had—a camouflage uniform, a blue dress uniform with a light blue shirt and dark blue pants, a pair of paratrooper jump boots, and a set of shiny dress oxfords. When I put them on, they cloaked my smallness and made me feel bigger than I truly was. I became part of something larger than myself, a piece of some greater whole. My mother had a blue name tape made that read ALEXANDER and had it sewn above the breast pocket of my new camouflage blouse. My dress uniform was fitted by a Japanese tailor.

My mom showed me how to go over the seams of my uniforms with a pair of small scissors and clip away the little wayward threads that occasionally erupted from the stitching. Alan sat with me in the living room with a boot brush and can of black Kiwi polish that smelled like wax and alcohol. He taught me to wet the brush from the tin lid filled with water and dab it into the dull wax and how to work it into the leather of my paratrooper boots in small circles. Attention to detail, he said. Go slow. Take your time. Get it right. Sometimes I would. Sometimes I wouldn't. But it was a start. Over the next decade, I would learn little tricks to make the toes of my boots mirror clean, like using cotton balls instead of the brush or heating the wax with a lighter. Sometimes I put in the time. Sometimes I didn't.

My mom took a picture of me in the living room a few weeks later. In it, I stand in front of the brown Lazy-Z-Boy with my hands behind my back. My new boots reach midcalf and are deep black against the blue carpet. The camouflage trousers hang baggy around my legs. The trouser legs are cuffed at the tops of the boots, something I would do over and over, even daily, when my youthful fantasies became real and ugly. The position would change somewhat over time, at the top of the boot or down an inch or two, but the behavior would always be the same. My blouse fits loosely, almost draping down my narrow torso. The flaps over the pockets are ironed against the buttons beneath, appearing as worn, faded eyes on the stiff fabric, a mark I would later deem a sign of a sloppy pressing job. My face is hairless and my lips pink; my eyes are wary and hopeful and slightly reddened by the camera flashbulb.

My hair was a deep brown and shaggy, due for a haircut. My parents had always kept my hair cut short, a staple of the conservatism of military circles, but Alan walked me into the barber shop at the Exchange that weekend.

"Thirty-five ten," I said to the Japanese barber, quoting the regulation number for the air force grooming standards Alan had taught me. The barber knew what to do without a word: *Tapered appearance on both sides and the back of the head, both with and without headgear. Hair will not exceed 1¼ inch in bulk, regardless of length and ¼ inch at natural termination point; allowing only closely cut or shaved hair on the back of the neck to touch the collar. Hair will not touch the ears or protrude under the front band of headgear. . . .*

The Civil Air Patrol was like the Boy Scouts in terms of promoting citizenship, leadership, and ethics. It was righteousness wrapped in military sciences; it was also sanctioned make-believe. We didn't carry guns or learn how to drop bombs, but they were out there, just beyond the horizon of adolescence. I pantomimed the identity, clocking the days until each Tuesday, when I would head to the old squadron building where the senior members, nearly all of them active-duty air force noncommissioned officers, taught classes on military customs and courtesies and basic military history.

On cool afternoons all that fall, I took the Civil Air Patrol cadet guidebook outside and practiced marching in the street in front of our house. I learned how to turn while marching, how to "mark time" and "about face." I learned how to salute, to bring my bladed right hand up along the center of my body until the tips of my fingers hovered near the outer end of my right eyebrow. I learned this was a custom grown from knights lifting the visor of their iron face masks to identify themselves to approaching allies. I also learned I was supposed to salute when passing officers, or else I might get my ass chewed, according to my mom.

I stood on the pavement between our house and the communal carport bellowing out drill commands with my preteen voice into the autumn air: "*Fo-ward, HARCH!*" and "*Tench-HUT!*"

"Use your diaphragm," my mom explained.

"What do you mean?"

"You have to project the end of each command using your stomach. Don't use your voice, use your diaphragm," she said. She seemed happy to teach me, but in retrospect I think she was also wistful, as if tapping into something that had been pulled away prematurely.

I became a zealot. It was hardwired into the landscape of my life and ideas of what I was supposed to be. I had seen the footage of bombs and antiaircraft fire on television. I had seen the war movies. I had already pledged my allegiance and sung toward the waving American banner. It was easy. So on Tuesdays I climbed into my uniform and Alan's white sedan and he drove me to the crumbling clubhouse on the base for another installment.

The cadets were entirely the children of the military—there was Joe, the blond sophomore whose father who was a navy submariner, and my friend Mark, whose dad was a navy intelligence officer. Justin's father was an air force master sergeant. We had aging veterans, like LaFleur, an air force retiree who wore the oak leaf clusters of a major and a former Marine named John who had fought with the Seventh and Ninth Marines in Vietnam. Later, when Vietnam became the specter of my teenage dreams, I'd ply John for stories whenever he came by and try to impress him with my knowledge of his war. Then there was Tony, the swaggering former infantryman. He strutted up the stairs of the old building, his uniform pristine. The weave of adults and cadets, and the military that bound us, was as much a social club as it was an instrument of basic military training and the village rearing of children.

We treated the base like our own amusement park. One afternoon, we took a government bus to the country north of the air base. I climbed off in my camouflage uniform with the others. Our boots crunched up the gravel path toward a small piece of high ground with a red-and-white tower that overlooked a large grassy field. An airman stood with us as a guide. He pointed east toward the ocean and the horizon.

"Look out there," he said. "Watch."

A speck approached from just above the sea. The familiar hiss of the Fighting Falcon began to echo across the sky. The ground a few hundred yards ahead suddenly erupted in a long string of violent brown geysers as the fighter jet strafed the earth with its cannon. The air sounded out with a long mechanic rip of the cannon but only *after* the shells had torn up the ground, a reversal of our action-movie expectations.

We cheered as the Falcon peeled off and snapped through the clouds out of sight, but the whole thing was strangely anticlimactic and I was left wanting more—maybe another pass, or this time a bombing run, something with fire and rock music—but it didn't happen. Instead, we climbed back onto the bus and rode to the Base Exchange and ate pizza.

Not long after, a handful of cadets and I stood in a control room next to a bay where a Fighting Falcon engine idled. The engine was bolted to a large cradle fixed to the concrete floor with thick steel cables. Its big air duct at the front was capped with a metal cage. The engine had been under repair. I stood wearing headphones and a set of foam earplugs in my ears. I felt the hissing engine beneath my skin.

I pressed the throttle forward. The burnished afterburner nozzle at the end of the engine faced a long, dark tunnel. As I opened the throttle, the nozzle tightened around the end of the engine and soon a glowing jet of blue flame reached down the tunnel. The inferno grew in length and intensity until it was streaked into a blue-white cylinder. The concrete vibrated beneath our boots. Our bones quivered. The roar was immense. The turbine fans inside the engine gulped air through the big metal cage at the front.

After a moment, the sergeant told me to back the throttle down and the air settled around my body. Another cadet came forward and took his turn at the throttle, leaving—just as I had—with a broad grin. We were thirteen and fifteen and even seventeen and we had controlled the energy of the multimillion-dollar engine of a fighter jet, touching the glory of everything the action can entail if tuned to its fantasy.

On a CAP-sponsored trip to Okinawa, I boarded an aerial refueling tanker one warm morning in the summer and took off across Honshu. The five or six of us were hopping a ride via "Space-A," or "Space-Available," transportation—a benefit given to military members and dependents with orders that permitted flight on military aircraft as cargo when there was room to spare. Midway into the trip, the crew chief came over and explained that a thirsty flight of Fighting Falcons had joined alongside to take on fuel. I walked down the cavernous cargo hold to the aft quarter of the plane with another cadet named Sarah. We climbed onto a pair of pads on either side of the airman operating the refueling boom. He lay between us with his chin resting on a small-cushioned platform and looked out a large thick window. The Pacific Ocean was blue and green below us and sparkled with sunlight. The Falcons were in formation, hovering alongside in near perfect stillness. The canopies glittered, but I could see the pilots clearly tucked inside their cockpits, their gray oxygen masks clicked against their faces.

The airman manipulated a joystick and the large boom began to extend from beneath the tail. A pair of fins painted black and marked with white squadron numbers jutted out from the end of the boom in a V. The first Falcon slowly rose to position directly astern of the refueler. The pilot nudged the craft up and left and right and down in subtle increments, speeding and slowing in hesitant shoves until finally the boom was aimed behind the canopy at a port on the fuselage. I held my breath as the boom and the jet touched with a slight jolt, and for a split moment I believed the boom would snap off. But they connected and fuel began to transfer. Once finished, the boom and the Falcon separated as a wisp of remnant fuel atomized across the jet. The fighter pilot slowly lowered his jet and fell back. I gave a slight wave and the pilot gave back a thumbs up. Then he turned the fighter on its side with a jolt of his hand and peeled away.

I closed my mouth and blinked for what felt like the first time.

There were encampments every summer. They functioned like military basic training but in miniature, complete with early-morning reveille to the sound of a bugle, physical training sessions, uniform and room inspections, and classes, all led by air force chaperones who would adopt the slightly neutered pastiche of the drill sergeant persona. This is something we begged our parents to pay for.

In Okinawa, we were given rooms in the dormitories. Once the encampment officially began, air force noncommissioned officers in CAP uniforms woke us before sunrise, blaring reveille from a stereo and beating a hammer against a trash can lid. My eyes were crusted with sleep. I stumbled out of my room in a T-shirt and shorts and stood at a mark along the wall.

Hertle was one of our leaders. On a given day, he was a genial, studious man, humorous. But now, walking the narrow halls as we stood in hazy predawn morning, he was terrifying, a squat toad of disdain, sneering as he passed each of us. During the next week, he lorded over us like a king over peasants toiling to drain some swamp for his pleasure. He was playing a role, but I still hated him for the first few days.

He ushered us through morning calisthenics and then marched us to the dining facility where we ate alongside airmen who would then head to work across the base. They watched us, kids in uniforms playing toy soldiers under the imperious helm of Hertle and the other adults, with a mix of pride and amusement. Hertle ushered us to flight simulators. We learned land navigation skills and how to rappel from the side of a tower. We were being given a look inside the room of the US military, at least the enlisted side, as a long, elaborate advertisement for some professional adventure on the other side of the hill. I was still a tourist in this world, not a true resident, and there were times when I felt conspicuous in my small pantomiming uniforms, but I was happy to wear them. It felt like belonging. The military can be thrilling to watch up close as an event, like a carnival ride to be experienced, but also beautiful in the presentation of its clinical precision and professionalism. The fodder for True Believers. This was the family business for all of us, and why wouldn't we be a part of this? How could we not? Look at this! Fighter jets and machine guns and heroes. Our uniforms were the universal tell, their creases the lines palm readers use to predict our futures.

But even then, my interest was becoming harder to sustain. I was fascinated by the uniforms and the structure and the identity, but the tools and weapons were beginning to feel too safe. That is the basic reality of the air force. The entire organization is generally devoted to a singular but necessary purpose: air superiority of a battlespace—a job for modern technicians. The product of its efforts mattered, but to me those efforts seemed largely air conditioned and technical, routine. The air force began to feel too pedestrian and manicured, military as a clinical idea rather than a mental state. It lacked intensity. Even the terminology was neutered some. Airmen would refer to living quarters as dormitories, as if the residents were college kids, instead of as barracks, where soldiers were housed. There was no story in any of it, just a job, and part of me, even then, was in search of a narrative with the characters I already revered in all the books I was reading and movies I was watching. In the air force, the only real flash, the glory, rested with the fighter pilots. But even they seemed removed. Switches began to flip in my head as I became a teenager. I wanted something dirtier, something deeper, under my fingernails. The machinery was no longer enough. I wanted an army on the march, shouldered with dark rifles and gleaming bayonets, the root story of the wartime experience. This desire lived under the surface at first, buried behind the noise of the fighter jets and hiss of the iron pressing starched creases into my uniforms.

I was shoving toward a style far more atavistic. I felt it one afternoon as school let out for spring break. The air base was holding a base-wide battle exercise. Airmen walked about with rifles on their shoulders and gas masks on their hips, grumbling over the inconvenience to their normal schedules. As I left school to board the bus home, a Black Hawk helicopter hovered a few hundred feet above the football field. Its sliding doors were open and a pair of machine guns jutted out from mounts on each side. Over the whomp of the rotors, I began to notice a familiar staccato that sounded out in short bursts. I looked up and saw puffs of smoke coming up from the barrel of the machine gun, the gunner firing at imaginary targets with blanks, just like the blanks I had fired a year earlier from a Humvee parked in the grass of an air base that no longer mattered to me, as if reaching out and reminding me of that moment, of the cordite smoke that had drifted into my nose and sparked wonder behind its racket. I pretended the gunner had riddled me with bullets and fell to the warm grass, my arms and legs spread out. I looked up and laughed.

CHARLIE

I think that Vietnam is what we had instead of happy childhoods.

—Michael Herr, *Dispatches*

Cory sits beside me in the shade of the Humvee near the big wadi that splits the Iraqi town like a no-man's-land—Americans on one dry bank, the insurgents on the other. It is nearing sunset, and before we hear the bullets overhead, Cory asks if I'll come to Mobile to spend a few days with him and his family after we get home. We'll get drunk with my uncle and my sister, he says. We'll go to the beach. You can stay with me and my mom and dad. His tells me his wife is cheating on him; he can feel it and he tells me he'll probably have to get a divorce once he gets home and his voice is a jagged edge of bitterness. It is an old story in this world, a story as old as the Alabama hills, the Dear John cliché. We are Americans in a war and we are bound to its clichés and in a few minutes we will be shot at and we will laugh at it like men and run and try to kill whoever is shooting at us because we are so bound. As we wait, we watch a bulldozer carve the top of a nearby hill for a new Marine outpost.

Before we hear the bullets and before the bulldozer and before we decide to hang out in Mobile after our piece of the war, we begin to clear the insurgents from our piece of the Iraqi country. I had come back from the firefight near the water tower to find Rebel Six spooling his battalion like an electric coil to fling it across the desert and into the valley to kill or run off the mujahideen as the Marines go house to house. His plan is to have engineers construct outposts inside the urban areas so Marines and Iraqi army soldiers can live and walk among the locals. An Iraqi constitutional

referendum is coming and Rebel Six wants democracy spread to the upper
Euphrates River valley as much as anywhere else.

I had found a photograph earlier in the day while Cory and I and a few
others searched a nearby house. The house had already been cleared of
weapons, but we were ordered by some rule-crazy staff sergeant to sweep it
again. Farming detritus and junk was all that remained. I found the picture
in a room full of bags of USAID rice. It was of a man standing in a black
thawb with a checkered kaffiyeh. He brandished an AK-47 in his hands like
a totem of pride and manhood and I remembered Alan in that picture with
his pistols. The man's face was splotched with a patchy beard and wispy
mustache. He looked stern and hard with the rifle in his hands, perhaps
an affectation, and I wondered if he talked shit like we did, if he was alive
out there now, somewhere with the same rifle, angry with us and ready to
kill us like we believed we were ready to kill him. I wondered if Rebel Six
wanted him to vote too. When I showed it to Cory, he called the man a
"hajji motherfucker." I put the photo in my pocket.

The war lives and we live in it and so now, in the shade of the Humvee
with Cory and Mobile and the bulldozer on the far hill, it begins. We hear
it high overhead as the sun begins to angle toward the Syrian horizon.
Cory looks at me and I look at him and without a word we know we
both understand. Shots register as flat, hollow snaps. We laugh at our
understanding, then grab our rifles and sprint toward the door of a tall
house nearby that serves as a command post.

We dash into the house, hooting in a frenzy of adrenaline. I feel light,
following Cory as if on a playground. On the first landing, a Marine we had
nicknamed Boomhauer from the King of the Hill cartoon has his rifle to his
shoulder, aiming through a broken windowpane. Rebel Six stands next to
him, giving instructions with his thick roadhouse accent.

"All right, you see him pop his head up right there by that door, you shoot
it the fuck off," he says like a coach providing instructions to his quarterback.

We hustle up the staircase to the roof where a number of Marines lean
against a short wall facing the wadi. Cory and I take up positions beside
each other.

"We think he's in that building out by the quarry," someone says.

The sad quarry sits in the center of the wadi. The big conveyor rusts near piles of stone and sand and a lonely brick building with three windows. A haggard captain stands behind us with the radio handset pressed against his ear. He calls in fire direction information to the battalion mortars.

A shot snaps by close with a hard CRACK. Heads duck. Eyes wince. Skin crawls. Chuckles and nervous laughter quickly follow. Combat is measured more by sound than by sight. How far away a bullet passes your body is measured by the loudness of the snap the bullet makes as it breaks the sound barrier. This shot is a whip that travels down my spine and settles in my bowels before it dissipates. Everyone lowers their stance behind the wall.

"I think he shot from that window, far one to the right," someone announces.

Time hovers. Perhaps in the quarry a man wipes sweat and rests his cheek on the wooden stock of his dusty rifle, which is aimed at the tiny figures perched along our roof. It's been a long, hot day. How many days must this go on? he wonders. Why won't they leave? Then he begins to chant softly to himself as he aims down the sights. He pulls the trigger.

Another shot snaps past us, but this one is much higher. We open fire with our rifles and carbines. I aim at the dark opening in the small brick building and squeeze the trigger. The rifle bucks against my shoulder and thin, bitter smoke from the chamber drifts into my nose. I fire a few more times before I flip the rifle to safe and lower it. We wait for another shot. The haggard captain finishes his call to the battalion mortars and within minutes a trio of shells crashes inside the quarry. We cheer and then fall quiet.

The sky is clear and hot. A dusty breeze drifts across the roof as we watch the brown mass of houses and the darkened windows and alleyways across the wadi. A Huey and Cobra helicopter combo clatter in from the south like relics from the fall of Saigon and pass low over the quarry and continue north. My knee throbs where it rests on the hard roof. I hand Cory a cigarette and together we smoke and quietly grow impatient. Boredom infects the energy and flattens the mood. Our joints begin to hurt from kneeling behind the short wall for so long. To the south, the lone Marine bulldozer takes off the top of a large hill where the new Marine battle position will be built. No more shots come from the little brick structure. Perhaps the mortar rounds have perforated the shooter's body with metal and left him bleeding on the dirt beneath the rusting conveyor. Or perhaps he ran away before the mortar rounds landed. There is no way of knowing.

The subtle click of a distant mortar tube firing across the wadi awakens everyone. The haggard captain presses the handset to his ear and listens.

"Incoming, gents," he says. He speaks quietly, professionally, just announcing the simple measure of day-job reality.

I look to the sky where an insurgent mortar round arcs its way somewhere, possibly anywhere, maybe here. Our roof is just as good a target as the next. The mortar round travels dumbly, completely blind to its abilities. It is a heavy inanimate object with explosives inside it, but it has no prejudices or complaints. It does not care where it hits or who. It is oblivious and thus terrifying, and those seconds waiting for it to strike fill me with a thick, greasy apprehension, like waiting for the verdict from a judge who is incapable of measuring my worth.

The round erupts on top of the big hill. It blossoms into a hearty plume of smoke and dust right in front of the armored bulldozer. The dozer jerks to a stop. The smoke from the shell begins to drift away. The driver waits a brief moment, just long enough to light a cigarette or put another pinch of Skoal behind his lip and skip to the next death-metal or country track on his iPod. Then he rumbles forward again and Cory and I and the rest laugh. We are Marines and these are the things we laugh at because we are alive.

VII

I climbed out of bed at sunrise and slipped on a pair of socks. Socks would keep my feet silent, but shoes might make noise. I had to be quiet. The door to my parents' bedroom was directly across the hall.

My bedroom door was closed, but I could open it soundlessly and step through if I turned the handle slowly enough. It was crucial to go slowly, especially at this point. I turned the doorknob until I couldn't turn it any farther. Only then did I begin to open the door. Our apartment tower on base was brand new; the hinges were silent. When the door was open enough for me to slip through, I stepped into the hall and padded past my sister's door into the living room.

The front door was the trickiest part. The door was metal and heavy. It sealed tightly against the jamb, creating a slight difference in air pressure between our apartment and the hallway outside. I knew if I opened the door too quickly air would rush down the hallway and rattle the bedroom doors. I might as well bang a hammer in that case. The trick was to open the door slowly and allow the air pressure to equalize. This had to be done twice—once going out and again when returning. But I am good at this. I have done this many times.

First, I turned the dead-bolt knob, slowly guiding the bolt to its seat inside the door. Then I grabbed the doorknob and turned it until it stopped, just as I had with my bedroom door. I pulled the door away from the jamb no more than half an inch. Air rushed out with a soft whistle. Once it was quiet, I stepped into the hallway and carefully closed the door behind me.

The hallway was clean. A room filled with storage cages was around the corner and down the hall. Unconcerned with making noise, I now ran to the door and stepped inside.

Our storage cage was on the right. Inside it were boxes we hadn't bothered to unpack, our luggage, my stepdad's golf clubs, and the boxes of his new Gateway computer that were colored to look like Holstein Friesian cows. I lay on the cold concrete floor next to the chain-link fence. There was a small dark space between the luggage and the floor, accessible through a gap under the fence. I reached my fingers into the gap and found the paperback book I had hidden there. I slid it out and fled the storage room back to my bedroom.

I lay down on my bed with the book. On the cover was a Vietnam soldier sitting on the ground in the lotus position. In front of his crossed legs, a pink flower grew from a ration can. A rifle was propped up against his chest, and his helmet sat low over his eyes. A village was on fire behind him. Above the title, *Meditations in Green*, the *New York Times Book Review* offered, "Brilliant, scarifying . . . Extravagant, rhapsodic and horrific . . . It has overwhelming impact." Below that, *Newsweek*'s opinion: "The best that any fiction about this war has offered."

I had beaten my mother's rules again. I opened the novel and began to read.

One afternoon the previous spring, a kid named Stuart handed me a stiff library book.

"You gotta read this, dude," he said.

The book had *Fallen Angels* written in hard red letters on the cover above a framed picture of five GIs strapped with jungle gear, weapons, and haggard faces.

"What's it about?"

"These guys in Vietnam," Stuart said. "I read it twice in a row."

I didn't know Stuart well. He had red hair and freckles and he strutted around the school like a rooster. Sometimes he could be cool, but other times he'd walk by and punch you or shove you into a locker door for no reason. An American Boy. His family would be reassigned within six months and I would never see him again, but in that moment he handed me a drug.

I checked out the book from the school library and afterward I sat in my bedroom with the window open and let in the breeze as I read the first two chapters. *Fallen Angels* is a young adult novel about a teenage boy from Harlem named Ritchie Perry who volunteers for the army and is sent to fight in the Vietnam War. He is assigned to a platoon filled with a cross section of kids from all over America: a charming tough guy from the Chicago South Side, a Jewish kid who wants to get into the movie business, a racist good-ol'-boy sergeant, and a smart lieutenant whose tragic death brings in a bumbling replacement, all led by a reckless captain who is more concerned with promotion than preserving the lives of his men. It was a simple novel, but it exposed me to a world I had never truly recognized despite all the uniforms I was surrounded by and had even begun to wear. I read those first few chapters and kept going. I wouldn't stop for three years. It was as if I were starved but didn't know it and, by chance and luck, had stumbled on a whole literary platter to satiate a hunger I suddenly felt.

Vietnam felt like the dark family secret buried in the vault of American exceptionalism. I quickly learned that the Vietnam War was the first war we truly lost. We walked, fueled by the terror of communism, into an ancient and complex culture trying to win its independence and for our troubles broke the moral, political, and patriotic spirit of America, began to expose some of its inconsistencies, and tore large rents in the fabric of our culture. For most of the seventies, Americans seemed unwilling to deal with the ethical implications of the war its country had escalated for the sake of protecting us from communism, the supposed threat, or for the sake of preserving a bloated sense of national prestige. After veterans came home, their experiences were then ignored by a culture of avoidance. But like all other American wars, the experience of Vietnam began to leak from the seams of our collective unconsciousness. Within a decade after the war ended, it reemerged in a wave of American-slanted art and commentary that forced an uneasy reckoning with it.

Fallen Angels was one of dozens of novels, memoirs, and battlefield accounts of the Vietnam War that torched through the American literary marketplace, peaking in the late 1980s with Oliver Stone's *Platoon* and Stanley Kubrick's *Full Metal Jacket*. The war was given life, realistically or otherwise, in everything from serious literary fiction like Tim O'Brien's *Going after Cacciato* and *The Things They Carried* and Larry Heinemann's *Close Quarters* and *Paco's Story*, to jingoistic action-adventure serials like *Saigon Commandos* and *Hatchet*, to memoirs and oral histories like Tobias Wolff's *In Pharaoh's Army*, Philip Caputo's *A Rumor of War*, and Al Santoli's *Everything We Had* and *To Bear Any Burden*. I shoved my *Star Trek* books into a drawer and replaced them with dog-eared paperbacks lifted from the book swap at the base library: *Body Count*, *The 13th Valley*, *Fields of Fire*, *Semper Fidelis*, *The Short-Timers*.

It was a history I was drawn to for its tragedy and even its criminality. I haunted the base library on rainy Saturday afternoons and flipped through big picture books of the war, gazing at faded color photos of grunts wading through rice paddies and inching their way up jungled hills or running bent at the waist toward helicopters waiting to airlift them to a fight on some nameless spot in the landscape. There was a visual clarity to Vietnam that hadn't existed for any other American conflict up to that point. World War II and Korea were black and white and a little out of focus. The low-intensity flashpoints of the eighties, like Grenada and Panama, and the Persian Gulf War were heavily sanitized and filtered through cheap patriotic public relations filters and Reagan-era action movies. But the ugliness of Vietnam was crystal clear, even if its geopolitical rationale, like the domino theory—the idea that the takeover of one country by communism would create the subsequent fall of neighboring countries—was murky and disingenuous.

Even as a teenager, just thirteen, with the history of America's failure in Vietnam so immutable, I felt the waste of that war in every story I read and every photo I saw in a history book. But instead of being sickened or disturbed by them as anyone might, I took a remarkable interest in the experience of its participants. Not for any patriotic reason, though that certainly hummed like a warm-up note in the orchestra pit of my growing obsession. Vietnam veterans, through their stories and fiction, showed me the sweeping array of emotions—from unconditional love to murderous Ahab-like rage— that soldiers feel in war, emotions strangely missing in my teenage life of thin friendships, bullies I was incapable of fighting, unrequited crushes, and a quiet divide that was growing between myself and my parents.

I could feel the war painted on the face of every single soldier, every little tragedy and horror, the fear and fatigue, the perpetual frustration, their bitter eyes filled with deep betrayal and blistering anger toward a lost war perpetuated simply for the sake of sustaining national pride. But there was love and respect among them, a certain stalwart leaning-in against the outrageous military and foreign policy stupidity of the war, the dangerously incompetent and even mean-spirited leaders who made unrealistic demands of their blood and body, their youth, and ultimately of their souls.

I fell in love with them like I fell in love with the fighter jets. It was easy. They were underdogs in a strange, collective sense. They were trapped between leaders who they generally felt were apathetic to the blood they sacrificed every day and the people at home who they felt were betraying them by protesting their existence or simply by living their daily American lives and treating the war as if it didn't exist at all. There was tragedy in the stories I read, but also endurance. The men and women were innocent and eager, raised on the illusions of glory of the Second World War, their fathers' war, but left to deal with the brutal realities of their own conflict almost entirely alone because the story of their war did not marry up to the action-hero image of the Greatest Generation. Their victories were cheapened by a myopic foreign policy and subsequent dubious military strategy that flattened them like Sisyphus's boulder as it crashed down the jungled slopes. They fought and died conquering hills named simply for their height in meters—like Hill 875, Hill 881, or Hill 937—only to abandon them to the vacuum of the jungle and the enemy once the grunts had choppered out their dead and wounded and only to spend more of their blood and bodies retaking these hills all over again months later. It didn't matter how hard they fought—the nature of the conflict prevented them from being truly successful, from winning. Winning was fundamentally impossible. Ironically enough, American national will was simply no match against the North's desire for Vietnamese independence. "You can kill ten of my men for every one I kill of yours," said Ho Chi Minh, the leader of North Vietnam. "But even at those odds, you will lose and I will win."

In every story I read, many of the soldiers, especially the infantrymen, often hated the military and counted every single day until they could leave it—in stark opposition to the quiet military careerism I was surrounded by—but nevertheless did the jobs they were asked to do and loathed, almost violently, anyone who failed to pull their own weight alongside them. They had foul mouths, they drank, they smoked marijuana, they pined for girls back home, they carried rifles and machine guns and grenades. They wore belts of machine-gun ammunition across their bodies and cut the sleeves from their jungle fatigues or just went bare chested under their flak jackets. They grew handlebar mustaches and wore beaded peace necklaces and Montagnard friendship bracelets, then hooked spent grenade rings around their helmet bands—grenades they had tossed at the Viet Cong guerrillas and North Vietnamese soldiers who were trying to kill them. Their language was raw, abbreviated, filled with a heavy slang that was a crossbreed of jive from Chicago and Detroit, redneck twang (undoubtedly a product of their lower economic status), military gibberish, and pidgin Vietnamese. It was a language all their own, never again seen before or after, now relegated to war-movie clichés and rotten 'Nam vet stereotypes: "*Xin loi*, man" . . . "Make sure you take your daily-daily. Don't wanna catch malaria" . . . "Drop some snake-and-nape on those mothers!" . . . "Come on, man. Let's *didi mau*" . . . "Hold on, brother. Just hold on, all right? Dust Off is inbound. You can make it, man. Just hold on" . . . "He's KIA, there just wasn't time" . . . And finally, the salve on their wounds: "It don't mean nothin'. Not a thing."

The wonders of Japan and the air force moved to the back of my mind. They were there, of course, but they lived just off the frame, on the far side of the barbed-wire fence that surrounded the base, in part hammered back by the angst of puberty but also taken over by my new interests. My mother and stepdad and sister continued to pack off to various festivals and sites, but I would stay home or just wander the base, haunting the houses of my friends or simpatico acquaintances, a desperate rogue state of sorts. Sometimes I would go to the Base Exchange where a pair of phone booths sat near the food court. I would climb in and call my dad collect and talk to him for thirty minutes or so. I thought it would be cool to call old friends in Utah, but I couldn't remember any of their numbers and the calls would have been expensive. They were all gone anyway.

My grades plummeted. It was as if something inside me clicked off once I became a teenager. School became a place I had to endure for six hours and afterward I would leave it all behind and come home to vanish into my stories. My mother, who would not tolerate flagging grades, banned all the novels and war stories from the house, believing them to be the key to my malaise. But like any prohibition, all it did was drive my interests underground. I snuck the books into the house and read them. If my mom knew, she did not say. My stepdad just wanted me to do well in school; he seemed to have no opinion about my interests.

Really, I just wanted to be left alone, even if I didn't, even if I subconsciously desired to belong to whatever clique or group thrived at school. Rebellion might be a righteous attitude and I certainly began to feel it inside me—a rebellious vibe against the notions of being accepted based on a choice of clothes or other teenage social whimsies—but belonging mattered to me. I had the Civil Air Patrol; I felt as if I belonged there. But everywhere else I felt like an outsider, and because I felt that way, I wanted to be left alone. While I might have been with classmates, might have hung out with them in their houses, played video games or watched movies with them, there was always this notion that I had to face, or at least acknowledge, even if silently, that I felt I was on the outside.

I lay in bed at night with my contraband books and escaped this feeling through the lives of soldiers. War stories aren't just about fighting, at least not the good ones. They're about enduring, putting up with our own human brand of ugliness. I couldn't remotely articulate this then, but that is what I loved about them. Soldiers were my sports heroes, playing on the worst kind of field. But they were not mere gladiators to me, nothing that mindless (though war-happy elements of American culture would make this the model years later). Instead, they had their rifles and their machine guns and their wits and their friends, their brothers, all up against forces beyond their control, enduring, surviving, waiting for it to end, all without the need for applause. To me, their endurance felt large, larger than the world, or certainly larger than my own world where I felt small.

Reading their stories was reading about freedom. Not freedom in any jingoistic or patriotic sense, but freedom from boyhood, from the confusion of needing to understand manhood, and freedom from finding an identity in an American culture I had never truly been a part of or experienced outside of the lens of the military. The modern military felt separate and deified, reduced to some kind of cheap one-dimensional Boy Scout image. The GIs in Vietnam I read about were raw and real, brutally honest. Their tales melded perfectly with the machine gun planted atop a Humvee on a patch of Utah grass, the fighter jets that had roared outside my bedroom window and torched the Kuwaiti desert with bombs and antitank missiles, the faces of young American infantrymen enduring all the various "times that try men's souls" playing against those military trumpets honoring those long-lost dead on our television.

The military was not wanton violence to me; it was a defense against such violence, a defense against people who believed they had the right to cast their shadows over others in violent ways, in both personal and geopolitical terms. The military was about protecting others, of being *for* the smaller *against* the larger, a mythology that lived inside me hotter than flares over a battlefield. It was a wholesome myth, one linked to old American notions of manhood, the kind of myths children are meant to accept. I believed it as a part of me, completely, even if I could not fully describe it. Years later, in my own war and after, I would learn how complicated this idea truly becomes in the face of executing violence.

I was never a bitter or vindictive boy. Or perhaps I was, the books about Vietnam the outlet for that brand of horrible energy. I do know I was unmotivated, perhaps even depressed, just looking for an escape from bigger boys and, in some ways, my family, and roiled with typical teenage angst. I never deeply considered the prospect of killing someone on a battlefield. Staying alive was more interesting. Many of the soldiers in Vietnam were simply survivors—of ambushes, land mines, and mortar barrages, of Dear John letters, of jungle rot, of inept commanders. They endured the moral injury for killing another human being and they survived the shadowy guilt of coming home when others did not and the darkness of living in the shame of the post-Vietnam American era.

The tales of Vietnam were twisted into a gateway drug; they anchored me to the naive perception that once I had come home from my very own little war I could sit on a tree stump somewhere, hold a cane between my knees, thump my chest, and say, "I was there," all without giving a passing thought to the battlefield horrors that might chew me up and spit me back out again, which is what many of the writers and artists of the Vietnam era were trying so hard to tell me. But I blew off their message, opting instead for the octane of their adult stories, for the helicopter clatter and 'Nam-era music, as I walked the quiet air base streets listening to antiwar folk music on my Walkman.

I playacted with my imagination tuned to military radio static, the chirp of jungle birds, and the whomp-whomp-whomp of Huey helicopters weaving across some distant valley. Then *BOOM!* Viet Cong mortar fire would drop me to the grassy ditches along the slow roadsides of base housing. *CRACK!* Guerrilla sniper fire would drop the imaginary point man and I would dive behind the nearest manicured hedgerow. *RATA-TATAT!* A North Vietnamese squad would erupt with Kalashnikovs and RPK machine guns and I would turn and charge toward them and yell, "Go-go-*GO!*" to my fellow grunts as cigarette-smoking housewives with bored toddlers tugging at their pastel capris cut me the side-eye from their front doors. But I just walked on until the next synapse fired and more imaginary enemy fire sent me screaming and running and diving once more.

I would marshal the troops, just a few neighborhood kids with sympathetic interests—there were always some around—and on sunny Saturday mornings three or four of us would ride the base shuttle to the woods northwest of the runway. Once off the bus, we changed into hand-me-down fatigues or whatever we felt passed as combat gear and set off into the brush with toy guns cut in the school woodshop or bought from the Base Exchange and grenades made from balled-up tinfoil. We played war, two versus two, hunting and stalking each other, patrolling the acres of dense woods until—*BANG!*—a small patch of woods echoed with crackling screams of *popopoppopoppop!* and *boomboombooomboomboom!* and *tatatatatatatatatatatat!* followed by "I got you!" and "You're dead!" and replied with "Bull-friggin-shit!" and other hollow vituperations. After we brushed the dead leaves from our bodies, and our casualties became whole again, we gathered and rattled off rapid-fire recaps of the little firefight with our voices put into manly stereo from all the adrenaline that came with it. Then we'd take a quick swig of water from our canteens, divide up, and start another war.

Sometimes we battled our imaginations. We crept through the woods like they were the jungles of the Central Highlands or the A Shau Valley of South Vietnam, moving through the trees until boredom outweighed reality and one of us yelled, "*Incoming!*" which meant mortars were falling. We dropped to the earth and sought cover around felled logs and tree trunks, protecting our heads with our hands as imaginary shells ripped apart the ground around us. Then perhaps a fake Viet Cong machine gun would crackle from a fake trench line nearby and we would turn and assault, throwing our tinfoil hand grenades from behind trees or calling in fake artillery barrages, then charge screaming, diving into the trench, and killing them with our fake bayonets.

Sometimes worlds collided. One summer afternoon, a dozen airmen palled around inside the base ski lodge for some sort of organized function. My friend Mark and I stumbled on them while play-patrolling through the woods and used them like a prop as we crawled to the top of a nearby grass-covered mound to report back to headquarters whatever our imaginations found. I wore a thick cartridge belt around my hips with a canteen that dangled on one side. A bandoleer stuffed with rocks and balled-up tinfoil to give it weight and shape was draped across my chest. An olive-drab Marine Corps octagonal cover sat on my head. Mark handed me the binoculars and pulled out a small notepad.

"Look for ranks," he said.

I peered through my cheap binoculars at the airmen standing near the smudged windows of the ski lodge.

"I think there's a master sergeant. Maybe a tech sergeant or a staff sergeant. I can't tell," I said.

Mark penciled in the information into the notepad, for no other reason than to do it. Playing the part. Suddenly a pair of airmen stepped outside on the walkway. Mark and I ducked our heads into the grass. I heard the strike of a lighter flint as one of them lit a cigarette as they spoke.

I slowly began to raise my head. "Dude. *Don't*," Mark whispered sharply.

"It's cool," I said. I didn't know what would happen if we were caught. Probably nothing dramatic. We were American kids playing war on recreational land on an American air base. At the worst, we'd be mildly scolded and sent away with jangled nerves, like after a brush with the school principal. I squinted through the thick grass and the loose vines and shrubs that covered the mound. The lodge was downhill. They would have to look up and focus specifically on the top of the mound and through the foliage if they wanted to see us. Next to the mound was a narrow road that led back to another road to the main part of the base, a short drive away.

On the airfield, Fighting Falcons hissed their omnipresent idle. But in my mind, the jets at the airfield weren't Falcons at all anymore. They were old fighter-bombers loaded with high-drag bombs and napalm ready to come melt the jungle at the press of my radio handset. The airmen below weren't airmen anymore; they were Viet Cong guerrillas gathering to overrun the nearby firebase. Only this time, I'd found them and I was going to call the fast movers to bomb them all. I pretended to push the key on the radio handset I held to my ear.

"Delta Six, be advised we are at location grid three-eight-two-one-one-five. We have in sight a platoon of Victor Charlie and we are requesting air support, over."

Mark snorted and smiled. We remained on the mound for another hour, watching and taking notes. Our evac plan—Mark's mom—was set to pick us up at around four that afternoon. When she arrived, she pulled her hatchback onto the road and stopped just beyond the mound. We gathered our gear and plastic guns and slithered down the back of the mound. Once we were out of sight, we stood and bolted for the car doors.

"Go! Go! *Go!*" Mark commanded, laughing breathlessly. His mother floored it.

While I was calling in airstrikes on imaginary villains, the world crackled with a blizzard of postcolonial wars. In the fallout from the crumbling of the Soviet Union and communism, Croatia and Bosnia battled for independence from Yugoslavia. The nightmare in Bosnia would ultimately remind the Western world of the clinical phrase *ethnic cleansing*. In Somalia, armed militias led by Mohamed Farrah Aidid attacked UN peacekeepers attempting to maintain some semblance of order in the country in the wake of the civil war. US troops sent to Mogadishu dodged sniper fire in the streets while struggling to feed a country starved by factionalism. It all felt vague and hazy, wars that ticked along in the background, relegated to the back pages of the newspapers and magazines, which lined the shelves of the bookstore at the Base Exchange, at least until the Battle of Mogadishu, in 1993. Suddenly I was introduced to the battered face of Chief Warrant Officer Michael Durant as he answered questions before the world and his Somali captors from a cheap mattress in a Mogadishu hovel. Then we watched the bodies of American soldiers dragged down the street, and inside us there was a sense of intolerable rage and shock at the act and I wondered if we were going to go to war with Somalia, full-scale war, to right that wrong. The details of the battle and our involvement there were just that—details. Americans were dead, and because Americans were dead, there had to be retribution. The causes of their deaths ultimately meant little, only that they were dead at the hands of an un-American other. But we didn't go to war in Somalia any more than we already had and whatever anger we felt dissipated.

A pair of no-fly zones were established in the northern and southern portions of Iraq to prevent Ba'athist crackdowns against rebellious Kurds in the north and Shia Muslims in the south. US sanctions levied after the invasion of Kuwait persisted after the war ended. Imports that might have helped the Iraq military in any way were restricted, even if they might have been useful to the civilian population there. Exports were also curtailed. The general idea was to limit Iraq's ability to rebuild its armed forces, but in doing so, the economy of the country was crippled by the draconian whimsy of what was allowed into the country and what was forbidden. Food scarcity became a problem. Eventually the Western world allowed Iraq to sell oil, its chief export, for food. Feed the cars of the world, the United Nations seemed to say, and the people of Iraq could eat.

Little of this filtered down to my ears. What made its way to me instead was our attitude of hubris toward Iraq, which we treated like a troubled child. Iraq was dysfunctional, nothing like the "bright, shining city on the hill" I had been taught America was in my thin, unworldly education, and the Iraqi people were supporters of a totalitarian anachronism. Because of its occasional tantrums, the American military maintained a presence in the Middle East and soon Alan was sent to Saudi Arabia for months at a time. His deployments became routine, every year or so, and were later extended to include bases around the Adriatic once America became involved in the various Balkan conflicts. All the angst of his absence during the Gulf War was replaced by an acceptance of this new routine. We missed him whenever he left, of course, but it didn't sting as much.

He was here one day, gone the next, and then in a few months he returned—just part of the tapestry of our existence. Iraq was bad and would always be bad, or so went the general notion, and because of its badness we would have to endure this. We accepted it, perhaps even cherished our role in it. Not in the way of martyrs but in the way of sacrifice and accepting the sacrifice because there was no other choice. Endurance. America had enemies and Iraq was one of them, perhaps the biggest one now that the Soviets were gone. It could have been any country—Iran and North Korea were certainly on the list—but Iraq was the biggest, the one that mattered in the consciousness of a teenager connected to the whims of geopolitical intrigue by family and by dreams.

Despite the best efforts of all those haunted authors and films, their work had shown me what I wanted to be when I was old enough. I could feel it out there somewhere. The draft that sucked so many of them into the armed forces and into Vietnam had been dead since the early 1970s, replaced by advertisements and enlistment incentives, like college and job skills, to fill the vacancies of an all-volunteer military. But I would not need all that, I thought. I just needed freedom—the freedom to be old enough to march into the recruiting office and sign the papers and finally, *finally*, step into the world of rifles and airstrikes, ambushes and patrols, of all that language.

I was locked onto a rail headed only in one direction. Any other choice was no real choice at all. There was no mystery to it, no question as to whether I would have my own little sliver of the American war story. Even if I understood the postcolonial flexing of much of Western military involvement from the end of World War II onward, it didn't really matter as long as I was allowed to participate or be a witness to it. Every single one of the fifty-eight thousand names etched into the dark marble of the Vietnam War Memorial in Washington, DC, signaled the myopic extremes of Cold War–era American foreign policy. I know I understood this by the time I was fourteen, but it was irrelevant in terms of my desires. I could not control what the American empire decided to do to, or for, another nation and secretly wasn't sure I even wanted to. Whenever it came time for me to go, I was ready to parrot so many men who hauled off to Vietnam, the men who arrived willingly, despite having knowledge of the flawed national reasons for being there, lugging their rifles and machine guns into the jungles filled with misery and death while someone somewhere muttered: "This is the only war we've got. Don't knock it."

DELTA

We each devise our means of escape from the intolerable.

—William Styron, *A Tidewater Morning*

I awake in the dirt with my rifle beside me. It is a clear night, and cool, the kind bonfires and whiskey and good music grow from. I pull off my poncho liner and sit up. I'm next to the Humvee among a scattering of abandoned houses that look gray and worn. Cory and Boomhauer and Airborne-Marine are asleep next to me. A radio beeps and crackles from inside the command post.

I've been awakened by a dog standing off to my left, maybe ten feet away. Its snout is down, its eyes up, in a question. It is a big dog with matted black fur, its ribs outlined by malnutrition.

Dogs are the eternal common denominator at night. We can hear them in the canals and around the dikes of the fields that line the river and out in the desert, baying and howling into the darkness in packs, telegraphing our movements and general business to the kingdom we vie over. I once watched a squad of puppies burst from the desert and run down a length of Humvees on a road as we waited for a Black Hawk helicopter to evacuate a wounded Marine. The little dogs yapped and skipped around us, climbed up our legs with their front paws, then skittered away in glee, taking the ugly energy of the medevac with them. We love dogs because they remind us of dogs at home, but we are also afraid of dogs because of their hunger and disease. Sometimes we must shoot them. It is a wretched thing, and when we do, it feels as if we have betrayed ourselves.

I grab my rifle and stand. The big black dog remains motionless. I do not know if it is sick or driven to some kind of madness from rabies. I do know that the others are asleep and I am awake and I cannot have this dog bite one of them. I am on its land and I am scared of it. It no doubt wants food, but I have none I am willing to share. It lifts its head and opens its jaw and pants easily. Then it closes it again and watches me and I don't know if it's contemplating an attack or simply my intentions. It makes no sound.

"Take off," I whisper at it, but it does not move.

I begin to think about all the concerns I have to consider when shooting a dog in the middle of the night. The shot from my rifle will certainly awaken the Marines around me. There might even be a moment of confusion as they try to figure out if someone mistakenly blew off his own toe or killed the point man of some mujahideen kidnapping squad baked right from our overgrown imaginations. Flashlights would reveal the emaciated mess in the rocky desert—the matted fur and the black gums with yellow teeth, the smell of dander and blood. There would be judgments and the lingering questions as to the shooting's true necessity. The body would also have to be dragged off and then I would have to bury it because it does no good to leave a body to decay in the middle of everything. Then, of course, I would have to bury it again within me. I do not want to shoot a dog.

I have already shot at human beings and will shoot at them again. I will never truly know if I kill anyone, but the action alone is enough; I'm already soiled. I am also certainly not new in this world. There is a red line reaching back to the marked-up walls of caves that shows arrows crossing into beasts and men, glorifying their destruction, or at least accounting for it. In war, we volunteer for the survival of our tribes and our kings, our emperors and despots and chancellors. We volunteer for our friends and our lovers and our warped ideas of God, for riches or land or sometimes for no reason at all. Every trigger we squeeze is an elective action with infinite motivations— some large, many smaller—and every time we do it, we volunteer ourselves on an altar of death. But right now, in this instance, killing a dog is too much.

I pick up a rock at my feet and toss it at the dog's front paws. The creature bolts across the desert to a patch of broken ground below. In the darkness,

I see other dogs lying about, a dozen or more moving subtly in the night haze, the ghostly apparitions of our own ancient history, canine Bedouins traveling across the dunes that outline the fable of some twelfth-century scroll. Some migrate silently across the dirt and rocks. Others lie in the dust and rest their snouts on their front legs. One chews at its fur. Whatever fears I have of any of us being bitten in the night by a lone dog are meaningless and futile.

I lie down and rest my rifle on the ground beside me and cover us both with my poncho liner. I fall asleep. When I wake, the dogs are gone. A gunner on a nearby Humvee ambles over after breakfast and tells us the dogs slept in a tight circle around Cory, me, and the rest, like a silent, protective wreath. At some point before sunrise, the dogs arose and moved away.

VIII

The tank column from the First Cavalry Division was stopped cold where the smooth hill met the floor of the Mojave. I sat on top of the long slope that looked into the broad valley. The tanks had appeared below like tiny beetles in the purple light just before sunrise. The moment they advanced, old US Army tanks painted with red stars and dressed to resemble Soviet-era armor snapped blanks from their main guns on the top of the hill while lasers that fixed to their bore sights signaled death to the crews of their targets. The training battle lasted less than ten minutes and then it was quiet.

The commander of a nearby tank pressed open the turret hatch and stood tall in the cool morning. He pulled off his helmet and ran his fingers through his matted hair. He lit a cigarette and rested against the back of the turret. His face was smudged with grime and sweat from the heat that brewed inside the crew compartment. He looked like a blue-collar knight perched in the rotating saddle of his brutal steel animal. He saw me watching from below. He addressed me with a thick grin, but I couldn't hear him over the rumble of his tanks' giant diesel motor. Then he tossed me a slab of beef jerky. After a few minutes, he flicked his cigarette into the desert, carefully lowered himself into the turret, and closed the steel hatch. I was fifteen and he was the coolest person I had ever seen.

I sat in the stiff passenger's seat of an open-air Humvee. I was dressed in my camouflage Civil Air Patrol uniform, wearing it with a whole new group of teenagers now that I'd returned to the United States. A cadet named Thompson, a nerdy fifteen-year-old from Riverside, and I had been paired together and assigned to an army lieutenant before sunrise. Thompson was unconscious in the backseat. He had remained awake for most of the cold twilight ride from the steel hut we had slept in the previous evening to our spot overlooking the valley. Once we stopped, he ate the stale coffee grinds from a Folgers packet that came with his MRE. He showed me the grinds packed between his brown teeth in a ridiculous smile, then fell into a surprisingly deep sleep. Even the booms of the tank cannons and the whine of a passing attack aircraft failed to awaken him.

The muscular lieutenant had said very little all morning. He ruminated in the driver's seat of the Humvee with a ball of snuff packed behind his lip. His job was to loiter around the army training grounds and serve as a referee for the war games. He carried a bulky laser called a "God Gun," which he used to reset the hit notification gear fitted on the tanks and soldiers. Our battles were essentially a giant game of laser tag and he had the power to resurrect the dead. It seemed some staff officer had given him the extra duty of chaperoning two pesky teenagers playacting as soldiers on what would otherwise be a slow morning in the desert. He didn't talk much.

In the early afternoon, the lieutenant drove us back to the main base and dropped us off with the rest of the cadets, mumbling "Good luck, buddy" before speeding away with a spray of pebbles from his rear tires. After an hour or so, our chaperones packed us into their cars and sped west, back toward home. Within a few hours of watching tanks play war in the California desert, I was stretched out on the couch in the dark living room in my dad's duplex in Palmdale. With a belly full of Carl's Jr., I was battling sleep while I futilely tried to decipher the chapter on offensive operations in a US Army field manual I had discovered on the shelf of an army/navy surplus store.

My mom and stepdad and sister were somewhere in Georgia, but I did not live with them anymore.

"The grass isn't always greener on the other side," my mother had warned me when I told her I was going to live with my dad. She had a habit of using aphorisms to punctuate a point: "It's six of one, half dozen of the other," she'd say, or "Life is hard; it's harder when you're stupid."

She made her green-grass comment as we sat in the living room of our apartment in the Misawa tower. It was late, around eleven. *Saturday Night Live* was on the television. I had just come home from a movie at the base theater. It was springtime and warm and I had walked through the dark streets of base housing listening to the Doors on my headphones, no doubt imagining Vietnam or the girl Brandi I had a crush on, and somewhere in that travel, I thought about my dad and about going to live with him when we rotated back to the United States at the end of the summer. "Back to the World," as the GIs in 'Nam called it. I had not seen my dad in nearly three years.

My mom's remark was not meant to suggest California would be somehow worse than where they were headed, which was another castle in the kingdom, this time in Georgia, where the air force was sending Alan. Aside from brief visits to Alan's father's place, I didn't know Georgia from anywhere else. She said it with a sense of unemotional honesty, suggesting that my life with my dad might not be better than my life had been with my mother and Alan and my sister.

But it was the belief I had built for myself slowly. While in Japan, a divide had grown between me and my family—namely, my mother. It grew, in part, out of my flagging grades and my parents' inability to navigate me through the struggle.

In modern terms, my mother might be called a warrior, but I always preferred the term *soldier*. Not in any specific way, as in a soldier of the US Army, but rather in a general sense: *soldiering, soldierly, she soldiered*. She demanded enduring, soldiering through.

She was the chief disciplinarian in our house, the drill master, the noncommissioned officer. "Don't cry or you'll get something to cry about" was a common refrain. She fed us and dressed us and protected us like a sergeant might. It was almost as if she were living in two worlds, the one she wanted and the one she had. She could be as harsh and unflinching as any NCO, but then her role as mother would intercede, creating a confusing dichotomy in the mind of an eight-year-old boy, and even a teenager's. For nearly all my time in Utah and Japan, I never fully knew when I walked through the front door of our house whether the sergeant or the mother would be waiting. Finally, on that Saturday night with Chris Farley inducing laughter from the television, I announced my desire to go to California to live with my dad. She took my decision passively, as if it were needed but not openly acknowledged.

My mother was born and raised in a military family. Her father, Don, had been in air force intelligence, as had her stepfather, and for much of her childhood she lived on or around military bases in the United States and in Europe, its servicemembers facing down the Soviets; her life was punctuated by the saber-rattling nuclear weapons tests that threatened mutual annihilation. My mother was a child of this environment as well as a participant. She enlisted in the air force in the late seventies. Pictures of her in basic training and at her follow-on technical school show her dressed in her starched olive-drab fatigues—a woman in uniform, a beacon of social progress. She took immense pride in serving in the defense of the United States and its Western ideals. My mother was in love with the uniform and the sense of order it brought from chaos. It represented discipline and commanded respect. She once told me it was about honor. My father and stepfather worked in their uniforms, but their fealty lived in the backdrop, a sort of quiet hum; my mother wore hers like a cloak. When she spoke about the military and about the people in it, her voice filled with a sheer, scaling pride that felt immutable and unavoidable.

She became a reservist after I was born. But at the start of the Persian Gulf War, when there was a chance that both she and my stepdad might be deployed to the Middle East, she left the service altogether to avoid the separation of our family. She was a military spouse from then on, her own service relegated to the back pages of our family story. She embodied the virtue that military service is just that, a *service*, something provided without flash or pomp. There were no medals or banners in our house, no bumper stickers on our cars. She put her uniforms in the closet.

But growing up, I always had this sense she was holding on to a remnant of the military service she had had to sacrifice on the altar of motherhood. I felt it when she gave me instruction on calling out drill commands as a CAP cadet or simply coordinated the daily efforts of our house. She would harangue me if my uniform wasn't ironed or if my boots weren't properly shined, all in a way that made her seem less like a mother and more like a drill master.

The military spouse lives in a perpetual state of aggressive compromise beyond the basic demands of marriage. The military is a third partner in the house, a jealous one, and its whims trump the needs and desires of anyone tethered to it. It's not that military spouses can't build fulfilling lives—they certainly can—but they must do so within the shifting boundaries of the military. Entire dreams can be cast aside by simple relocation orders or deployments, and spouses are constantly pulled in three directions, even if only unconsciously, by the demands of family, their own goals, and the military. While the average servicemember has to endure the physical and emotional hardships of deployments and even war, the spouse left behind risks sacrificing slivers of their dream. It might not be a sacrifice in battle, but it's a sacrifice nonetheless. The roads to the courthouses outside every American military base are partially paved with the bones of dead marriages from spouses who ultimately found that sacrifice too much to bear. After my mom left the air force, she went to school to become a nurse, but no sooner did she complete her training than she had to relocate to Japan, a place where there was little demand for her services because the military handled nearly all medical needs on the base. While she never complained, and seemed disdainful of anyone who would, I always sensed she felt the sting of her sacrifice. It seemed to produce its own tension in our house and its toxicity drove me to get out of her way.

It was Southern California sunny as my dad pulled away from the airport. I had landed at LAX in the morning, after some twelve hours airborne, and said a stiff goodbye to my mother and stepdad and sister. Now I sat in the passenger's seat of his red Audi and watched the United States flow past the window while Counting Crows played on the radio.

The world outside the windows seemed bright and dreamlike, but that might have been from the jet lag. America seemed huge in the car window, familiar and comfortable, sprawled and relentless, compared to the almost quaint confines of Japan. I could feel the country's immensity in the broad, packed lanes of Highway 101 and Interstate 5, the dun horizon littered with houses and big signs for McDonald's and gas stations. Giant rapacious malls and department stores, stretching endlessly, reached for my wallet. But I wanted all of it—the restaurants and the sun and the gawdy billboards; the palm trees and convertibles and the surfer girls; the desert breeze and morning ocean fog; the California movies and California television and California music. I wanted to go to the beaches and through the hills, to hit the Sunset Strip and cruise along Mulholland Drive and the Pacific Coast Highway, and there in the seat, hands on the wheel and shifter, was my dad—*right there!*—after three years apart. Sometimes I stared at him. I wanted to put the dream in my pocket, wholly, and believe I was home.

When we pulled into his duplex in the desert valley of Palmdale, I dropped everything into the spare bedroom, *my* bedroom now, and was happy to see the two model jets still suspended from the ceiling where I had hung them when I visited three years back. That night, I tried not to let jet lag crush me into the couch cushions while my dad plucked at his big Martin guitar.

We did not talk about why I was there. In fact, much of the energy that propelled our previous visits was missing. He was slightly tense and dour, as if caught in a net. I would come to understand this later, but not yet.

The military was always there, the thread tugging at me in the background, directing my judgments. I was outside the castle walls. Officially. I could not explain what that meant in the moment. I suppose it meant nothing in those first few days, caught as I was in flash imagination of the California dream. But over time, I began to notice the reality around me. The weeds that lived in the cracks in the side street gutters. The abandoned empty lots, broken by stunted shrubs and tumbleweed. The neighborhoods baked almost flat by the perpetual sunlight. It felt dirty somehow, unformed, missing a substructure—a cheap judgment, which I now understand came from living on manicured military bases. It is also true that I was nervous.

My nervousness was compounded when I began my sophomore year at a school that stood in stark contrast to the gentility of my school in Misawa. I quickly learned my new school was helmed by a menagerie of threadbare teachers, their altruism dulled into cynicism under a barrage of teenage threats. Deputies patrolled the grounds alongside campus security. A month after I arrived, while hanging outside my next class with a tall girl named Tori, we watched a squad of security guards and a few policemen sprint across the campus to the large basketball and handball courts near the back corner of the property as shrill whistles from loudspeakers drummed us back to class early. An argument between one faction or another had driven the hard-asses of three races—Whites, Blacks, and Hispanics—to line up on three sides of the blacktop and charge at each other like a cross between the Battle of Hastings and a San Quentin prison brawl. My new world beyond the moats made me anxious; it felt too loose and chaotic and even violent. Also, I was too socially naive to navigate it. I didn't have the language or, for that matter, the toughness.

Compared to Palmdale, life inside the castle walls of the military had been like living in a vaguely socialist environment. Everyone was paid the same based on rank, irrespective of race or gender. There was access to affordable healthcare and decent schools. I never felt uncared for or worried that I would go without a meal. There were also few drugs and little violence outside of parental corporal punishment and jackass bullies, neither of which were unique to the larger military world. My biggest concern had been war or military interventions abroad that might rob me of my stepdad, even if temporarily. Now, in Palmdale, I could feel my inexperience in classrooms of teenagers, some of whom were witness to and shaped by fear—a fear, I now understand, that was born from trying desperately not to become chaff beneath the classist and racist millstones of American society. The California dream was gone. It's arguable it ever existed at all; I had only wanted it to.

I think about Peter in this instance. Peter was a peaceful boy who lived with his father, mother, and younger sister in a small three-bedroom house not far from Palmdale Boulevard in a neighborhood built in the 1950s during the postwar housing boom. The front lawn was more weeds and broad patches of dead soil than grass, and the driveway was split and cracked.

Peter sat behind me in math class. He was shy and wore his sandy-blond hair short, almost in a flattop; the frames for his large glasses were a decade out of style. He resembled a short-sleeved government office worker. Peter and his friends—Stephen and his girlfriend, Shannon; Erik; and a taciturn underachiever nicknamed F-Man, a name given presumably for his academic prowess—huddled together on the awkward floe of high school. We became friends, too, and most of our days not buried in classrooms were spent in front of computers. Peter's eyes came to life in those moments as he tinkered with the guts of old circuit boards or kept them fixed to the glow of a monitor as a new system came to life.

Peter's father had worked in the aerospace industry. Heavy hitters like Lockheed Martin, Northrop Grumman, and NASA had been giant employers in the valley. Lockheed Martin had designed the U-2 and SR-71 spy planes and the F-117 Nighthawk stealth fighter at its research facility on the west side of the airport. Palmdale had once grown fat on the back of Reagan-era defense budgets, but those days were gone after a rare drawdown in spending after the Cold War. Now Peter's father pulled shifts as a security guard, working until early in the morning, coming home when Peter was asleep, then heading out again while Peter was at school, returning from one moonlighter and heading right into another.

Once a month, Peter and his dad tooled in their Ford Pinto to Redondo Beach, where an electronics swap meet was held in the parking lot of an old TRW Inc. building, and sometimes I joined them. Peter's father was an amateur radio operator and he and Peter often talked in esoteric terms about transmitters and amplifiers and radio circuitry while I picked through old computer motherboards and graphics cards and old proto-laptops with green digital screens. I always felt like an interloper in those moments, stealing energy from their rare father-and-son experience. Afterward, we cruised through the Angeles National Forest into the Antelope Valley. When his dad dropped me off, he made sure to ask me for gas money before they sputtered back to their life.

Their house was old and crumbling. They had projects in the garage, like an old truck that they could never finish because of time and money. His family seemed to be clinging to the world with their fingernails, or at least that was how it seemed to me in comparison with our surefooted military existence. His mom was a mercurial woman who, planted in an armchair in front of the television, was a fixture in their living room. In a screeching tenor, she'd demand that her son make her mayonnaise sandwiches or refill her drink. One afternoon, while we pecked away at his computer, she freely berated him in front of me when he didn't move fast enough. I sat next to him, listening as my skin crawled, eager to appear invisible.

"She does that all the time," he said quietly once he returned. "All the time 'Get me juice' and 'Make me a sandwich.' Nonstop. Like I'm a fucking slave." He shook his head, his eyes dark.

Peter seemed psychically exhausted. We talked about the future, in the way of teenagers, but he seemed unsure of what the future meant in any tangible sense. College was out, locked behind a financial and experiential wall. All this made the military even more appealing to me, and more righteous, a way out, and yet for Peter it wasn't. Peter had no direct connection to the military that I knew of, nor did many other kids I met in Palmdale. I was an oddity. He viewed the military as a construct of extremes far too draconian to be acceptable—all the drill sergeants and yelling and projection of hypermasculine intensity, never mind war. Who wants to receive a paltry paycheck in exchange for getting chewed out by a superior and then possibly being left to die in some alien place chosen by the whims of foreign policy? Poverty was not enough to motivate Peter to consider the military an option.

"I couldn't handle someone yelling at me," he said when I suggested it. "I don't think I could deal with it."

The military stereotype was something I was happy to play into when it suited me—namely, with dumb teenage gags. One Saturday morning, my dad took me to a swap meet at the racetrack in Santa Clarita. While sifting through booths of old clothes and cassette tapes and novelty knives, I came across a vendor hawking a genuine Vietnam-era helmet and a dummy hand grenade. The helmet cost ten dollars. It had a faded camouflage cover that was lightly torn in places. The chin straps were soft from age. I made a helmet band from an old bicycle inner tube and slipped it over the top of the helmet cover like the pictures of the Marines I had seen fighting in Hue and Khe Sanh.

The grenade was harmless, just an iron body with a blue spoon and a metal pin, a paperweight, but it looked real enough. It usually never left my bedroom, but one summer afternoon I put it in my book bag and biked to my friend Erik's house. A big kid with a fleshy face and a grin that narrowed his eyes into slits, Erik was energetic and gullible, prone to outbursts and wild flashes of lark. We lounged on the back patio of the house, two bored teenagers. I was hungry.

"You got any of those burritos left?" I asked.

"Naw, we ran out."

I went inside the house and returned with the grenade hidden against my side. I held it out and put a finger through the pin.

Erik gawked. "What is that?"

"It's a hand grenade. What's it look like?" I said. "Now what do you have to eat around here?"

He shot up from the chair in a panic and stood with his hands in front of him. His face trembled with cross of humor and fear.

"Where did you get a friggin' hand grenade?"

"Who cares?" I said. "Just get me some friggin' food or I'll blow this place up."

"*Oh my God, we don't have anything!*" he cried.

I remained calm. "You're lying. I know it. You better find me a burrito or I'll pull the pin."

"*There's nothing here, I swear, please don't blow us up!*"

"How much money you got?" I asked.

He began to frantically search through the pockets of his big cargo shorts.

"Too slow," I said. I pulled the pin and tossed the grenade. It knocked against the concrete at his feet. Erik bellowed a hard scream and bolted around the corner of the house.

But he soon returned. He sat down in his chair and held the grenade in his hand. "It's heavy," he said, then: "Dude, let's get Peter the same way when he gets here."

Peter arrived an hour later, but when I tried the same gag on him and tossed the grenade, he merely shrugged and rolled it into the gravel around the porch with his big sneaker. He looked at me with a spark behind his big eyeglasses. "What kind of psycho owns a *real* grenade?"

I was a teenager, mindless, a prankster around people I was comfortable with, aloof or shy around people I was not. I respected Peter and Erik and the rest; they seemed to be struggling in ways I could not entirely fathom. But I had also come from a world they had seen only through whispers of popular culture and I felt a light thrill in playing up to it. My experience with the military up to that point had been little more than aggressive tourism, but I believed I was onto something bigger and better than whatever I was seeing in Palmdale. I couldn't understand—and gag grenades aside—why anyone would favor a world I perceived as crippling, impoverished nothingness over what I felt mattered dearly in my heart.

In James Webb's Vietnam novel *Fields of Fire*, which I had first read just before moving to California, a young and poor street tough nicknamed "Snake" looks at a newspaper photo of US Marines sacking the Imperial City of Hue from the North Vietnamese army and thinks to himself, "There's some mean motorscooters for you. Uh huh. Well, I'm gonna get me some of that. Bring me home a medal. No more mopping up other people's pee." The popular notion that poor Americans volunteer for the military solely to get out of some economic hole is cheap and one-dimensional. It's also one of those snide rhetorical tools used by gentry to denigrate the military, especially the enlisted ranks, as a repository for the American lower class.

In fact, the military appeals to one's vanity; it is a vehicle for self-respect. While the paychecks and college money all matter, an inherent personal resolve, a sense of worth, must account for something in a desire to join the military. Money is not enough to risk death. People will, however, risk it for pride.

IX

In the summer a year after I arrived, my dad took me to Disneyland. Then he took me to the airport. I was leaving California.

We packed up his new red Jeep Cherokee, which had replaced his Audi after a car accident, and left his Palmdale duplex for Anaheim in the late morning. We checked into a Motel 6, my dad's go-to lodgings for overnight stops. He held no reason to look for an alternative motel, not even a better one, if the big blue sign with the red 6 was in eye shot. I unloaded the Jeep into a room where the smell of disinfectant and industrial laundry detergent and old cigarette smoke hung from the wallpaper. The pair of beds were draped with brown floral spreads that looked like couch upholstery from some sad-ass seventies-era basement. I tossed my gray suitcase and book bag onto the bed. The springs groaned, but I didn't care. It was only one night and then I would be gone.

Motel 6 and Disneyland were the only stops en route to the airport, a distraction to kill time before I awoke in the morning and boarded a plane and left. My dad never said much about how I was too old for Disneyland and neither did I. I don't remember caring much; it was all for kids and the lines were too long anyway. Our trip felt like the afterthought of the California dream.

At some point in my time in Japan, my dad had come to hate Palmdale and California. All that desert, its relentless tan and brown, had triggered some internal flight response, or maybe a latent sense of wanderlust fueled a deep ire. His hatred coated his mood. It forced a groan from his throat at odd moments whenever we drove around town on errands. He'd look out the window and mutter a grinding "I just want to get the hell outta here" at the windblown buildings and trash fluttering across the gutters on a typical desert afternoon.

My dad had an amateur interest in history and indulged me with conversations about Vietnam and the military, discussions that would never have happened with my mother or my stepfather. We talked about the Gulf of Tonkin resolution, the Tet Offensive, and all the other details I had to bottle in my mind and sneak into my Misawa bedroom. He introduced me to films and documentaries about Vietnam, like *Apocalypse Now*, *Vietnam: The Ten Thousand Day War*, and *Dear America: Letters Home from Vietnam*, in ways that were neither jingoistic nor judgmental—it was simply a point of connection between us. Otherwise, I was left to my own devices. I went to school on winter mornings, walking up Avenue R as a fast wind tumbled down from the Sierra Pelona Mountains and Mount McDill. I sat in my classes—there, but also not there, both nervous and uninspired, numbed by a sort of teenage shell shock. Then I'd meet up with Peter and we'd pal around a computer lab, disassembling old IBMs, rebuilding them into our own images, amazed by the colors on the screen and video game battles we fought with them, hiding, unsure of where we were headed, lost in our own tangled teenage circuitry. Sometimes I'd head to the library and read about war; other times, I'd just go home and watch *X-Files*. Then my dad would come home and tell me how much he hated the place. Or he'd sit in the living room and stew with a bowl of pasta and watch television, his mood soured by overcooked torment.

The grass was not greener, as my mother had suggested. Or at least it wasn't the lush green fairways I had grown in my own mind, watered by the short blasts of adrenaline my dad had offered whenever he'd fly into town to see me for a weekend. After I moved in with my dad, I quickly came to understand that my childhood fantasies of his life were just as incongruent as the life he believed his was *supposed* to be but never saw come to fruition in California. It was why we went to Disneyland and it was why I was leaving.

"I just want to get the hell outta here," he'd groan again.

To him, the eternal cause of his woe was the FAA. He was an air traffic controller at the big control center that handled bulk air traffic over much of the Southwest. Every shift, which typically stretched late into the evening, my dad sat in a room lit only by the green glow of the radar scopes and the backlit buttons and dials and strange maps of Southern California that were crossed with lines delineating restricted airspace and various flight plans marked with esoteric codes and jargon I would never understand. If the demands of air traffic control bothered him, he never showed it. But the bureaucratic side of the job—the administrators and policies and paperwork and general water-cooler malaise—all seemed to wear on him. At the point when I moved in with him, he was allowing his feeling of stagnation to keep him from building any kind of real life for himself in Palmdale. He accepted me into his house because I was his son and he was my dad, but he cashiered opportunities that he perceived might lock him into the desert permanently, like long-term relationships and marriage, and spoke about a new life for himself in some other city like a convict eyeing parole. He wanted to go to Denver. He talked about it as if it were some kind of spiritual panacea, as if moving there would cure his ills. He seemed to think that happiness was just beyond the next hill, if only he could reach it. He marked time and hoped for an escape.

My dad had spent his childhood in the dust bowl of southern Oklahoma. His mother scraped out a living as a hotel maid to support him and his two brothers. There wasn't much money to go around, no child support or alimony. Pining after some kind of adventure or at least the simple promise of wider horizons, he turned to the air force immediately after high school. His two brothers stuck around. They didn't have much use for the military.

He had no father to send him off. His own father was a ghost, a cavity in my thin understanding of family. His name was Bob, and throughout my childhood I knew nothing about him, other than that he had been in the army. On the rare occasions I'd ask my dad about him, I always got a stony response, just a word or two to demonstrate his utter lack of interest in the topic, followed by a quick change of the subject. It wasn't just that Bob didn't exist; it was that Bob wasn't *meant* to exist, as if a substructure of resentment had been intentionally laid to rot the image of the man from our minds.

Years later, after I became a Marine, I was overwhelmed with a desire to know *something* about the man. Military service has become ancestral in the American narrative. War is a family business; the son picks up where the father has left off, applying his own texture to it. I wanted to put on a uniform and go off to war in part because my stepdad had done it in the Persian Gulf and my grandfathers and related kin had done it in Vietnam, Korea, World War II, and further back still. They did not always serve because it was their dream but more out of necessity and simple obligation, part-and-parcel duty of being American. Children see their parents performing their duty and they believe it worthy and want to be in service to it too. Military service is a fairly easy choice when surrounded and reared by it. But for me, it had also become a narrative of bloodline and history that I felt I needed to understand. And so I was curious about my absent grandfather.

I spoke to my uncle Eric, who was far more indulgent of any conversations surrounding my grandfather than my own father. He explained that Bob had run out on my grandmother, my two uncles, and my father when they were children. Bob was in the army then. He moved to Germany, remarried, then started a whole new

Alexander franchise somewhere in western Arkansas. His previous family was largely forgotten.

I was not angry when I learned this. Anger was not something I was comfortable with yet. I could be notionally angry at an enemy pointed out to me by my Marine leaders or by the president, but I could not drum up anger for a figure in the lost halls of my family whom I had never met or seen and who had no agency over my life. His absence had been the status quo. But I wanted to hear his voice, to know he was real and alive and not some avatar of resentment and abandonment. I wanted to fill in the gap, to understand more about where I came from. I sniffed around the internet and made awkward phone calls to anyone with my last name in the area. Cell phones hadn't yet swamped the landline market, so many folks still had their numbers listed in phone directories. After a few calls, I landed on a man named Jim.

"Hi, I'm Jerad. I'm trying to track down Bob Alexander."

The voice on the other end was cheerful, an older man. "Oh yes. I know Bob. Who is this again?"

When I told him my full name, he boomed through the phone that he was in fact Jim, my great-uncle, and knew exactly who I was and who my father was. I had never heard of him. He was a stranger, but at the moment I was elated.

Jim explained that he would have to contact Bob first and check with him. He didn't explain why. He promised to call me back and quickly hung up. He seemed motivated to be helpful.

My phone rang about ten minutes later. It was Jim. Bob had apparently given some kind of casual okay because Jim gave me a 1-800 number to call.

"It's a direct line to him. He'll answer."

I knew no one who had a 1-800 number. I had no idea what it meant, aside from some vague idea that it might have been a clue to his financial status, and for a moment I panicked, thinking Bob might assume I was after him for money. He might have owed it to my dad and uncles as a reparation for his absenteeism, but I wasn't interested in that. I just wanted to talk.

I dialed the number. Waiting, I pictured him in a dark office in the back of some broad house, an older man sitting, very grandfatherly, in his leather lounger amid old books and wood paneling. He wore a cardigan and collared shirt and his hair was short. Maybe he wore glasses, maybe not, but his face, smelling like my dad's aftershave, was chiseled in stone by wisdom and time. I wondered what life and history he might unlock for me with our connection, what veil he might pull back on his actions and the legacy of our lineage.

"Hello?"

Before I called Bob, Jim had emailed me a copy of a family tree that reached back to the late eighteenth century. Reading the list of names and dates of birth and death felt like looking into a room full of strangers who might have been happy at my presence if they had known I existed. My family, at least the family I knew, was small. No more than maybe twenty souls, most of them spread out across the country, a product of military service at the generational level. I had family in Maryland and Georgia and Oklahoma and Texas, people I had seen a handful of times and some not at all. Names with no faces.

Now here was this document. I scrolled down it on my computer in my barracks room as I drank a beer, awed and yet frustrated. Every Alexander I had known was listed, mainly my dad and my two uncles and some cousins. And there, farther down, was an entry for me. It took me a moment to find it, however, because my name was misspelled "Jarrod." I never learned how my name got there, but it spoke a quiet meaning. They knew of us. They knew who we were, maybe even where. And yet I had had to find *them*, to seek them out directly. Whether their silence was intentional or the by-product of shame or guilt, it did not matter. They knew of us and had done nothing.

"Hello," I said.

My conversation with Bob was ultimately meaningless. I learned little about him and nothing as to why he left so many years ago, and I did not have the language to ask, or perhaps the courage. I am supposed to show these things as I write, the language of our conversation and the revelations it brought, but I will not show any of it, because after I hung up, I realized he had said nothing. The words were empty, just twenty minutes or so of forced, mindless pleasantries. He was as absent in his speech as he was in his actions.

We spoke once more, maybe twice. Each time was the same. Then so-called War on Terror began and I didn't call him for another year. When I finally reached out again one bored night, I found the number had been disconnected.

I began to better understand my father's stony resentment. Jim, my great-uncle, when answering my phone call, announced that he "knew" me, but then I saw my misspelled name in his family tree and I began to feel that resentment too, if subtly. If Jim knew me and knew my family, why the silence in the absence of his brother's responsibility? Why know *of* us but not truly *know* us? His lack of moral courage, and the seemingly total lack of accountability, made our exclusion seem concrete, deliberate. Blood had thinned into water. And so my family in southern Oklahoma lived as orphans, alone and separate, removed from the legacy the Alexanders had cultivated since the inception of America.

Years later, I explored the family tree and discovered that the Alexanders on Bob's end of that broken chain also held a legacy of military service, one that seemed to stretch back as far as the American Revolution. I would wonder what stories I might have known, what they might have told one another about their connection to the earth of America by virtue of their service. What stories did they tell about Christopher Columbus Alexander, a rifleman in the Forty-Sixth Illinois Volunteer Infantry, who saw action at Fort Donelson under Ulysses S. Grant, and about Emery Alexander, who was killed in February of 1945 while fighting with the Ninety-Fourth

Infantry Division? What bond was shared among the living? Did they tell one another the stories of their wars, passing them down from one generation to the next, a litany of horrors and glories molded and pressed into American narratives of patriotism? American history is complicated, but it is ours, and I feel moments within it are worthy of pride. But the stories of these Alexanders are not mine and I cannot take ownership of them. They were denied to us the moment Bob abandoned his sons. And me.

I could rationalize the divorce between Bob and my grandmother. Chemistry changes and love dissolves. My grandfather was in his early twenties during his marriage to my grandmother. He was a soldier and had presumably seen combat in Korea as an artillery forward observer. A combination of youth and the drudgery of soldiering in the dust bowl of Oklahoma could produce a rotten foundation for a marriage for anyone with dreams of something, or somewhere, else. But for Bob to abandon his children, shoving them aside to start some new franchise, hiding behind a new life, was unconscionable to me, maybe criminal, certainly amoral. I knew that even then, during our stiff and abrupt phone conversations. How does a man do this? How does a man turn away from three boys, robbing them of the joys and lessons of having a father?

Grudges are unhealthy, perpetuating themselves to no real end. I spent time shuttling away any anger I might have felt over the separation from our American lineage that Bob's abandonment created. But there is a part of me that knows I can wade into that anger anyway and offer a decisively American *fuck him*, and I would be righteous in doing so. Sometimes I do.

My dad felt this anger inside him too. In every place he's lived he has maintained a den where he spends most of his time sniffing out deals on Amazon and eBay or watching videos on YouTube. During a weekend visit with him, we were absently plucking at his guitars in the quiet darkness when I mentioned I had spoken to his father.

He did not look at me, but the temperature around him seemed to drop. My dad could be restless, easily agitated, but nothing in his speech had ever revealed any real anger. That day, it did.

"I don't want anything to do with it," he said. "I don't want to know anything about it. I don't want him to know about me or what I'm doing or where I'm at. You do what you want, but I don't want my name even mentioned to him. I need you to understand that. Do not say anything about me to that man."

I sat silent, stunned. It was the most I had ever heard him say about his own father, and every word of it signaled a thinly checked flood of anger and resentment, that vat of bile churning just under the surface. The air in the room held its own breath, then sighed when my dad finally changed the subject.

We would never see any semblance of closure, no final accounting for his abandonment. Sometimes closure is impossible by virtue of human failings. Bob would die in late 2016. I found his obituary only through a Google search on a slow workday. I read that he was survived by his two sons, two strangers named Mark and Patrick, and his litany of grandchildren and great-grandchildren, all of them mysteries to me. There was no mention of my father and my grandfather's two other sons, my uncles Eric and Donald-Gene. Or his half-dozen other grandchildren, for that matter. We are strangers too. Over time, my family's anger would abate into something more neutral and retrospective, removed by time. Still, when I think about it now, when I really look down into that vat, I can reach out and touch that anger, and when I do, it is scalding.

But looking back at sixteen, walking through Disneyland at the end of the California experience, I can see my dad viscerally and filtered through the memories I have of him in that era: the dark brown hair, the mustache, the polo shirts and shorts and sneakers, and the sunglasses with the nylon strap, which he used to hide a pair of deep brown eyes. I have no doubt my dad remained in my life not simply because I was his son but because his own father had not. This was especially true in the early years of my life, after my parents divorced, when he seemed to struggle with his own role as father, when my mother graciously allowed him access to me even after he had left me alone in the house so he could go to a party. He did his best, flying in for birthdays and holidays, keeping me connected to my grandmother and uncles. And yet now he would soon take me to the airport and put me on a plane, out of his life.

As the end of the school year closed in, my dad began to see his own way out. It came on slowly, a loose idea that formed in the loopholes and caveats found in the tomes of FAA rules and regulations and the human resources malaise of the Average American Bureaucracy. His idea was to send me to Georgia to live with my mother, then appeal to the FAA for a hardship transfer so he could live closer to me. Once he was settled in place, presumably after a year, I could move back in with him. Anything to get out of the desert. Sometimes I wonder if that gut-gnawing tension I saw in my dad in Palmdale, that failure of the machinery of self-made contentment, might have grown from the same root that led Bob to run toward whatever lights he believed he saw. Sometimes I wonder if that same tension lives inside me too. Sometimes it scares me.

I had not thought about the next year or what would happen when this school year ended. In retrospect, it seemed inevitable that I would not stay in Palmdale, regardless of what I wanted, if I had even known. I was not present or aware enough for that. I know I didn't want to leave and was resentful about having to return to my mother, but I don't remember having any real control over it either. So we went to Disneyland and back to the Motel 6 and the next morning we drove back to LAX, where I had landed a year ago. It was sunny and I saw Brian Austin Green from *Beverly Hills: 90210* walking from the terminal. He looked pale and was hiding from his celebrity in sunglasses and with his collar pulled up around his neck. I watched him walk toward baggage claim and I offered a short wave. He waved back just as simply, then disappeared into the crowds, taking California with him. When my dad returned from the bathroom, he promised to buy me a new computer. Then he put me on a plane, and when I landed in Georgia, it was dark and raining. I don't remember if I said goodbye to Peter.

ECHO

There was no harm in taking aim, even if the target was a dream.

—John Knowles, *A Separate Peace*

Rebel Six is a good officer. His Marines love him and he loves them back.
He is a southern boy. Born and bred. He dips tobacco and smokes cigars
and talks to his men with a roadhouse twang that gives him an instant
organic credibility with the blue-collar gentry of the enlisted ranks. He is
an American student of war, a scholar of concepts like "centers of gravity"
and "lines of departure" and "axes of advance." He has at his fingertips the
culmination of a century of American firepower. He loves a good gunfight,
respects the necessity of aggression in winning one, but he also demands the
grind of civic engagement. He is as much of a Marine as a Marine can be, a
True Believer, and someday Congress is going to make Rebel Six a general
because of it.

But for all his machinations and knowledge, he has no power over the
roadside bomb. The insurgents build them from old kerosene and propane
tanks, cell phones, watches, cheap copper wire dug out of walls and the
ground, pressure plates made from plywood, explosives taken from old
Soviet-bloc hand-me-down munitions carted in from Syria, Jordan, old
Palestine, the Balkans, and Chechnya, weapons that were built to kill us
in Western Europe. They make them for ideology and religion. Sometimes
they make them for anger and sometimes for money. Some are meant to be
triggered manually with a cell phone. In Iraq, a cell phone is a weapon and
sometimes we kill people for having them to their ears while watching us
in odd places, like from rooftops or empty street corners. Other bombs are

*just buried and forgotten. Sometimes their own taxis nail them. Sometimes
children find them while playing soccer in the street. Sometimes we find
them first and sometimes we don't.*

*A man is wounded or killed through a random application of physics
and bad luck. One afternoon, I stand on a roof with my rifle against my
shoulder and listen to the heavy staccato of rifle fire in other parts of the
city. A whistling comes in long and fast from my left, its pitch growing. It
is the fragment of something—a bullet or piece of concrete set loose by
explosives—its trajectory absently decided by wind and friction, random
data I have no agency to question. One set of variables and I might not see
the fragment at all. Another set of variables and the fragment might strike
my left cheek. Maybe it hits my temple. Instead, I look around and giggle
nervously after it clips the top of my rifle and takes a sliver of plastic from
the handguard with it. I am lucky.*

*The bespectacled Marine mechanic I know is not. He shows me the burn
on his shoulder where a bullet grazed him. When he does, I see the deadness
of it in his eyes, as if he's seen past the darker side of some equation beyond
his control. And there is the Marine I meet who has been shot in the head
by a sniper. In a twisted sense of irony, his name is Snipes. He lives because
his helmet saved his life, adjusting the mathematics in his favor at the last
moment, the bullet piercing only his wits. Another Marine, who stands next
to me on a rooftop one gray afternoon, is shot in the chest. He is spared by
his rifle buttstock and the thick ceramic plate in his body armor, but for a
long time he sits inside the house on bags of USAID rice and frets when his
buddies keep asking if he's okay. They might stop if it weren't for his pale,
wide eyes that drill into the gray concrete of the foyer wall, silently running
the numbers of his own impermanence. Another Marine is shot by an AK-47.
The bullet has found the right trajectory to firmly enter his body, giving him
a jolt. "I got shot in the butt-tocks," he hollers, our own Forrest Gump, as
he's carried from the roof.*

*But the roadside bomb is another matter. We might tolerate the wayward
bullets and the mortar fire, at least as much as we must, but there is no*

stomach capable of completely extinguishing the fear of the bomb. It is a bile that lives in the perpetual inches in front of every front tire.

Stevens is a boy who has been set permanently into the past tense by a roadside bomb. It happened in the middle of the day. It was hot, but not. Stevens had driven a Humvee down a dirt track with two comrades near the river during Rebel Six's offensive. Stevens was popular. He was a scout sniper, and in the warrior culture of the Marine Corps, the scout sniper is an electrolyte of manhood. With a tanned, tough body, blond hair, and Christian virtues, he cut the one-note figure of the American warrior. But that was also meaningless. A collection of 155 mm artillery rounds had been buried in the dirt track in front of him. Each round was nearly two feet long and about six inches in diameter, about the same as a can of Folgers coffee. Each shell weighed nearly ninety-seven pounds and had a blast radius of roughly thirty meters. When fired from artillery, the shells issue a sighing warble that grows into a shriek before impact, an unnerving sound. When they strike the earth, their explosions erupt from the ground in flash-fire geysers of dirt and smoke and shatter into nearly two thousand hot, sharp metal fragments.

A propane tank, the kind used at backyard barbecues, had been buried with them. It's impossible to say if the whole kit was buried haphazardly or with care, but I can deduce it was buried enough to remain hidden because the big front driver's-side tire of the Humvee rolled across the fresh dirt, across a pressure plate that closed a cheap circuit and triggered the bomb somewhere between a bored lunchtime sigh and an empty thought.

Everything moved in milliseconds. The electrical current set off the explosive compounds, and hot gases expanded into a blast wave from the ground at supersonic speeds—into the tire and through the suspension and the armored floor. The shock wave reverberated between metal and bone, canvas and Kevlar. Cans of snuff and field notebooks and bits of MRE trash and entire cans of ammunition were tossed as if pebbles. The men inside were thrown about, too, their heads and limbs flung against the windows and metal seat frames and the thick metal floor. The overpressure stressed *the resistance and elasticity of the lungs and eardrums; brains recoiled against the inside of their skulls.*

Humvee armor provides some protection and many roadside bombs fail to kill anyone. But not this bomb. The shrapnel ripped through Stevens's body—through the fabric of his camouflage uniform and into the granular, spinous, and basal cell layers of his epidermis, through the sebaceous glands and erector pili muscles and all the little nerve endings that once sent the signals of soft touches from his body to his mind. Bits of metal, large and small, carved jagged paths into his collagen and his elastin fibers through the small blue veins and bright red arteries that moved oxygen and nutrients to all his cells. They cut through his muscles and tendons and ligaments, stretched and shaped by the Marine Corps and American boyhood. The shrapnel pierced the metal containers of the propane tank and released all those pounds per square inch into an inferno that rammed through the holes made by shell fragments The flames reached into the vehicle until they blanketed Stevens with a fireball of expanding gases, reducing him to a marker of flesh and blood and bone. He is still a Marine by the virtue of our mythology, but he is no longer among us. He is now an article of pain, pride, sorrow, and even retribution, another picture in the book of American martyrs.

I see Rebel Six now, just moments after it happens. His command post sits on the western side of a new outpost dug into a small hill—just a large industrial pop-up tent under a small canopy of camouflage netting. Inside, the big map of his battlefield sits on an easel and little pushpins with multicolored flags taped to them represent the location of his men.

The tent fills with a cloud of grief and bitter sadness once the death is revealed. Airborne-Marine bursts from the tent with his face completely awash in tears and snot. He sobs uncontrollably, groaning and speaking to himself with a staccato of searching words. He buries his face in his arm and lets his body shake against a nearby water trailer. Most of us swallow our grief and shock and anger to regurgitate later when there is more time and maybe alcohol. I stand a few dozen feet away with a cigarette drooping down from my mouth stupidly. I did not know Stevens. I had seen him around, perhaps back at Camp Lejeune, but we had never spoken. And yet I am a Marine, too, and this Marine is dead. He is dead and it hurts us all.

If only the circuit hadn't closed. If only the bomb makers had blown themselves up burying it, or the artillery shells had been duds. If only Al Qaeda operatives in Iraq had decided to forget about this sleepy little nowhere river valley. If only our kingdom weren't so terrified of the world and self-righteous enough to exert its power on this land. If only we hadn't come here at all. Maybe this dumb little war would have been skipped and these Marines, these volunteers, these Americans with mothers and fathers and bank accounts and hopes, wouldn't be wounded and killed. Maybe Stevens would still be alive. But he is not. He is dead and there is nothing Rebel Six, or any of us, can do about it.

Rebel Six steps out of the tent and drops his heavy frame onto a small camping stool under the camouflage netting. His body has lost some of its toughness, its larger-than-life air of confidence. He has just lost a man as if he has lost a piece of himself. Our eyes meet. His are wide and wet, but he does not weep. I can see the weight of his sadness in his bright sky-blue irises. His mouth is closed, his jaw slightly clenched. I am not sure if he wants to berate me for staring or transmit some thought to me.

I wrestle with my reaction. I wanted to be him once, when I was much younger, to command troops on some battlefield. But as I stand and watch Rebel Six sitting on his stool in the hard shadow of death, I can see the totality of the burden of ordering men to chance the mathematics. I can see it pressing down on him. As I see it in those moments, the burden appears like the artifact of some old childhood dream dug up from my mind. What does your power mean for you now? I wonder of him. What did Stevens's life mean? Did he truly die for freedom and liberty, or was he sacrificed on the altar of a patriotic vocabulary? What do we gain with the memory of his loss other than another martyr to service? What noble insight? What will we earn with these pains? But I ask Rebel Six nothing. I turn and walk away.

X

I ran through the woods behind my new high school, number three in as many years. It was fall, 1997. Rain had fallen that morning, but now sunlight slanted between wet amber leaves and gray pines. A cool snap in the nostrils. Tree sap and musty decay. The trail was slick, but the black rubber soles of my boots gripped the Georgia earth and the brown pine needles. I was at the front of the column of teenagers with a duffel bag on my back. A sandbag inside pulled the ungainly green mass toward the back of my thighs as I ran, forcing me to pitch forward until I was nearly doubled over. The straps cut into my shoulders and threatened to put my left arm to sleep.

The trail looked unused. I didn't know it was here before now, but it didn't really matter. All I had to do was run to a specified point marked with a flag, turn around, and run back. Teammates ran behind me with a stretcher and large plastic water jug. One boy carried another boy over his shoulders as if he were wounded. A retired army master sergeant with dim eyes waited at the trailhead with a stopwatch, recording our time. We were all students and cadets in the Junior Reserve Officer Training Corps—another American outlet to playact as soldiers: running through the woods, dressing as a facsimile of an American GI, pretending, marking time. But in just a few months, I'd wear the real thing. I'd get my dog tags and helmet, my rifle and flak jacket. Another volunteer for the empire.

I made it to the turnaround point, touching the tree with the flag and running back down the trail. After a few dozen yards, I came across a felled tree that I had crossed earlier. I quickly sat on the log and swung my legs to the other side and kept running.

My hands suddenly felt as if they were being stabbed. Three fat wasps were jabbing their rotten stingers into my skin, two on my left hand and one on my right. I bellowed and frantically swatted my hands clear. I must have stirred up a nest of them somehow, perhaps buried in the dirt or a tree. The trail had seemed long unused.

My hands throbbed. I flicked them as if trying to wick away the poison. I had a mild teenage love for profanity and exercised it when I knew I could get away with it, careful to avoid the ears of southern Christian piety. Now I ran down the trail blathering a stream of unfiltered gibberish into the pines.

A freshman in a camouflage uniform stood just off the trail. He had a big camcorder on his shoulders. Recording the race for posterity. I saw him plainly but continued my litany of teenage vitriol.

I only slowed my cursing once I made it out of the woods. I kept running. My shoulders ached. Sweat poured into my eyes. My hands were on fire. It hurt to ball them into fists and I felt woozy. The pain must have registered on my face because the retired master sergeant with the stopwatch, who normally stood with a dull face as if devoid of thought, looked at me wild eyed, his mouth slack jawed, as I tumbled across the finish line and tossed the amoebic duffel bag to the dirt and shoved my red hands into his face.

"You bother to send anyone down that friggin' trail beforehand?" I said.

He mumbled something about grinding aspirin powder onto my hands, but I walked away. It was a useless question. Others tossed themselves across the finish line. No one else was stung, but I wasn't surprised. Alan and I had spent a few weeks the previous summer working in the yard on a series of projects. While trimming bushes and plucking weeds, I had discovered a terrible symbiosis that existed between me and the insects. I was routinely slapping and swatting away flies and bees and mosquitoes as they angled their hunger in my direction, which all built to a moment when I found myself inadvertently standing on an anthill, the little monsters chewing on my ankles and calves and eventually my hands as I tried first to brush them off, then stripped off my clothes in a tortured dance while expelling another staccato of self-neutered profanity. Alan had laughed and laughed . . .

I sat on one of the water jugs, nursing my swollen hands. I quickly calmed down; I wasn't much for prolonged anger. There was no way anyone could have known about the wasps. I felt a mild venomous grease on the back of my tongue, but I didn't care much. I dug the notion of being able to power through.

The freshman with the camcorder returned with the rest of the cadets. He approached me awkwardly. "So I, uh . . . I got you on tape dropping those f-bombs." He spoke softly, like one kid warning another over the impending doom of an approaching angry parent.

I thought about it a moment, but only a moment. I was nearly eighteen, wearing the uniform of a proto-American soldier. I looked up at him.

"Fuck it."

I had lifted off from California and landed back in King Suburbia, this time in the humid South. My life was now palmetto bugs and cul-de-sacs and college football games, kids who said "yes sir" and "yes ma'am" in class. The high school was a mixture of military kids and upper middle-class southern debutantes. Polished teenage girls in preppy school gear sped off in glossy convertibles that beamed the promise of their parents' credit limits. Boys and even men dressed like out-of-work Baptist deacons on Game Day—khaki pants and polo shirts and loafers and visors with logos of the Masters Tournament or the University of Georgia. Women with cheeks the color of gin and who dressed in floral prints said, "Well, bless your heart" with a dash of veiled horror and church-pew judgment. Whenever I told them I had come from California, they looked at me as if I were from some terrifying land of hedonism and drugs and whatnot else their pastors had warned them about on Sunday mornings.

Georgia was a peaceful, sedate bubble compared to California. We lived off base, deep in quiet, manicured suburbs. There was a steady rhythm in our house, a sense of completeness. Our neighbors were mostly civilians. My parents didn't socialize as much with other servicemembers. Not out of spite or disdain but simply because of the distance. Instead, there were trips to the lake and weekend yard work, church every Sunday and family dinner afterward. My life quickly became a menagerie of teenage daydreams and experiences—best friends and awkward flirtations, summer vacations and the petty dramas of high school crushes. I made good grades. My sister moved toward middle school and pined over *NSYNC and the Backstreet Boys. Alan inched toward retirement. The routine deployments overseas continued unabated. My mother had taken a job as a nurse in a pediatrician's office. She was happier than she had been in Japan and Utah, guided by purpose.

She was also soldiering through the slow death of her father.

My grandfather, Don, lived with his second wife, Gail, in Texas, and split time between Fort Worth and a cabin on the shore of Lake Palestine, near Tyler. Gail had been his childhood friend and for a short time, after he enlisted in the air force in 1953, they sent letters back and forth in a way that held the promise of one kind of future. But she was young and beautiful and he was away, so she married the high school football star and had three children and for nearly twenty years endured the torture of an abusive marriage. Don married an Englishwoman while assigned to the United Kingdom and had two children, one of whom was my mother. I did not know the nature of the relationship between my grandfather and my grandmother, but I knew that he went to Vietnam in 1968 for a yearlong tour and divorced while he was there. I also knew that the Vietnam War was killing him twenty years after the war had ended.

Don's death began in a lab in Chicago a decade before he put on a uniform. During World War II, the Department of the Army commissioned chemists at the University of Chicago to begin experiments with a pair of herbicidal acids—2,4-Dichlorophenoxyacetic and 2,4,5-Trichlorophenoxyacetic—for their application in destroying crops and vegetation over battlefields. The compounds worked specifically on cereal grains, such as rice, and on broadleaf weeds by copying the behavior of the plant's hormones, causing abnormal growth and loss. The various combinations of these compounds produced a series of defoliants known as the "Rainbow Herbicides," because of the color codes given to each type: Agent Green, Agent Pink, Agent Purple, Agent Blue, Agent White, and finally, Agent Orange.

Rainbow Herbicides were never fielded in World War II or during the Korean War. The perception of their effectiveness grew from their use in the 1948–60 Malayan Emergency. British Commonwealth troops hoping to dispose of communist guerillas by desiccating the jungle hiding their sanctuaries and eliminating their food supply sprayed herbicides on a small scale with effects that seemed positive to the sensibilities of military leaders. Later, their use was adopted in South Vietnam to combat the National Liberation Front (aka Viet Cong) and the People's Army of North Vietnam. From 1961 to 1971, the Dow Chemical Company, Monsanto, Hercules Inc., and a half-dozen other US companies canned more than four hundred thousand barrels of herbicide at the request of the US government. The military called the operation Ranch Hand, and for ten years the US Air Force, along with the US Army and its counterparts in the South Vietnamese military, sprayed twenty million gallons of concentrated defoliants over large swaths of the countryside.

American transport planes loaded with herbicide would come in low at first light, before the warm air could rise from the jungle, and disperse the spray. The crews did their job to "protect and serve the Constitution of the United States." They cannot be blamed. As far as they knew, everything was kosher, just another weapon in the arsenal of freedom. At a predefined point over the jungle, they turned on the spray booms fixed to each wing and began dispensing herbicide over their planned track. The booms could cover a strip about eighty yards wide and ten miles long. They flew in formations, depending on the terrain. Sometimes three ships in echelon, maybe four. Sometimes it was just a helicopter or two fitted with spray booms. The herbicide drifted into the jungle, along with an embedded carcinogenic by-product called dioxin. The leaves turned brown over time, and at the first heavy rain or gust of wind, the dead leaves would fall to the jungle floor. Sometimes the aircrews had to make the same trip two or three times to wither down the layers of jungle the previous passes had exposed. Sometimes the agent settled in rivers and in the village wells from which Vietnamese children and old men sipped on hot afternoons. Sometimes grunts on patrol hiked their way through the spray tracks and smelled it in the barren trees. Sometimes they dug their foxholes into the saturated earth and slept in it.

Somewhere in my grandfather's Vietnam tour, Agent Orange became a part of him too. He was assigned to the Cam Ranh Air Force Base on the South China Sea, which was tucked into a narrow peninsula that formed the eastern line of Cam Ranh Bay. The air force cantonment was just north of the airfield, along the beach. I picture it as a remote tropical paradise hidden from the mainland by lush green hills to the west. The Vietnamese have built resorts there since, but in 1968 the war was at its ugliest. The Tet Offensive had wracked the country and sent the American efforts tumbling into the light of its own folly. The base served as a major hub for fighter jets and logistics. My grandfather worked at Cam Ranh as an intelligence analyst in the nearly futile effort of identifying communist targets so American airpower could "bomb them back to the Stone Age," as the American general Curtis LeMay once described it.

The mangroves and jungled hills surrounding the perimeter of large installations were routinely defoliated to prevent the Viet Cong from using the cover as an infiltration route. I can't help but picture my grandfather, somewhere in his midthirties, strolling along the duckboards of the cantonment or around the hangars and workshops near the airfield, maybe walking out of the mess hall on a random humid evening and looking inland to see an American aircraft gassing the tree line with Agent Orange, or just seeing barrels of it lying about the airfield bound for one destination or another, carted by tractors with ONLY YOU CAN PREVENT A FOREST stenciled on their flanks.

He came home and retired and settled down as an electrician in San Antonio. Gail called him not long after, on the whimsical suggestion of her mother. They had not spoken in nearly twenty years, but something sparked between them in that moment and later that year they married. He became a beloved stepfather to her son and two daughters. Not long after they were married, while my mother was just beginning her own military career, he built a sprawling lake house with a cathedral ceiling, including a darkroom where Gail could develop her photos from her world travels as an art history professor. It was a warm place, comfortable, a refuge for his wife and children and eventually grandchildren. He traveled with Gail, chaperoning college students to Egypt and China and even to the Soviet Union, and together they circumnavigated the globe, relishing its arts and culture.

The Agent Orange buried in his marrow went off like a grenade while I was in Japan. Similar grenades had been going off all across Vietnam since the end of the war—children and even grandchildren being born with birth defects and cancers—and had long begun to ravage veterans in the United States. Thousands of vets and noncombatants alike had become casualties of the war without knowing it until years later, long after the war was over. I have little doubt Don spent his yearlong tour without firing a shot, but the war mortgaged his life for another twenty, then finally collected right about the time I was falling in love with all the GIs who had fought there.

He was diagnosed with multiple myeloma, its roots traced back to the dioxin he had been exposed to in Vietnam. I didn't know what that meant. I wasn't sure what to ask, or even if I was allowed to ask anything at all.

It was difficult to completely fathom the tail-eating cruelty of it, all decorated with patriotic window dressing. We did this to ourselves and others—"fratricide" and "friendly fire," as it's called in the military. But as I clicked toward my own enlistment, I knew, even if subconsciously, that being in the military meant being susceptible to death not just by the enemy but by the hands of people who sold America its weapons on a bottom-dollar carpet of national defense. I carried a tacit understanding that my life was subject to the whims of the weapons America saw fit to lob against its enemies. Enlisting in the military, the simple act of showing up regardless of the risks of gas or dioxin or depleted uranium (the latter a Persian Gulf War problem that we were just beginning to understand), fueled a toxic nobility around ideas of service. A substructure of skepticism was forming, or perhaps had already formed, and was baking itself into my dream of being an American soldier on the front lines. I knew that America might have me killed just as it was killing my grandfather: up against the wall of its own myopic foreign policy, either immediately, in war, or later, through some installment plan. I accepted it, in fact, as part of the work, a part of the story. A simple job risk.

I would go to football games on Friday night with friends, sometimes dressed in my uniform, sometimes not. When "The Star-Spangled Banner" played, I'd face the flagpole on the north side of the field at attention and salute. The flag would unfurl as the drill team cadets pulled it up by the lanyard; the brass swivel snaps tinkled against the aluminum pole. I listened to the music and felt the familiar swelling inside me—a balloon of pride and awe. I knew that I wanted to be Over There, and that desire felt almost physical. But my desire was not pure, singular patriotism; I wanted to be a part of the military as a way of separating myself from the average American. The military felt like its own entity, removed from society and placed on a pedestal, a statement of complete national identity in contrast to the pettiness of the chaotic cultural and political landscape.

My mother was pragmatic about the illness and death of her father. That was her way. His death came on slowly, assuredly. There was time for her to prepare. I navigated my junior year of high school and then the summer came and I helped my dad move from California to Virginia, his release from purgatory having finally come through. But I did not stay with him. I was sick of moving. I returned to Georgia and somewhere around then, when summer was grinding out its last days before my last school year, my grandfather called. There was a lot unsaid, but what can one say in those moments? How are lives and lessons distilled through cheap telephone speakers; how much wasted time can be packed into bytes of data and stuffed into the bandwidth of cables? He told me he loved me. He said that much. I could hear his hurt behind the soft gravel of his voice. I did not cry. He did not either.

He died in August, surrounded by family in a sunlit alcove added to the cabin he had built. My mother and stepdad drove to Texas just before he died and then again right after. I asked my parents to take me, but I was told he did not want me there, that I should remember him as he was, not the shell that cancer had reduced him to. I'm not sure how much of that is true. I do know Don was not a religious man, that he viewed religion as a shackle on human thought. He chased away padres who came sniffing around looking to use his mortality as a fulcrum for conversion. While I grew up in something of a Christian house—my mom and stepdad took my sister and me to church every Sunday—I was quietly proud of him. His body was cremated, his dying wish.

Before Don died, he told my mother another wish: "Don't let Jerad join the army."

. . .

I stood in front of the bathroom mirror and tugged on the thick wool blouse of my green US Army Class A uniform. A block of spurious ribbons were affixed squarely above my left breast pocket. A little tab sat in the center of the right pocket with a black nameplate above it. I checked the black tie, centering it in the collar. This was a ritual that differed from the day-to-day jeans-and-T-shirt vibe I tended to default to on a standard school day. It added a formality, a sense of purpose that straightened my spine some whenever I wore it, even if this uniform was only a placeholder for the real thing, a tether to my future. Then, my eyes still bombed with sleep, I walked downstairs and out onto the dark driveway and waited for my friend Scott to pick me up in his Pontiac with "Mo Money Mo Problems" blasting into the predawn morning.

The cadet program was run by a retired army infantry officer, a lieutenant colonel named Ramsey. He was a graduate of West Point, class of '71, and he wore his status like a crown, jeweled by the sparkle of his big class ring. He was a small, lean man with eyeglasses, but he wore aviators when he was outside in the sun. During our military class periods, he watched as we marched outside the school cafeteria from the wooden steps of the trailer that served as the staff office.

Ramsey was a student of military history. Books on the American Civil War, World War II, Korea, and Vietnam lined a long single shelf along the ceiling above his desk. But he wasn't terribly inclined to indulge me in any discussion of my favorite subjects outside the classroom. He was not mean spirited or dismissive. My passions kept interfering with his routine—and we were simply separated by class. He was an officer and spoke to me as a commander, not as a teacher. He was pleasant but reserved, distant, as if some stopwatch were running in his mind with only so many minutes allotted to my presence, and when my time was up, he'd shoo me away with airs of bristling disengagement.

Ramsey represented the archetypal American military officer and its lineage. His father had been at West Point and landed on Omaha Beach right after D-Day during World War II and fought through the end of the war. Once, when Ramsey was discussing the Persian Gulf War, he referred to himself as "unlucky" for not having been deployed to support it. While I was getting stung by wasps, Ramsey's eldest son was sweating his way through his plebe year at "the Point." I had met him only once or twice in passing. He had the humorless arrogance of a prep school upperclassman, a snobbery I tended to avoid. His younger son was on his way to the Point as well. They all had seats at the table in the court of the American military aristocracy. The perfect military family. The Achievers.

There was a proto-officer cabal among the senior cadets, a loose factory producing junior military leaders. They were good kids mostly, tough and honorable, the Best and the Brightest. In the afternoons, I went on runs with one of them, a kid named Kevin, who pined for a commission in the navy. He wanted to become a naval aviator and fly jets from the decks of aircraft carriers, a dream he would ultimately achieve. We pushed and cajoled each other on long jaunts through the neighborhoods and fields behind the school, not far from the trail where the wasps nested. He was in better shape, but not by much. I was light and could push through the runs with a certain ease, dashing over the hills during our afterschool physical training sessions.

"Just go to college," he said one afternoon after I had told him I was looking to enlist at graduation. "The enlisted guys get treated like crap."

It was a refrain I heard often in those late years of high school, and though becoming an officer seemed like a remote fantasy grown from the way I idolized some of the commanders of American history—men like Joshua Lawrence Chamberlain, Ulysses S. Grant, J. Lawton Collins, Patton and Bradley and Schwarzkopf—it was something I wanted truly. But it felt impossible: there were no Ramseys in my family, no one I could latch on to as an example. Starting out at the bottom also held a strange allure, simple and noble—or at least that's what I told myself and others. College would always be there, I said. Even if I went nowhere else in the industry of the military, I would always know what it means to be surrounded by the core of the American military identity.

Kevin and I ran on, making it to the green farm field that served as our turnaround point. The autumn sun lit the field; the leaves were just starting to turn. We turned, running back the way we came. Despite any admonishments from the cabal, I felt hope and excitement for the future, a fantastic sense of peace at finishing school and marching off to the army. It just seemed right, even if I had no idea what that world would look like outside the topical necessities of marching and uniform inspections and esoteric military customs and courtesies, like saluting and addressing officers as "sir" and "ma'am" whenever I spoke with them—none of which were remotely new to me.

The hard truth was that I did want to be an officer, to put on the shoulder straps and bronze bars of a second lieutenant of infantry. But I was scared. Not of officer candidate school or anything else. I felt I could shoulder my way through any military pedagogy; the military has an indomitable way of teaching what needs to be taught. I was scared of college, of my own ability to keep myself motivated through four more years of school. I didn't even know how I'd pay for it, or if my parents, who seemed as eager as I to see me off to the service, would support my ideas. I thought perhaps I was worthy of the honor, or could at least measure up to it over time, but it seemed lost over the horizon of my flagging self-confidence. Quite simply, I was tired of school. I just wanted someone to hand me a rifle and let me fall into the story.

We began to run faster as we neared the finish line—a natural unspoken competition formed with our speed and energy. Acid began to burn in our legs, our lungs blew air in hard gouts. Kevin began to pull ahead of me. I pushed to keep up.

Kevin took off as we reached the final turn around the football field. The distance between us widened by yards. I grabbed every bit of power I could and shoved it into my legs, but Kevin's endurance was deeper and he bolted. The gap widened more and everything seemed impossible. Lieutenant Colonel Ramsey, US Army, West Point class of '71, stood nearby, his aviators gleaming the in afternoon sun. He silently watched Kevin blast across the arbitrary finish line. I snapped across the line seconds later. Ramsey remained silent, his face a slate of internal calculations and judgments. He turned and walked away.

I never learned why Don hated the US Army. I knew he had worked in intelligence, which is often a joint venture with intelligence specialists of other branches, like the navy or the army. Perhaps somewhere in that experience he witnessed the army acting in ways he found heinous—"Let's put some napalm right on those slant-eyed fucks" or anything else I'd read about in cheap novels and seen in tawdry films. The tired clichés of the Average American Grunt. Vietnam was a portal of American ugliness, a collection point for everything the American ego could produce. But whatever he saw, he never described it. To anyone. Such is the silence after war.

My mother was quiet about my desires to enlist in the army; she respected my free will enough to allow me to make my own choices. Not that she had much say, anyway. I would be free to enlist in whatever direction I chose once I turned eighteen in the spring of my senior year. But a subtle tension formed in our house, a clashing of desires both internally and externally. I was going into the military, a direction she supported absolutely; but she was also beholden to a promise, a seemingly righteous one. When I began communicating with an army recruiter, just months after Don died, my mother issued mild sighs and eye rolls whenever they called the house or if their presence was mentioned. My grandfather's legacy hung over the conversation. The army seemed to hold no honor to my grandfather or my mother, a judgment that seemed arbitrary and meritless.

No doubt they would have been pleased if I had joined the US Air Force. It was what they knew. But I didn't want that. Unless I was a fighter pilot or perhaps a pararescueman, neither of which interested me much, I would be relegated to a desk somewhere or a mechanics' bay, hanging on the trailing edge of the American narrative. There was nothing inherently or even specifically wrong with any of it—the air force has earned its place in the American military landscape. But I didn't want to spend an enlistment maintaining the torque on the bolts of a horizontal stabilizer or filing reports in an air-conditioned office. I had already seen that. It all felt toothless.

My mother had no reason to worry. The army ultimately proved to be its own deterrent, tripping over its feet in a rush to get me to enlist. My recruiter was a luckless sergeant from some administrative field, exactly the kind of work I wanted to avoid. She called incessantly to check on me, making sure I was okay, that I was happy, constantly expressing her concern for my well-being. She wasn't concerned in an authentic way but rather as a salesperson making sure I was still on the hook for that fancy new car. But when I mentioned my interest in joining the infantry branch, preferably with an airborne option, she flatly refused. No slots available, she said. Completely full. Let's put you in water purification. Have you thought about being a chemical operations specialist? Great fields!

I knew she was full of shit and said as much. The implied suggestion that only idiots and the insane go into the infantry, men with terrible scores on their enlistment exams and no other options, was blatantly insulting nonsense. Were Audie Murphy and Senator Daniel Inouye morons? How about Oliver Stone or Samuel Fuller? What about authors James Jones and Norman Mailer; Robert Leckie or William Manchester? Were they all obtuse people? Was every rifleman in the Union army or the Allied Expeditionary Force of World War I or of Bradley's First Army in World War II, a half-wit? It felt as if the army should be applauding its volunteers, welcoming them for their time and effort, not belittling the intellect of soldiers who choose dangerous occupations.

It's arguable she was trying only to spare me. But I did not want to be spared. She tried to blunt my disapproval with promises of college money and a short enlistment period—smoke and mirrors meant to attract working stiffs hunting for a job skill and a leg up on their education. She wanted me to enlist at the earliest possible moment.

My mother agreed to sign any papers I handed her, but it began to feel wrong somehow. The sergeant's salesperson veneer began to rub off, revealing a pushy clerk anxious to scratch a notch somewhere on her desk, to up the scoreboard no doubt buried in the back of the recruiting office. I wondered if there were some super recruiter brought in every quarter to pep up the team, like Alec Baldwin in *Glengarry Glen Ross*. ABC: Always. Be. Closing. Coffee is for closers only. I tentatively agreed to the enlistment physical, choosing military intelligence for my occupational field, but when the time came to meet her at the recruiting office for the drive to Fort Jackson, in South Carolina, for a day of poking and prodding, I flaked.

"What's wrong?" she asked when I called to tell her.

"I just need to think it over some more," I said.

She huffed impatiently. I knew she wanted to cajole me, but after a moment of silence, the greasy saleswoman oozed through the phone. There was no leadership to it, no call to action or the beacon of some adventure. She might as well have been selling timeshares on a backwater lake in Missouri somewhere. Or life insurance.

"I understand," she cooed. "Take all the time you need. I can probably get you in the next physical. Should I put you down?"

I stood at the phone in the living room. I stared at the wall. I stared at the phone cradle. I stared at the fake brass frame on my stepdad's desk chair. I stared at the black spiral phone cable and ran my pointer finger through its loops. I had to unravel myself from it when I finally hung up. I said a few soft words and we never spoke again.

"I had a nightmare that you were dead in the desert."

Melanie told me that while we stood outside in the cold. She lived in an apartment with her mom and stepdad near the interstate. She had told her mom we were going to walk around the complex, but instead we had gone to make out beside the AC unit.

Melanie was a teenage hippie with long blonde hair. She had been seeing some other boy before me, but that ended, and on New Year's Eve we had made out in my friend Scott's bedroom during a low-key house party.

She liked strange crystals and stories about witchcraft. I didn't really know what that meant, other than I felt it was supposed to clash with my hazy Christian upbringing. She was filled with the angst and sappiness of a teenage romantic tragedy. She had a thing for Baz Luhrmann's *Romeo + Juliet* and James Cameron's *Titanic*, which I refused to watch as a sort of petty rebellion against pop-culture sentimentality. But I thought she was cute and maybe a little dangerous in her own teenage way and she liked to make out with me.

Melanie meant it when she told me she'd dreamed I died in the desert. She believed her dreams had meaning and even opened the window to some kind of future.

"You were lying in a ditch or something," she said. "You were wearing tan camouflage and had a big hole in your chest."

I wasn't sure I believed in any of it. Maybe her dreams did have meaning; maybe they didn't. I had told her about my plans of becoming a soldier. Maybe her nightmare was just an extension of those conversations, some sort of overblown psychic link mixing with the news of American forces deploying because of another Saddam

Hussein tantrum over UN weapons inspections and sanctions. Or maybe she made the whole thing up. I had no way of knowing, but I was keenly aware of the irony of dying in some trench in a wasteland I had willingly walked into. I also felt her terrors were overly sentimental, just part of the pop-culture lore surrounding the military— the epic poem of the dying American soldier ad infinitum.

I smiled and poked at her fear. "It must have been from a .50 cal."

"I'm serious," she said. "You could fucking die."

I shrugged. "Maybe." I hated these kinds of conversations—death and violence and blind stupidity, a forced look at my dubious invincibility. I had no control over whether I'd die. None of that mattered in the larger scheme of my own fantasies. It was meaningless at that point, anyway. I had no idea where I was going.

"You need to do *something*," my mom kept saying. "Make a decision."

She was right, but she was also wrong. I didn't need to do anything. I could have sat on my hands for a few weeks, maybe even a few months, maybe even through the year. The military would always be there. There was nothing prodding me other than my own desires and whatever expectations my parents had of me.

I don't remember when the US Marine Corps came into my mind. It might have been from something subliminal—a magnet of the Marine Corps crest stuck to the side of a fridge or maybe a passing bumper sticker with MARINES written with hard yellow letters on a camouflage background. I had all but forgotten about the US Marines; their stories had been buried beneath all those I had read of GIs in Europe during World War II. But they came rushing into focus, charging like happy ghouls through the slime of the army's recruiting efforts, almost chasing them away with the point of their bayonets.

I had had little interaction with the Marines in high school, just a quick brush with a recruiter in the school cafeteria a year before I was eligible to enlist. The army, navy, and air force had all called me, no doubt by virtue of the fact that I happened to be a high school senior and had done well on the armed forces aptitude battery, essentially an SAT-style exam for military service. But the Marine Corps hadn't. As far as I knew, its recruiters hadn't contacted anyone. The army had long cornered the market in my high school, such as the market was. I didn't even know where the Marine recruiting office was located. I annoyed the navy recruiter when I called to ask for the Marine Corps number. When I finally reached the Marine recruiter, he seemed somewhat dispassionate about my interest—not dismissive, but not convinced either. He agreed to come to my house to meet me and my parents and talk.

The recruiter's name was Canty. He was stern but genial, a former artilleryman who had turned in his lanyard to become a drill instructor for a few years before finally becoming a recruiter. He arrived warrior tall in a starched khaki shirt with staff sergeant stripes sown to its short sleeves and blue trousers with a red stripe running up each leg. He told me the red stripes were meant to honor all the officers and noncommissioned officers killed at the Battle of Chapultepec during the Mexican-American War. We call them Blood Stripes, he said, and when he did, my mind overloaded on ideas of glory. His chest dazzled with a kaleidoscope of ribbons, including the Combat Action Ribbon, which I would later covet and quietly worship at its altar. There was something taut and expeditionary about him, as if he were still sweating out the dirt from a dozen outposts and dangerous misadventures—the sweat of conflicts in the brush fires of an empire. The exotic mysteries behind his experiences were tantalizing.

He had explained all the usual trappings of modern enlistment in an all-volunteer military, mainly the GI Bill and job training, but I knew those were givens, the bennies of providing honorable service. But I wasn't going to be sold on the fiscal decorations of showing up. He no doubt saw that as I eyed the uniform and explained my past problems with the army, which made him wince with a certain empathy that I was convinced was organic.

He did not ask me to enlist. Instead, he asked me *why* I wanted to enlist, a challenge, a question that stunned me at first, as if it suggested my interest alone was somehow unworthy of the Marine Corps. His time would not be wasted on dilettantes. I had to earn his approval. It was a recruitment tactic for sure, but one that grabbed me by the throat. I suddenly felt a strong desire to measure up, which is exactly what the Marine Corps wanted. Its recruiting slogan begins with "The Few . . ." which nails down a sense of exclusion, that one must measure up, *earn* the right to be a Marine, which is at the core of a conscious separation the Marine Corps holds from the average American who has *not* earned that right. The average American is simply Less, and as Canty sat in my parents' house and demanded to know why I wanted to enlist, I knew I had to prove that I was worthy of being More. And that was an anchor of my interest: Was there something more, something larger than myself, I could attach to and become greater than the sum of my parts? He made no requests of me when he left that night; he wouldn't even hear of any commitment from me. "Think it over, talk with your parents," he said. "Call me in a few days if you're still interested."

Canty could have sold my own kidneys back to me after that. By the end of the week, I had set a date for the enlistment physical, a week from Monday.

I was initially nervous announcing my intentions, but my mother and stepfather flocked to it immediately. "I prefer the Marines over the army," my mom said. "It'll be tough, but at least they're honorable." My stepdad had worked with the Marines on his various deployments and thought them intense people but utterly professional.

My dad, however, was furious. I called him at his house in Virginia after I made my decision. He had little to say about me joining the army in all the years I had considered it, but the Marine Corps was another matter entirely. The military is tribal when at its most petty, and every service builds its own distortions of the others. Most are nonsense, but some are true. My dad had been in the air force, the "softest" of the services. It has the shortest basic training and a healthier quality of life—a cushier existence by any military definition. It is sedate and technical; it demands more of the mind than the body. For my dad, anything else was an extreme to be avoided. No doubt he was nervous about my safety. But I did not want safety. I also didn't want to be bored. When I told him the news, he blew up on the other end of the line: "Why the fuck would *anyone* join the Marines?"

The physical was held at a facility ninety minutes into South Carolina at a backwater army fort near Columbia. Canty picked me up from my house the day before and that evening I rode up in a van with two or three other Marine enlistees. I knew no one. I spent the night in a cheap motel near the fort, where enlistees of all services were gathered, rooming with a nervous twentysomething on his way to Fort Knox, Kentucky, to become an army tank crewman. He spent the night pacing the room and the sidewalks outside, smoking Newports, terrified of the uniformed monsters he believed were waiting for him at basic training. I didn't have much to offer him. When I told him I was going into the Marines, he told me I was insane.

I boarded a bus before sunrise the next morning and was taken to a large brick building inside the fort. The entire facility, called the Military Entrance Processing Station, or MEPS—one installment in the blizzard of acronyms to come—seemed to be a magnet for bureaucracy and impatience. Everyone from the janitor to the doctors operated on some short-tempered wavelength, ushering enlistees in cattle-like groups through physical tests, foot inspections, and endless medical history questionnaires. Blood and urine samples were taken. There was an almost pathological fear of marijuana. Examiners interrogated enlistees to the point of obsession and threatened expulsion if THC was found in anyone's history or urinalysis results.

I made it through most of this fine. The problem began with my right ear. I was given a standard hearing test at some point in the mayhem of examinations: a soundproof booth with headphones and a button to press whenever a tone emits in the ear. Thanks, no doubt, to an unprotected exposure to fighter jet afterburners blasting by my bedroom window, a low-grade tone always hummed in my right ear. It was never obtrusive, but it was present enough that I always slept better on my left side because my right ear didn't pick up as much sound.

I had never considered it a problem, but whatever numbers I registered for the bored technician caused her to believe otherwise. When I came out of the booth, she handed me my results in the form of another acronym scribbled on the government-issued form: DQ.

Disqualified. I stared at the form with uncut disbelief.

"Can I take it again?" I asked.

The technician shooed me away. "I ain't got time to be running you through my booth again. Go sit down before I get the sergeant over here."

The air in the room was indifferent. The nurses and rule-crazy technicians moved on without me. It did not matter that I was turned down to enlist in the US armed forces. It didn't matter if just for now or if forever. Something in my body failed. I could run. I could see perfectly. I could think and reason and compute. I could speak. I was ambitious. I wanted to be there. But none of that mattered anymore. A few mild and arbitrary tones missing from one ear over the other, some benchmark not met, and now I was found lacking. The machinery moved right on by. I was faceless. I had no reason to expect otherwise.

I left the physical with everyone else and rode home in the van. I sat in the far back and did not speak to anyone. No one spoke to me either. If we had once been together, now we were separate. They had been sworn in and I had not. My insides felt scooped out and tossed to the side of the highway. I stared out the window at the passing blue sky of early spring. I registered none of it. Afterward, at home, I sat with my mom and Canty in our living room. The room was dark, the funeral parlor of an idea. Canty left after a few words coated with thin pity. I went upstairs and shut the bedroom door and sat down at my desk and vanished my face into my forearm and cried like a boy.

What else was there?

College was the natural and assumed direction of nearly everyone in high school. The entire high school experience of most of my friends in Georgia was aimed entirely at getting into college. The military was an oddity reserved for the zealots in the JROTC program and the children of soldiers, who were often the same. But now I had neither.

I had tried to enlist but was rejected. At least according to the Big Fish in the pond of the enlistment physical. But they had left me an option. "He has to get an ear exam," Canty explained to my mother. "Then he can retest at the end of the week. On Friday."

To call it a miserable week would be like beating a gong inside the temple of the obvious. I felt as if I were wearing some green cloak of shame everyone could see billowing behind me as I walked through the halls between class. I wanted to cave into myself whenever someone asked how the physical went and I withered into desperation as I explained the issues with the hearing exam and saw the pity glaze over their faces. Whenever someone cracked a joke—"Didn't make it, eh?" or "Not good enough, eh?"—an inner rage grew in me that twisted my face into violent knots and I had to bite the inside of my mouth to keep from spitting anger and tears.

I had no idea what my future would be. I perceived any suggestions put forth by my parents as hollow and cheap, second class, without meaning. I couldn't see the world past my high school graduation. When I think back on this time, I think about the teenager Finny, from the John Knowles novel *A Separate Peace*, which I had read the previous year in English. Finny falls from a tree and breaks his leg, crippling him. He dies at the end, trying to make his leg right, to become whole again. I don't know if there was anything I could have

done to make my ear work properly, but I know how much I would
have put up with to try. I know how much I would have given of
my life. The alternative was unacceptable. What would I have measured myself against if the military found me unfit permanently?
Surely there were answers. I know that now. But in those long hours
between Monday and Friday, I was terrified. I had wrapped the military identity, or at least my estimation of it, around myself so tightly
that it had become its own straitjacket.

In the end, it didn't matter. Early Friday morning I went to a doctor
in Columbia, near the processing station, and had my ears examined.
On the drive up, the recruiter, a Marine sniper named Clark, looked
at me in the rearview mirror. "Just press the fuck out of that button,
dog. No one gives a shit about your hearing once you're in. Fuck, man,
we all end up deaf anyway. If you ain't cheatin', you ain't tryin'."

I didn't have to go through the entire process again. I went straight
to the hearing section. The same cranky technician was at the controls and I sat on the stool inside the soundproof booth after she
called my name. I put the stiff headphones over my ears and picked
up the hand button. The technician spoke to me through a micro-
phone, instructing me to press the black button whenever I heard
a tone.

Every neuron of my concentration went to my ears. A series of
tones registered in my left ear, loudest to softest. I heard them all
and pressed the button each time. Another four tones sounded out
and I pressed the button four more times. The tones sounded off
in increments that I could closely guess. After a bit more noise in
my left ear, the technician switched to my right. I heard the first
tone and the second. I pressed the button for each. Then I pressed
it again for the faint third tone, waited, then pressed it a fourth
time. I went slow. Easy. Don't rush. Listen. If you ain't cheatin', you'
ain't tryin'.

I was sweating when I came out of the booth. The technician said nothing. She made some notes on my government-issued forms, then handed them over.

"You're good," she said before calling the next name.

I looked down at the sheet. I had passed. Qualified. My insides rattled. I exhaled the fumes of the past week and drew in fresh air. I felt light. I could have kissed the technician, but she was busy with the next recruit and she would no doubt have been mad anyway. I turned with a thick, stupid grin and walked away.

Minutes later, I was sworn into the Delayed Entry Program, an administrative holding pen for enlistees awaiting their high school graduation. I was taken to a wood-paneled room with pictures of the president and secretary of defense and various military officers hanging from the walls. A navy ensign performed the oath of enlistment at a podium near an American flag. He seemed mildly bored, just getting through the day. I stood with a half-dozen other enlistees in a loose formation. He snapped at us to raise our right hands and we recited the oath.

"I, state your name . . ."

"*I* . . ." Our names blended together in a mumble.

"Do solemnly swear . . .

"*DO SOLEMNLY SWEAR . . .*"

"That I will support and defend the Constitution of the United States . . ."

"*THAT I WILL SUPPORT AND DEFEND THE CONSTITUTION OF THE UNITED STATES . . .*"

"Against all enemies, foreign and domestic . . ."

"*AGAINST ALL ENEMIES, FOREIGN AND DOMESTIC . . .*"

When we finished, I felt huge. I walked out under the Friday sunlight in a daze. The van ride home was too small for the energy I carried. My legs rattled. A few hours later, I lay on my bedroom floor, my eyes starry with pictures of the flag raising on Mount Suribachi and grunts running through the streets of Hue City while "The Marines' Hymn" blasted from my stereo into the spring air.

Spring blew by in a frenzy. I went through the motions of classes, lunch hours, weekends with friends cruising around stone bored through the dark streets of suburbia, dates, make-out sessions in the backseat, puppy love, grasping for time while letting it pull me forward. I wore my future on my sleeve. I made no promises. No love carried permanence. Everything was coming to a final point and all the marks in between were the cataloging of youth. Then graduation came and I ran from the school, dove into Scott's car, and sped off with a middle finger blasting into the warm air.

On the day before I left for Marine boot camp, my friends and I packed coolers and headed out to a nearby lake, about ten of us. What were we doing and why were we doing it? we asked ourselves and one another. Where were we going? I was going into the US Marines, the only one in my entire graduating class to do so, because I wanted it more than I wanted a sense of sedate normalcy of the American Dream. I was going into the Marines because I believed the identity I had built around myself demanded it. I felt special and privileged, even somewhat saintly.

Canty arrived the next day and I said my goodbyes to my sister and my stepdad, who was tall and proud. Alan shook my hand. "Don't let them change who you are," he said. My mom hugged me. "Just listen and move fast when they tell you," she said. They walked me through the kitchen and out the side door where Canty waited, no doubt suffering through the awkwardness of a son being pulled from his family. I felt an undercurrent of anxiety as I walked to his car, as if passing through some psychic membrane that separated me from home and the world as I knew it. It was hot. As we pulled away, I looked back to see my mother as she stood in the doorway. She seemed to be crying.

FOXTROT

A man loves a thing. That don't mean it's gotta love him back.

—James Jones, *From Here to Eternity*

Airborne-Marine sidles up with a war story.

"You guys hear about the staff sergeant from EOD?"

He says this in the early evening. The sun lowers to the berm of our new outpost in the middle of town. Shadows stand and stretch. Nearby, a mortar section plants its black tubes into the earth. Soon they'll thump parachute flares over the broad wadi that divides our town from theirs. Cory and I say no as if it's a story we don't care to hear. It's not because we dislike war stories, though they are tired in this world. We just don't like Airborne-Marine all that much. We don't trust him. He is a sycophant who tries to buy his friends with rumors and gossip culled by eavesdropping. He stands in front of us with his angular wraparound shades with orange lenses, the same style Rebel Six wears. He doesn't get our memo and tells us the war story anyway.

He tells us about an Iraqi who approached a Marine platoon wearing a suicide vest. How anyone knew he was dressed in a suicide vest when they first saw him is beyond our comprehension; no one seems to have asked and neither do we. It is a truth learned only after the fact, but a truth nonetheless. According to Airborne-Marine's gossip, the bomber took cover in a building after Marines fired a machine gun at him when he refused to stop. A big Marine tank idling nearby followed up with a tank round and, as the story goes, reduced some of the building to rubble.

At its worst, death is discussed flippantly by the braggarts and know-it-alls, whose offhanded comments are baked with a mean sense of teenage bravado and glazed with an American middle school pastiche. A platoon sergeant laments how he watched a tracer bullet go through an insurgent running down an alley. The bullet went clean through, he says, laser through, like a geometric ray, and bounced off the concrete in front of the insurgent as if it had passed through air. The staff sergeant was mad about the bullet not doing the thing a bullet is supposed to do, which is kill. He spoke about the bullet in simple terms, a failure of ballistics, and about a desire for a heavier, larger bullet, like he wanted a better wrench or a more powerful drill.

There is the corporal I meet who brags about killing a man in Afghanistan. He tells me this as he guards Iraqis one cool morning while they are voting in one of their elections. A man brandishing a weapon came up to the perimeter the corporal was guarding one day. The corporal tells me he shot him with his rifle from the guard tower and treats this story like a button of pride pinned to his body armor, something he'll brandish at parties once he's home. A few friends later tell me that the man the corporal shot was less a hardened Taliban fighter and more an eager teenager; the boy was turning in a firearm he had found. According to the lore around the battalion, the boy had come to the corporal a day or so before and told him about the weapon. The corporal told the boy to bring it from his village to turn in. When the boy did as he was told, the corporal shot him. The whole thing was buried to avoid the scandal. That was the story.

Aside from the clinical vocabulary of prosecuting enemy forces, most of us say little about the dead or the actions that make humans dead. But death as an action and a story always bleeds between the seams and makes liars of our composure. There is the lieutenant colonel from civil affairs I witness sitting in a room with two Iraqi women who are demanding the Americans compensate them for destroying their home with a bomb. You did this, they tell him through a translator. We were innocent and now you must pay us. The colonel looks at them with a stone face, barely concealing a sneer. We're not paying you anything, he says. The courtyard of your house was used as a mortar position to fire on coalition troops. You should consider yourselves lucky. After the women leave empty handed, he takes me into his office where he shows me pictures of a girl who suffered from spinal bifida. He was trying to send her to the United States for surgery. One afternoon, the colonel asked her grandfather, her sole living relative, to retrieve documents from home. But the grandfather was old with poor eyesight, and while he was driving through the narrow streets, he failed to see the squad of Marines patrolling ahead, signaling him to stop. In their fear, they leveled their rifles at the vehicle and killed him.

In a breach of military etiquette, he looks at me with wide, pleading eyes. "What am I supposed to do, Sergeant Alexander?" he asks. "What am I supposed to do?" But there is nothing I can say.

Then there is the story of the lance corporal who sits with me and sings "allahu akbar" over and over again, as if possessed by the words. It's what they say when they kill themselves, he says to me. He is a young boy, blond with a heavy face under his Kevlar helmet. He had been on patrol with a rifle platoon days before. A suicide bomber behind the wheel of a car crashed through a wall right in the center of the platoon. The bomb detonated, but in a royal flush of fate, no one was killed. Except for the driver, of course. The lance corporal tells me the driver's spine was blown clear through the car and landed against the wall nearby, its vertebrae intact, still in its column. He tells me this with a wide-eyed franticness, an amazement, a grueling wonder that courses across his eyes as he gently rocks in his seat and mutters "allahu akbar" over and over and over and over and over. "It's what they say, Sergeant."

In Airborne-Marine's story, which is not his own, he tells us he heard the suicide bomber was still alive in the rubble with the bomb wrapped around his body. We don't question any of this. A story fills in the seconds, kills time. Whether or not it's true means little. The sun is setting and soon the mortars will fire parachute flares every ten minutes or so with loud metallic thumps near where we sleep.

Motivated by our interest, Airborne-Marine brings in the EOD staff sergeant he opened with. He stands next to the Humvee with his orange-tinted cop shades, his thumbs tucked into the armholes of his body armor. "So then I guess the hajji gets trapped in the building," he says, "and they have to send the EOD staff sergeant out there to deal with it."

The tenor of his voice changes now, as if he is speaking of a death-metal saint, a legend, some kind of knight in camouflage. Airborne-Marine idolizes US Navy SEALs and Marine Corps Force Recon and all the other pop-culture icons we've made from our wars. Airborne-Marine is like most Marines in that he likes the characters of our stories to bandy around with a dose of fuck-you élan, not flaunting the rules outright but certainly possessing enough charisma and specialized technical acumen to sanction small deviations from the rules and regulations we are all bound by.

The EOD staff sergeant is a member of another acronym in an institution practically suspended on the weight of its own bland alphabetic jargon. EOD stands for "explosive ordnance disposal," a deceptively inert title for an occupation that requires either steel nerves wrapped in ceramic or a death wish quietly authorized by a higher military power. In basic terms, EOD technicians climb into bulbous armored suits with thick padding and waddle into the middle of highways on the suspicion of explosives and attempt to disarm them or rig them to detonate in a controlled environment. Often, the bombs are wired to blow on the command of a spotter and all too often the technicians are blown to a smoking ruin of Kevlar and viscera by a set of eyes watching with a cell phone from a nearby window with a mouth muttering "allahu akbar" to the heavens. EOD technicians are typically loved as "hard dicks" and "motivators" and "badasses" in the gun club culture of the Marine Corps.

Airborne-Marine tells us the staff sergeant went out in his bomb suit to the remains of the building that had collapsed around the bomber. He tells us that the staff sergeant got as close as he dared to the man with the suicide vest, which was, according to the storyteller, close enough to speak with. Airborne-Marine tells us, without a beat missed, that the man begged to be rescued from the rubble, as if the weight of all the concrete that pinned him had also changed the polarity of his beliefs. But we snicker at this notion, too, as if we are somehow immune to any wayward drift of our own hubris.

"Anyway," Airborne-Marine says after lighting a Camel, "the staff sergeant packed a bunch of C-4 near the motherfucker and blew his ass up."

Cory drops his own cigarette to the dirt. "Sucks to be him," he says.

I laugh too.

XI

Ken said we were going to war the evening the towers fell in New York City. Afterward, we hugged like brothers, then smoked cigarettes in the last air of summer and listened to Fighting Falcons patrol the vacant American skies. Three days later, Congress issued a joint resolution authorizing the president of the United States unilateral access to use the military at whim. The gloves are off, our leaders said with relish. The leash has been cut. We were Marines and one way or another we wanted this. It didn't matter how or where or with whom as long as we were there to earn a piece of its story.

Ken was tall and wily with sergeant stripes pinned to the collar of his camouflage uniform. He was from Kentucky, under the shadow of Cincinnati in a poor part of town. Shotgun-house poor. His daddy had been an army radioman in Vietnam; one of his high school teachers was a retired Marine colonel. He had been raised with the banner of the military and American war draped around his shoulders.

I was a corporal in his squad. We were both infantrymen, "killers" and "warfighters" and "shock troops." At least that's what the Marine Corps called us. But we were not. Instead, the Marine Corps took our rifles and helmets and gave us gas masks and stretchers, charging our unit with evacuating Americans exposed to chemical and biological weapons attacks from terrorists and madmen. We were based in a sleepy outpost on the banks of the Potomac in Maryland, a short drive south of Washington, DC. We spent our days training like fire-fighters and hazardous materials professionals. At night, Ken gathered the squad—me and Fields and Naugy and Big Joe and the rest. We blasted into DC or Baltimore or just the local redneck bars and drank ourselves into a chaotic haze, then returned zapped on adrenaline and youthful stupidity to run it off for four or five miles, leaving behind a trail of sweat-stench that reeked of beer and vodka and cigarettes. Our eardrums rang like bells from the nightclub Outkast and the morning Marine Corps cadences of violence and glory. But as much as we said we wanted it, we were not going to the war.

Still, we held out hope. We tooled into the heart of Capitol Hill in a column of white government trucks and buses before sunrise at the beginning of October. Letters filled with anthrax had appeared in mailboxes in Florida and New York, at the offices of Senators Tom Daschle and Patrick Leahy in Washington DC, and at a nearby congressional mail facility. No one knew where the letters came from. We set up our tents and tables and equipment in the broad courtyard of the Rayburn House Office Building, just south of the United States Capitol and across the street from the Longworth House Office Building. Our officers pulled us together and explained our role: to go office to office inside Longworth and collect dust samples from a few surfaces in each room and from the carpets with a special vacuum. Senator Daschle's office was inside Longworth and the entire building was assumed to be contaminated with anthrax. Those selected to go inside would wear full-body HAZMAT suits with gloves, boots, and respirators.

We wanted to go inside Longworth, to say we walked the halls of a US congressional office complex filled with a biological weapon—the fulfillment of duty and the acquisition of personal bragging rights. We had taken scores of anthrax vaccine boosters. We learned the symptoms anthrax could cause: sores on the skin with large black ulcers in the center; inflamed lungs that fill with fluid; bloody vomit and diarrhea if the bacterium entered the gastrointestinal system; lesions in the intestines and in the mouth and throat. We knew it could certainly kill us and we wanted to be in the room with it because we knew that it could. In our military world, to be near a thing that can kill you is equal to riding the leading edge of history. It was a means of demonstrating our worth in this world, a quiet, personal challenge of bravery, a point of pride, a chance to sweat in the suits four or five hours, maybe six, to show our toughness in the absence of bullets and bombs that would soon fall in Afghanistan and who knew where else. Longworth became our own little battlefield.

I eagerly dressed in my gear when it was my turn. Marines doted on me as I prepared—securing my gloves to my suit with high-grade duct tape, ensuring my boots were on comfortably, checking the charge on my battery pack. I put on my mask and turned on the purifier. Stale air blew against my face. The lenses tunneled my view and flattened the contrast. I stood still while a Marine taped the hood of my HAZMAT suit to the edge of my mask and closed the flap around my neck. Then, sealed against the biological threat that might kill me, I walked toward Longworth alongside my partner, a hulking sergeant nicknamed Big Baby.

Ken and the rest of the squad were responsible for decontaminating us when we came out of Longworth. They set up black rubber containment pits the size of kiddie pools and used sprayers to soak us with high-test hypochlorite—a high-powered bleach normally used to clean pools—before they cut us free from our suits. Someone joked that we might all end up with cancer because of it, but no one laughed.

I passed Ken and the squad in their rubber pits and flashed them deuces as we made our way to the door. Big Baby and I were assigned to the second floor. The elevators were out, so we carefully climbed a broad staircase. We moved slowly, placed each step deliberately. A tear in our suits would mean a panicked dash out the building and a thorough decontamination involving a rinse from a fire hose, a squad of pills, and a bevy of follow-up appointments with navy doctors.

A tall Marine staff sergeant named Poole waited for us on the second floor, ready to direct us to our line of offices for the day. Poole was a soft-spoken, genial man, a combat veteran of the Persian Gulf War and Somalia. It was rumored that he spent his entire time inside Longworth with a large wad of tobacco packed in his cheek with nowhere to spit. We laughed and groaned at the thought of swallowing, but we also thought Poole was hard core and we respected things that were hard core. As we reached the top of the stairs, we found him bouncing a large ball of rubber bands against the marble wall.

Poole assigned us to a length of rooms and we began to work. Every office appeared as if its inhabitants had been beamed aboard a starship or had just vanished in a puff of smoke. In their mad dash, the congresspeople and their aides had left everything in situ. Computers were still on with the last website they had visited up behind their screensavers. Phones rang. Televisions were on. Fax machines spit out paper from constituents.

The work wasn't difficult beyond the clumsiness of moving in a thick plastic suit and breathing filtered air. I lugged the small vacuum room to room while Big Baby wiped dust samples from varnished oak desks and dragged the vacuum nozzle on the carpet. The walls were covered in awards and state flags and pictures of the sitting representatives in handshake shots with Bill Clinton, George W. Bush, Ted Kennedy, Bob Dole, and Newt Gingrich. There were snapshots of the smiling faces of Boy Scouts and Shriners and church leaders. There were plaques and law degrees from some of the best schools in America. Sports memorabilia—little pennants from the University of Arizona and Notre Dame, signed footballs and baseballs—sat on bookshelves lined with bound bills and law books and bordered by ficus trees.

I briefly sat in a congressman's plush leather chair. The novelty of sitting behind the desk of an elected official of the US House of Representatives was not lost on me or even on Big Baby, who just wanted to get through the day as quickly as possible and go home to his wife and children. We were coming back tomorrow, anyway. But it was impossible not to feel our nearness to the epicenter of American power. Any other day we would be locked away as trespassers, but today we walked through these abandoned offices entirely sanctioned, certainly resentful of their presumed political pettiness but also secretly awed by their patriotic opulence. We were lance corporals and corporals and sergeants and staff sergeants from a million lower-middle-class nowheres across the American kingdom, and people like the people who sat in the chair we helped pay for had a nasty habit of killing people like us overseas for reasons no one bothered to fully understand. I grew up knowing it. I had little doubt Big Baby knew it as he bagged the next sample or that Ken knew it, too, as he waited for us to come out. The same went for every Marine in the courtyard on that cool October afternoon some five weeks after the towers fell. But despite that, we knew that we would go and kill and die or just come home shattered for America because we were Marines.

Big Baby finished and soon Poole sent us back outside. Ken and the squad cut us from our suits and the cool air felt crisp against our damp skin. Once I had cleaned up, I smoked a cigarette in the shade of the Rayburn building and watched other Marines come and go from Longworth. Rumors began to float about Marines calling up porn sites on office computers, of calling home from phones on the desks of congresspeople. None of the officers seemed to care. It had to be expected. We were in our late teens and early twenties and we were going to take advantage of this, for the stories to tell later.

I worked with Ken in the decontamination pits on our last day outside Longworth. Toward the end of the day, a Marine from the squad returned from inside the building with prizes lifted from a congressman's office. He handed them to Ken, who quickly dunked them in the bleach solution and hid them. He returned to share them once the last Marine had left Longworth and the decontamination pits had been closed for good. His prize was a handful of long cigars, each tightly wrapped in sealed and properly decontaminated plastic.

We smoked them just before we left for the day. This was our own little war after 9/11 and we felt like victors. A decade later, the FBI pinned the whole anthrax act on Dr. Bruce Ivins, a middle-aged microbiologist and defense worker. His guilt was never proven; he committed suicide before charges could be filed. We would never learn his motivations or if they were truly his at all. But in the barracks we did not know about Dr. Ivins. It didn't matter. The finer details of its madness would be left to people in suits with high-powered pistols and shiny badges under their jackets. Eventually they pumped the building full of chlorine gas and the whole thing was forgotten. I promised never to tell who stole the cigars. A few days later, US ground troops invaded Afghanistan and we all celebrated the Marine Corps way by getting terribly drunk. That was how my war began.

Compared to the air force and even the army of my childhood, the Corps felt like a profession—one where the rituals of an ex-cop biker gang blended with tomes of traditions and rituals to rival any Ivy League frat house. Its story is a culture of guns and the fantasy of single combat, mano a mano, the hard-core David against the anti-American Goliath, a culmination of bravado and glory and blind exceptionalism. DON'T TREAD ON ME. PRAISE JESUS AND PASS THE AMMUNITION. BOMB ALL NONBELIEVERS BACK TO THE STONE AGE. DON'T RUN; YOU'LL ONLY DIE TIRED.

Everything begins at boot camp. There is no other way. I went to boot camp at Parris Island, a sandy thumb in the Port Royal Sound eighty miles south of Charleston. I tooled in a van with a dozen strangers from the enlistment processing facility at Fort Jackson toward the Carolina coast. It was a flat, nervous ride. No one spoke. We arrived at the receiving center just as the sun set. The sky was thick amber. The drill instructor waited for us as the vans stopped in front of the large receiving building. He was dressed in green wool trousers and a crisp khaki shirt. His brown campaign hat—a "cover" in Marine parlance—sat on his head with its wide, round brim angled slightly forward and covering his eyes. He stood still, a lightning rod stabbed into the concrete. Massive bronze letters tacked to a chrome facade on the building read THROUGH THESE PORTALS PASS PROSPECTS FOR AMERICA'S FINEST FIGHTING FORCE. UNITED STATES MARINES.

A few in the van began to suck wind to mask their panic. I sat frozen, terrified. I felt dread. For months, years even, I had been fed terrible stories of Marine boot camp. Now I was here, at the end of one life and looking down the throat of another. I had asked for this, but whatever interest I'd had about becoming a Marine suddenly felt foolish in that moment. And yet the drill instructor on the sidewalk, the first of many, was here to take me through. A teenager ahead of me moaned "oh fuck" over and over.

Groans in the van intensified as the drill instructor began to approach. To say he marched would cheapen his movements. I had seen plenty of marching, but none of it looked like this. He glided across the sidewalk toward the van in a strut. He leaned his upper body back at his waist, giving him a taut appearance, like a cobra flared in arrogance. Every movement was precise, deliberate, and yet effortless as he advanced on prey who were both terrified and awed in the same moment. He was merely playing a role, but it was a role he took seriously, far more seriously than any banker or middle manager or average government official. It was a role that required that he change himself, his core, into something atavistic and yet professional. When he jerked open the door of the van and opened his mouth, my life ended and I began to play a role, too, if clumsily.

Wilkinson called me a "nasty civilian." He promised he would wring this nastiness from my bones like a plague that had soiled his land. He was a Marine and I was not, and that distinction was all that mattered, a military division between high and low cultures. But he offered that if I—or rather *we*, the mob of teenagers that made up the eighty-odd souls of my training platoon—worked hard enough, we just might become US Marines.

Wilkinson was one of many drill instructors who made this promise, but of all those I encountered, he was the worst, the meanest. He was also the best. By no measure did he look the part of the burly cliché of a Marine drill instructor. He was short, almost diminutive, five foot eight at most, with narrow shoulders and thin, hairy arms. His face had a sort of dopey look and a heavy five-o'clock shadow that was barely kept at bay by shaving. A clinical disdain oozed from his capillaries, punctuated by a perpetual scowl and a scar that ran down his chin. His reedy voice squawked when he yelled and would invariably break, but what he lacked in baritone he made up for with a tonal apathy that was cold and biting and felt completely absent of any regard. He was an incongruent force of will but one that demanded instant obedience.

I was made to understand that somewhere beyond the shell shock of boot camp, I might walk across the parade deck and be called a Marine and then be let loose on the "nasty" chaos of the American culture better somehow, supposedly more refined, or at least *defined* by, what the Marine Corps wanted. They were grafting their identity onto us—that of the toughest, loudest, and meanest motherfuckers on the planet. The drill instructors dangled before us a part in that story every day as they stripped pieces of us and replaced them with ethos and pride and cheap snarling arrogance.

By design, the drill instructors were the epitome of the poster Marine: starched, pressed, crisp, intense, devoted, hard, disciplined, encyclopedically knowledgeable about Marine minutiae, and unflaggingly aggressive to a point just shy of violent. They were human allegories for infantry combat. If a recruit made a mistake, thereby exposing himself, he was pounced on and disciplined through a litany of calisthenics, which served as a stand-in for enemy fire. Often, the whole platoon was disciplined for the mistakes of the individual.

The instructors were men and we were expected to be men too; in a very real sense, becoming a Marine meant, at least to them and certainly some of us, becoming a man. (Women were trained separately on another part of the base by an all-women cast, almost entirely removed from us.) But we were eighteen and nineteen, most of us, and though we were technically adults, we were certainly not men, not yet by their standards, and so they needed to wring our boyhood and our civilian nastiness from us and make us useful and whole—Marines.

The drill instructors attempted to strip away any distinction between race or class, aside from the divide between commissioned officers and the enlisted. Racial categories for White and Black recruits were clumsily reduced to *light green* and *dark green*—terms meant to reclassify race into simple shades of the broader Marine identity. Any notions of the individual were reduced to a mere function of a larger whole. The word *I* was eliminated from our vocabulary. Instead, we were commanded to refer ourselves in the third person—"*This recruit* needs to make a head call, sir" or "*This recruit* does not know, sir." Any utterance of the first person would call down the drill instructors like a time-on-target barrage. The implication was simple: you, by yourself, mean nothing; we, together with you, matter more.

While we ran, we sang cadences in glory of death and sex combined into an ugly violent refrain:

I wish all the ladies
   I WISH ALL THE LADIES
Were holes in the road.
   WERE HOLES IN THE ROAD.
If I was a dump truck
   IF I WAS A DUMP TRUCK
I'd fill them with my load.
   I'D FILL THEM WITH MY LOAD.
Singin' lo-righ-ley-o . . .

And:

A little yellow birdie with a little yellow bill
A LITTLE YELLOW BIRDIE WITH A LITTLE YELLOW BILL
Landed on my windowsill.
LANDED ON MY WINDOWSILL.
I lured him in with a piece of bread
I LURED HIM IN WITH A PIECE OF BREAD
Then I smashed his fuckin' head.
THEN I SMASHED HIS FUCKIN' HEAD.
Singin' lo-righ-ley-o . . .

The Marine Corps spiritualizes battle and eschews war. Per the Corps, battles are won by heroes, and wars are started by geopolitical villains or, worse, crooked politicians. On many days, my platoon gathered around a drill instructor as he recounted tales of Marines who in World War II, Korea, and Vietnam had died on the altar of brotherhood, saving their friends and killing the enemy. Even if they were terrifying, the battles were vehicles for heroism and legacy, its participants the role models of what we could become if we were True Believers. America has thousands of these stories on paper, millions of others buried by time, but exemplified nonetheless when the recruits cried out "TARAWA!" when asked to recite the toughest battle in Marine Corps history or "TUN TAVERN, PHILADELPHIA!" when ordered to name its birthplace.

I yelled these words and others too. But I was certainly not the meanest motherfucker on the planet, or even the second-meanest motherfucker on the planet. I was a nervous, skinny kid who had fantasies of carrying a rifle in a war. I stumbled my way through boot camp neither excelling in any particular sense nor lingering with the "boogers" at the bottom of the platoon's Darwinian social structure. *This recruit* was decidedly average. I ran when I was supposed to run, screamed when I was supposed to scream, marched and shot my rifle and recited the famous bloody battles of the Marine Corps, many of which I already knew from my hours of nighttime reading and daydreaming.

The cultish nature of Marine Corps boot camp quietly scared me, but I was also awed by it and proud to be around it. It seemed to marvel in itself to a place beyond vanity. We were all boys trying to be men, and the lewder instructors talked about how much sex we might get if we became Marines, as if the blue trousers and navy-blue coat with red piping of the Marine dress uniform was a magnet for barflies and bored housewives. One gunnery sergeant routinely suggested that as Marines we might become "twists of steel, with sex appeal" once we were turned loose in supposed fleshpots full of college girls. These instructors also taunted us about how our girlfriends back home were being fucked, routinely, by some limp-wristed spiritual boogeyman named Jody, a nasty civilian we might have to go home and "get some" against by beating his ass with our new combat training. My high school girlfriend had broken up with me just days before I came to Parris Island, a decision I had begrudgingly empathized with. But it didn't matter. Inside the fantasy, I wanted to find her Jody and beat his ass, too, even if I knew this absurd story was little more than a tired, bad photocopy of some World War II fable.

Boot camp had filled me with the spirit of the Holy Marine Corps before sending me off to service the needs of the president. I was taught brotherhood and comradeship, told about Marines who gave their all, about teamwork and selfless sacrifice for the greater good, about virtues and the Core Values—Honor, Courage, and Commitment. I was taught Motivation, Dedication, and how to have a Positive Mental Attitude. Wilkinson and the other drill instructors called the world outside the Marine Corps the "Real World," as if what we were doing was somehow so bizarre and unusual and spectacular it could only be considered unreal when compared against the drool of the average American life. As our training days clicked toward the end, I became a young monk in the draconian monastery of the Marine Corps story, supplicated before the legacy of American power and ready to sacrifice myself on the dais of patriotic buzzwords. Twelve weeks later, I stood in front of the Iwo Jima Monument and sang "The Marines' Hymn," then wept unabashedly as Wilkinson stepped in front of me, shook my hand, and called me a Marine. Lee Greenwood's "God Bless the U.S.A.," the same song I chorused with my elementary school classmates after the United States bombed people in the desert, hummed in the background. I graduated a week later. My mom and Alan and my dad came, along with other family. They took pictures of me in my uniform. I stood at the position of attention in every picture. I had done it so much over the past three months I didn't know the difference. Afterward, I climbed into my dad's Jeep in my dress uniform and sped into the world believing *this Marine* was better than everything America could possibly be.

But on a Saturday night a few weeks later, I came to understand my place in this new world. I walked down Marine Boulevard, in Jacksonville, North Carolina—a military town that sits like an oxpecker atop Marine Corps Base Camp Lejeune. Blistering Harleys with tuned aftermarket carburetors blasted loud and fast past check cashers and army/navy surplus stores. Strip clubs and cheap bars lit the cracked pavement with gaudy neon signs for ladies' night and one-dollar Coors. Marine Boulevard was a main nerve filled with tuned sports cars and big shiny trucks, their bumpers and back windows lined with stickers that read like patriotic death threats:

Carpenters hammer nails.
Plumbers fix pipes.
Marines kill people.

And:

Give war a chance.

I wasn't old enough to drink, not legally, and so I walked toward the Economy Inn where a few friends were rumored to have holed up for the weekend with alcohol. A kid named Irvine walked beside me in a blue Parris Island physical training T-shirt. Tucked into jeans and cinched down with his uniform dress belt, this was the same shirt his drill instructors had worn every time they crushed his body on the physical training field the previous summer. Next to him, another young man and a gaudy Marine Corps T-shirt, the kind of shirt an insurance salesman from Topeka buys when he's in Vegas for the first time. I don't remember what I wore, or maybe I'm just too embarrassed to remember—no doubt my combat boots or a boot camp T-shirt, too, or a shirt Alan had given me when he came home from one of his deployments. We all looked like tourists.

And here they come! The Fleet Marines, two-year veterans roaring from behind at high speed, romping the accelerator of a big-block V-8 rolling on massive knobby tires that crushed down the wide boulevard. As they came up alongside us, a loud voice burst from the extended cab.

"Die, you Boot motherfuckers!"

A beer bottle smashed on the cracked pavement and sprayed glass and foam up the entrance to a Waffle House parking lot. Its thrower leaned his whole torso out the window and in the streetlight we glimpsed a sneering mouth. The Marine wore a polo shirt and his hair was skintight on the sides. His eyes were tuned in a testosterone rage. He flashed a pair of middle fingers like invitations to a frathouse beating before the driver sped him away.

It might seem strange, but the Marine Corps became easy to hate. The Marine Corps does this on its own. In a way, Marines are supposed to hate it. Love comes later, growing from the camaraderie that forms in suffering the military experience together and is eventually bound by nostalgia. But for a new Marine private, sometimes there is hate. It is an impure hatred, childish, more hyperbolic than logical, a resentment that comes from feeling duped. "My fucking recruiter tricked me" was a refrain I often heard in the barracks of infantry school. Whether that was true or not was entirely inconsequential. I can't claim that Canty ever lied to me. But the drill instructors in boot camp did, even if it was merely a lie of omission.

I began to see it in boot camp. No one knew what to expect after graduating, aside from the standard requirement of attending advanced training at one Marine base or another. During classes, recruits routinely stood up and asked, "This recruit would like to hear what the Fleet is like, sir," referencing the nickname for the Marine Corps operating forces. Wilkinson or the other drill instructors would snap, "You'll find out when you get there," and quickly change the subject, as if they'd been asked to reveal classified intel. But someone would always ask again. Our experience was only of boot camp, and if boot camp was any metric of what was coming, we wanted to at least pretend to prepare. But we learned nothing.

The marketing and lore of the Marine Corps built the act of "earning the title" of a US Marine as an end state, an achievement of energy and discipline and time. And they were right. I had arrived in boot camp and had become a Marine, an honor I was proud to have earned, and still am. But earning the title also masked a fundamental truth: it was only the first gate of acceptance, not the final. I was still just a "Boot," a new guy, without form, a dilettante, at least to Marines outside of the boot camp fantasyland.

This was quickly, if dumbly, demonstrated by a clerk at the receiving center at infantry school. I had arrived in Jacksonville with a few others the night before. I cabbed to the school the next morning, my orders in hand, and began the laborious check-in process. The clerk, a young lance corporal from some administrative office, ruled from behind a desk in the receiving area. A hulking red-faced sergeant stood guard behind her. He bayed like a cranky mule whenever

Marines asked him questions whose answers he deemed obvious. I sat nearby, drinking water for an inevitable piss test—the never-ending hunt for marijuana. The lance corporal called the name of a private I knew to her table.

"I think he stepped out with a couple other Marines, Lance Corporal," I said.

Her face screwed into a sneer as she leaned forward across her paperwork. "Motherfucker," she said. "You ain't Marines. You're just *students*."

Her remark, patent nonsense, exposed her own bloated sense of self-righteousness. But it also signaled a theme that would be repeated in the yelling and screaming of infantry instructors to come, never mind the drunken beer-bottle histrionics of grunts in town: my dreams of acceptance as a new Marine should be considered folly. I was a Marine, I had earned that much, but no Marine proves it only once. The Corps' aggrandized self-perception as a spartan culture demanded proof constantly, almost as a pastime, which it achieved by turning itself into a millstone and grinding its youth with an endless and exhausting test.

I joined a rifle company in the Sixth Marine Regiment after infantry school and for eighteen months trained for a deployment overseas. We spent or week or two at a time traipsing through the damp wilderness around Camp Lejeune—patrolling, living in fighting holes, attacked by chiggers and hypothermia, playing war against other Marines or just imaginary enemies, their identities dependent on whom the news had deemed Bad Guy of the Week, typically Iraq or one of the Balkan countries. I was living in a sardonic comedy of absurdities pulled from war novels and matinees. In the absence of a real enemy, it felt as if the peacetime Marine Corps was content to chew its own tail. My battalion commander seemed like a modern-day Colonel Cathcart of *Catch-22*, working us recklessly for a chance at a promotion. Our sergeant major was a bullet-headed anachronism whose sole sales tactic to encourage Marines to reenlist was to tell them—usually while screaming—that they wouldn't amount to anything in the Real World.

In my unit, *out* became the operative word—we wanted out, to be out, away, elsewhere, maybe in college or just working a job somewhere, not humping a pack and a rifle in an infantry company, a job they had all volunteered for. "I fucking hate the Corps," some would say. "I cannot wait to get the fuck out," others moaned. It often felt like we were doing mindless things for the sake of paperwork or to satisfy the whims of officers or, worse, just so we appeared "hard"—like pretending to assault a clearing surrounded by deep swamps in the middle of a cold January night or dropping men to heat exhaustion on long hikes in the dead center of a humid Carolina summer, all to appease the colonel buzzing around in the helicopter above us.

The barracks was a *Lord of the Flies* ant farm of bottled testosterone. Walking along its catwalks felt like walking through a conduit of blue-collar male identity in America—country and death metal and grunge and hard-core rap blasted into the night as empty Coors tallboys piled up in the big aluminum trash cans. Men drank nightly, then arose at five-thirty in the morning to the wretched cackle of the barracks intercoms announcing reveille and orders to fall out for morning physical training. Marines strutted up and down the catwalks as if fixed on some elevated missions for the commandant; others just wiled away time in their dark rooms, sleeping under their racks to hide from the martinet corporals and sergeants who were hunting for bodies for work details, only to reappear for evening formation and then to drink away the night once more. Every Thursday night, the barracks was taken apart like a rifle, cleaned, and reassembled for inspection. Grunts hauled off to the Seven-Day Store and wheeled out cases of beer on dollies, then returned to the barracks to get blasted drunk while scrubbing their showers with bleach and spraying their crumbling furniture with thick coats of Pledge or Endust. Boots like me wandered about in our physical training gear, ushered by one impatient corporal or another, as we cleaned the laundry rooms and mopped the hallways and then, before sunrise, lined up and walked the grass in front of the barracks to pick up all the cigarette butts that had been flicked into the night.

At any given moment, the guttural echoes of a commonplace ass-chewing were audible across all three battalions of the regiment. You could hear them across the night, and when you did, you laughed a little and said something like "Someone's getting lit the fuck up" or just a quiet "Get some." We laughed because it was part of our reality, part of our world, and much of our world meant avoiding those ass-chewings, even though they were inevitable. But the ass-chewings were only a part of being new. I heard stories from friends in other rifle companies of young men being ordered to run calisthenics under hot showerheads or to mop the sidewalks on rainy days. I heard crazy apocrypha about a Boot being tied between a pair of mattresses and tossed to the quadrangle from the second or third deck and about Boots who were ordered into their gas masks and forced to clean their bathrooms with a dangerous combination of bleach and ammonia. The general attitude seemed to orbit one chief idea: I suffered when I was new and therefore you, too, must suffer this rite of passage. It was frat-house absurdity on a merry-go-round, pushed by people who arguably hated it just as much as I began to.

The noise of the Marine Corps left me threadbare—the testosterone posturing, the repetitive work parties, the humping of an automatic weapon through the woods for no apparent reason, the being left in the dark, the never-ending cleaning of the cinder-block confines of my crumbling barracks room, the homesickness. I lost my appetite for the military narratives I had devoured as a teenager and replaced it with everything the military wasn't. I fell into Jack Kerouac and William S. Burroughs, authors who would have nothing to do with the Marines. I lounged about the barracks reading Hunter S. Thompson and Tom Wolfe and George Orwell, imagining myself on the edge of a desert highway somewhere around Barstow in a "very fast car with no top" or as a free agent, like Ken Kesey, packing off on a cross-country bus tour with a squad of psychedelic misfits. When I think about it now, I realize I was drawn to this theme of running, being free, or just fleeing myself. Or perhaps just trying to. I bought a cheap car, a white Pontiac four-banger, and drove home to Georgia every weekend I could. As I blasted away from the base on a Friday afternoon, my stereo pumping rock into the summer air, I wondered what it would feel like to leave for the final time, to flee into the Real World, maybe head to the softness of some college. I had wanted to be in the Marine Corps, to be in the infantry, to be a part of that world—or at least the image of that world I had formed in my mind. Sometimes I had wanted it to the point of desperation. But then driving south, away from Camp Lejeune, I felt inside I might have made a mistake, that perhaps I should have done something different with my life. But it was a feeling that was hard to stomach and I felt like a fool for thinking it.

One Friday afternoon in my first Marine summer after boot camp, on the way out of Jacksonville, I stopped at a McDonald's across from one of the military base housing developments. I went inside and placed an order. I was anxious; I wanted to get down the road. Time mattered. Weekend hours always burned faster than the weekday minutes. I took my tall paper cup to the fountain drinks.

I heard a reedy voice behind me. "Weren't you one of my recruits?"

My insides rocked with fear, a Pavlovian response that snapped me right back to the squad bay at Parris Island—the cadences and the cult, my old boot camp world collapsing into this new wretched one. I felt a strong impulse to stand at the position of attention.

I turned and it was indeed Wilkinson, the drill instructor. He was in civilian clothes. He smiled pleasantly and asked me if I'd eat with him.

I wish I had been older than I was then. A few years might have done it, maybe even one or two. But I had just come from a field exercise. My legs were chewed raw with chigger bites and my face was sunburned. My body was sore. I was young and resentful of this place. Too young in my impatience. Wilkinson stood before me with an invitation. He was a Marine, the real thing, a cardinal of Motivation and a Positive Mental Attitude, and he was asking to sit with me. Driving later, I told myself I had just wanted to go home and maybe score some drinks and forget the Marine Corps. But in truth, I withered in front of his presence; it was too much. Not because I didn't measure up but because I didn't care to. I didn't feel worthy. I was not Motivated; I did not have a Positive Mental Attitude. I muttered my thanks but said I was in a hurry, then climbed into my car and fled, and felt ashamed.

However I might have felt, I was now one sliver of an international contingency plan. The Soviet Union was long gone, but there were still plenty of antagonists. An empire with tentacles wrapping the globe will inevitably land on a few troubled spots, like Bosnia, Albania, Kosovo, Liberia, Sierra Leone, and East Timor. Should an American interest—real or perceived—come under the thumb of some Stone Age cleric, or maybe just the ire that remained in the wake of colonialism, I would load my magazines and board a ship or a plane and maybe fight, for better or worse. Iraq was always a hard standby, a natural default state. A few Salt Dogs—the jailhouse nickname for the grunts who had already pulled one deployment overseas—told stories about how they had been sent to the Persian Gulf to rattle sabers as the United States and the United Nations squabbled with Saddam Hussein over weapons inspections. They were unabashed about their fear of dying in another war with Iraq. They said that when they returned to the States men were kissing the first American earth their feet touched. A platoon sergeant in our company routinely beat us over the head with these fears. "Something is going to happen," he would say. "I can feel it!" He would prove to be right, if off by a few years.

My battalion boarded amphibious assault ships and cruised across the Atlantic and into the Mediterranean for six months, steaming from port to port, waiting for the news to tell us what war to fight. In the meantime, I made stops in Spain and Turkey and Italy and Greece, drinking, walking through the streets of Barcelona, making out with a girl in a park in Tarragona, haggling with traders in Marmaris, marveling at the way the green mountains sparkled against the blue waters of the Turquoise Coast. I stood on Mount Vesuvius and walked through the ruins of Pompeii, laughing like the teenager I was at the erotic art and awed by the statuesque bodies of Romans petrified into place by the pyroclastic nightmare that had killed them. But I was still a Marine and so I sailed to North Africa and the Middle East, and instead of seeing the Pyramids, I flew with my company to the Egyptian desert and trained to kill Iraqis or terrorists or whoever else deserved our national judgment.

Our firepower always felt like a saving measure against our collective angst about the Marine Corps. We routinely trained with live ammunition and explosives, and through their display, many became silent lovers of this weaponry even as they feared it. I watched wide eyed as sepulchral red machine-gun tracers slashed across a dark night sky or as the ghostly haze of parachute flares ignited the broken woods of a Camp Lejeune live-fire range. I felt something inherently animalistic buried inside weapons of war, similar to when I fired guns as a kid, but far more visceral, intense, raising my heart rate and flooding my veins with endorphins until my skin tingled. We ran through the ranges, rushing and diving to the earth, firing and changing magazines, screaming commands and exhalations, sweating through our flak jackets, the gun oil and smoke coating our hands and faces with a fine sheen. During one range, a machine-gun team fired long strings of live ammunition into a set of bunkers we were preparing to assault. Our own Colonel Cathcart ordered the team to fire at a target dangerously close to our path. I huddled on the ground with my squad mates and watched the bullets pass before us—a line of death just a few feet away. I could hear their sounds—*SNAPSNAPSNAPSNAP!*—and while we were horrified and angered that we would be so foolishly put at risk, I felt excited by their presence.

In Egypt, near the World War II battlefield of El Alamein, I watched shells from Marine artillery erupt on the night horizon while we ran through a complex live-fire drill. Tracers snapped down the barrel of my squad automatic weapon across a desert ignited by our handheld flares and the glow of high-explosive shells cratering the distant landscape. In the Israeli desert, while I slopped a rag over the dinner tables at the field mess, my company ran a massive exercise with the Israeli Defense Force, supported by Marine attack helicopters. A corporal in my squad later told me just how badass it was to watch their miniguns clattering overhead, sprinkling the earth with hot brass.

We were practicing the realities of facing the battlefield. We didn't want war, certainly not. We would have rather been home or drunk or having sex. But I felt awe at the spectacle and destructiveness of our own firepower. By the time I neared the end of my deployment overseas, my unit, even the loudest of complainers and detractors, had been honed into a razor of professionalism. We always walked away tired but electrified, chattering joyfully with one another. Even if we hated the Marine Corps and talked about how much we hated it, there was always that sense that we hated it because it was easy to hate and popular to hate but that there might be something more to this work than simply our collective desire to leave it. While the Corps might produce its own misery, that misery also formed bonds. I would feel slivers of this years later, in various civilian office jobs, but never again would it compare to the bonds grown from the combination of suffering and adrenaline in the face of incredible danger. It is a bond that makes the average world, the Real World, seem small and sometimes meaningless.

But we didn't experience its intended purpose: war. Instead, we returned home. Somewhere toward the end of that experience, my hatred for the Marine Corps lessened, almost imperceptibly. Or maybe I just accepted "the Suck," the old pejorative the Corps was sometimes called, for what it was.

I knew that I could be a competent Marine, and if a war came, I could be a part of that story too. But three months later, I was out of the unit, transferred with a dozen others to Maryland. Just drifting along with "the Needs of the Marine Corps," as the saying went. When the war did come at last, Ken and I watched it in the Maryland night sky as fighter jets carved paths above our cigarette smoke. I watched on television as the Marines invaded Afghanistan, and because I was finally a Marine, I was jealous.

GOLF

It doesn't matter how many Mr. and Mrs. Johnsons are anti-war—the actual killers who know how to use the weapons are not.

—Anthony Swofford, *Jarhead*

We file out of the outpost on the Syrian border under 1,001 Arabian stars of a cool predawn November morning. Our boots hiss through the dirt as the column moves past earthen barriers and razor wire. Dogs howl our arrival out beyond the firmament.

I see the lights of the distant city as we enter the wasteland. Husaybah is a big black spot on the maps of Rebel Six's liberation plans back at headquarters. It is the mouth of the Iraqi ratline, a supply train running guns and money and foreign insurgents across the Syrian border all the way to Baghdad and Beyond. The city is packed with homegrown insurgents and foreign fighters looking for The Shit. The city is the prize, an urban nightmare with the hearts and minds of thousands of Iraqis waiting for us to liberate them from beneath the sandal and scimitar of Iron Age rhetoric. This is our story. Inshallah!

A pair of Marine guards manning a small gate at the exit high-five and jealously whisper, "Get some" and "Kill bodies" as we pass.

The column stops just outside the walls and a Marine private first class is called forward from the column. I stand in the twilight as the staff sergeant reads a promotion warrant with the help of a red-lens flashlight, and the plucky lieutenant pins the black-metal lance corporal stripe to the collar of the Marine's dusty uniform. The new lance corporal beams proudly, his teeth gleaming in the darkness. We are near the Line of Departure—the invisible line between peace and battle. All the stories and anecdotes, lessons of heroism and valor, circle in the night like ghosts on the far edges of the darkness. Someone says that he'll probably remember this for the rest of his life. We believe it.

We are pressed, at least in part, by the instruments of American history. We stand at the border of an urban landscape in a foreign country and seek to take it, liberate it, seize it from some dark blot in the valley below the firelight of the American castle, dubious as it may sometimes be. We're all proud to stand on its parapets in the face of a town filled with people who we believe desperately want to kill us and know we are coming to kill them for all the words we ascribe to as our virtues. Battle is legacy in the fantasyland of our world and we want a piece of our own to take home with us.

We rush into the city not long after, accompanied by awkward jundis of the new Iraqi army, dashing across the desert past bits of trash toward the first line of houses at the city's edge. We are nervous. We know nothing about the houses we are commandeering. The Iraqis of these first homes quickly awaken to find hard flashlights beaming in through their windows and rifle barrels wagging in their faces.

I step into one house with a rifle in my hand. I see an older man on his knees, beardless and with eyeglasses, his haggard face glazed by fatigue and resignation. His wife and children, a little boy and a girl, cry in the children's room. It is four in the morning. They are scared. But soon they calm and a few Marines play with the kids as the navy corpsman looks them over. The mother of the house makes chai in the kitchen. She is passive and guarded. Afraid, surely, but calm. We might not be friends and we might be an evil, but we all seem to believe there is another evil in this town somewhere and we must do this to hunt it down. This is the story we tell ourselves.

Fighting begins at sunrise. The insurgents in the city have awoken to see hundreds of Americans on their rooftops. The air clatters and snaps with bullets as I stand on the roof with a Marine named Kemper, a southern boy with an easy air about him that hides a deep reservoir of inner confidence. I can see the lines on his face that will come when he is older, in charge of *some business in middle America or perhaps working as a sheriff's deputy in some backwoods county. Whatever he might become, right now he is a Marine.*

I huddle with him and his squad behind the wall of the roof. A couple of riflemen hunker nearby. Both of them have canted their eyes upward, looking toward the top of the wall with the corners of their mouths curled upward slightly in a mix of wonder and terror. I look up too. It is a strange sensation—to look at the sky with its soft blue glow and wispy traces of autumnal clouds and know right there, just a hand reach away, an extension of the arm, is a place where shaped pieces of lead snap by in high definition. They fill my ears with hard CRACKS! that prick at the electrodes of fear inside my skin and make my cheeks twitch. The bullets are impossible to see, but I can sense them up there a few feet away, as if altering the code that compiles the picture of the sky. Nearby, a mortarman writes on a ragged slip of paper, "Hi Mom, I'm getting shot at," and he holds it up while his friend takes a picture. We laugh.

The fire slackens. On the roof of the next house, a machine-gun team sets up its long black gun and aims down a long road. Somewhere farther in the city, an insurgent pokes his Kalashnikov around a wall or a corner or perhaps from a dark window and crackles off a scatter of bullets down an alley toward us. The machine gunners have a loose idea where the insurgent could be. "See that friggin' ox cart thing?" the sergeant asks. "Like, just to the right of that . . ." One of the gunners squeezes the big black trigger and sends a burst down the alley.

Almost immediately, the insurgent fires back. Then the gunner talks back with another burst of his own. The two guns chatter back and forth, striking out at each other with hot, primeval words of hate and vitriol. But neither one is quite sure of the position of the other. After a while of snapping back and forth, the gunner stops responding. Like a sad child, the insurgent fires again, hoping to draw the machine gun back into the conversation, but the gunner spits tobacco juice off the roof and listens to the rueful complaints. The insurgent then seems to give up too. We leave the family in the house below and move into the city. What more is there to say?

XII

I met up with Ken in Cincinnati the first Independence Day after the War on Terror began. We spent most of the time drinking in the bars in Mansion Hill, on the Kentucky side of the river, then tooled to the Ohio side to the nightclubs in the central business district, blowing cash with a friend of his from high school named Billy who had just finished a four-year tour as a Marine in Hawaii. On July 4, we gathered at the VFW Hall in Covington with Ken's father. The hall had purchased a few hundred dollars' worth of fireworks and put us to work blasting them over a large pond behind the building. I was initially nervous about the cliché of Vietnam veterans snapping into those flashbacks depicted in war movies as we began to fire off bottle rockets, but that was absurd and I felt mildly ashamed for defaulting to that stereotype. After we ate hot dogs and charred hamburgers from the grill, we gathered our gear.

We started small. Bottle rockets and firecrackers mainly, but we quickly graduated to large dazzlers that blasted colored sparks across the grass and into the gray pond. We began tying bottle rockets together for louder bangs while young boys along the sidelines oohed and ahhed at the crackles and glitter of the sparks in the clear sky above the water. The more we drank, the more it became a game. Roman candles were now guns we shot at imaginary enemies. When some multishot whistler or whiz-bang tipped over and began to fire its cheap projectiles at us, we dove behind the coolers or the table, huddling and laughing with our heads covered by our arms as if under mujahideen mortar fire, or maybe North Vietnamese or Iraqi Republican Guard, whichever suited the fantasy. When Ken was peppered with a shower of harmless sparks, Billy yelled, "Corpsman up!" and pretended to treat his shrapnel wounds. After a defective industrial shell shot just a few short feet into the air, then exploded into a cloud of yellow sparks across the lawn, I yelled, "Incoming!" and laughed when we dove to the ground. The neighborhood kids laughed too. When we ran out of fireworks, the pond was coated in a gunpowder haze and our fingertips were burned, but we were drunk and did not care.

America was at war and somewhere out there was the prospect of combat, the door that might open into our own version of the American Dream. War meant surviving and Ken and I wanted to go to war, to witness and survive it. We weren't deranged; we didn't pack ourselves into the gym or strut about like American action heroes, at least not any more than our identity as Marines would allow. We usually laughed at the archetype anyway. Instead, we waited.

Combat videos started making their way back to the States. I sat at a computer in our headquarters building and watched grainy footage of Marines in the cold desert twilight. Somewhere in the blurring distance was a target—Lord knows what, perhaps a truck full of Taliban. The video suddenly sparkled as tracers snapped across the desert as white spheroids, their light overpowering the sensitive night-vision optics. I looked for enemy shots and they were there too—twinkling meekly inside the tumult of our overwhelming suppression fire. I watched, awestruck, and played it a few more times, imagining myself there in the cold, maybe afraid, but alive. There was combat. *Now.* Not buried in the pages of some GI account of World War II or Vietnam, or locked into the flash of Hollywood pyrotechnics, but alive and authentic—a Real War.

What is it like to be under fire, to have another human being shoot at you or lob high-explosive projectiles across the sky to land in your midst? I wondered this often as I lay in my rack in the barracks at night reading or watching *Band of Brothers* and *Black Hawk Down*. Thanks to my Marine training, I knew what bullets sounded like when they passed overhead, but to be under fire from some outside agent, whether malevolent or impoverished and desperate, was a whole other matter. I knew most of the words art and history has used to describe war and battle—*horrifying, terrifying, insane, chaotic, deadly*—but their meaning had long been flattened inside me by ideas of patriotism and glory and the American history I had been raised by. Or maybe I just ignored them, too, using the arrogance of my youth to repel the realities of war-story vocabulary. I wanted to experience combat, its adjectives be damned.

If I wanted, I could be done with the military; my four-year obligation was nearly over. I could have gone to college on the GI Bill, joined the ranks of the Real World, whatever that meant. But the war would have floated out on the unanswered periphery of my identity, and I knew that that singular lack of experience would have festered. So I signed the papers and took the oath of enlistment once more. Somewhere out there was the war.

I considered joining the Fifth Marine Regiment at Camp Pendleton, in California, once my time in Maryland was through. I had completed advanced training as an infantry squad leader. I liked the idea of staying in the infantry, but I also had a long-standing interest in photojournalism and writing and had even done some work as a stringer for the base newspaper at Camp Lejeune. Every military branch has its own media department, mainly for the purposes of public affairs. I had no interest in being a shill, but this seemed like a job that, at least on paper, sent its people to the leading edge of the Marine Corps to record its actions for history and legacy. There was something special about capturing the experience of war and putting it down, like Hemingway, Mailer, Jones, Crane, and Tolstoy, a tradition all its own. Gustav Hasford, the author of the novel that became *Full Metal Jacket*, had been a combat correspondent in Vietnam.

Even Hunter S. Thompson had been a military journalist for a short time. The bean counters of the Marine Corps allowed me to change fields as an incentive to remain in the service and months later, in January 2003, I stood on the bluffs overlooking Onslow Beach on the Carolina coast as a combat correspondent.

It was sunny. A cold wind snapped in from the bay. A navy beach-master stood nearby with a pair of orange semaphore flags in his hands. Beyond the surf, a landing craft approached the shore pro-pelled by a set of large fans that pushed sea spray into the air behind it. The speeding craft slowed as it crossed the breakers and stopped once it pushed far up onto the sand past the waves. Then the pilot killed the big fans and let the air from the black bladder that held it aloft.

A gathering of navy assault ships rested at anchor in the bay like the gray silhouettes of castles. Helicopters clattered among the larger of them, ferrying troops from a nearby landing zone. Humvees and trucks waited in rows behind the bluffs. After a few minutes, their engines came to life at the holler of NCOs. They filed onto the beach and onto the landing craft one at a time, guided into posi-tion by loadmasters in green jumpsuits eager to get moving in the sunlight.

They were all on their way to Kuwait for the big buildup of American forces preparing to invade Iraq. I was not going with them.

While Iraq had been the chief spiritual antagonist of America since the end of the Persian Gulf War, short of it being some neoconserva-tive fantasy there had been no real intention to invade the country before 9/11. The United States seemed content with economic sanc-tions. But even if Secretary of Defense Dick Cheney stated after the Gulf War that "we were not going to go get bogged down in the prob-lems of trying to take over and govern Iraq," anyone in uniform who had any understanding of history and the proclivities of American anger knew, even if only unconsciously, that Iraq was going to be a target of our ire after the World Trade Center fell.

Fighting war, especially preemptive war, represents a failure of foreign policy, a failure of every other institution of its defense, a failure of society. Countries that fail to grasp this tend to lose more wars than they win. I didn't agree with the spirit of this war. A few Marines I knew didn't either, at least in private. Most others were eager, however. Ready and willing. "Fuck Iraq," they said, "we were attacked!" which was also not an uncommon sentiment among vast swaths of Americans in the Real World. As a result, America was going to bury a country with American bombs for a list of reasons that were inherently dubious, despite any humanitarian or patriotic claims put forth by our government, our media, or our public intellectuals. But despite how I felt about the justifications of the war, of course I was going to go. I was a Marine. Bombs would fall in Iraq regardless of any protest, and if they were going to fall, then I was going to bear witness. It felt shameful not to.

But I was not going.

I had arrived back at the Marine base from Maryland just weeks before the first troops boarded transports and steamed across the Atlantic. I was a newly minted combat correspondent, a sergeant, a former infantryman with advanced training in chemical and biological weapons protection, but I was not going. There is always gate-keeping at nearly every level of the military—some of it dictated by time and experience, or merit, all reasonable criteria in theory. But sometimes it's governed by bureaucracy, cronyism, and appearances, and somewhere in all that I was stuck, thanks to "the Needs of the Marine Corps."

The base felt hollow once the bulk of the Marines left. The lines to the front gate, logjams that normally stretched for miles on a standard Monday morning, had thinned to a narrow trail. I could walk into a barber on Sunday and get a seat within minutes rather than wait the usual hour or so. The local newspaper flagged concerns about bars and tattoo parlors faltering without the biweekly paycheck of thousands of Marine lance corporals. There was a sense of deflation and even bitterness among those who remained. While there may be a few men and women who wear a uniform while at the same time opposing the war, this is not the case for most in the military, especially those who launch the missiles and pull the triggers. It's madness to want to go to war, and yet collectively, in masses, it becomes honorable, even if the reasons for the war are not. Part of this comes from a duty to serve larger principles: democracy, freedom, justice, liberty, the litany of virtues with meanings open to interpretation. But there is also a chemical, almost primitive attraction, something as old as the first caves of humanity, to being at its leading edge. I understood it then and I understand it now. To miss it feels like being gutted by a love that is rejected.

A Marine gunnery sergeant was asked to give a talk to a banquet hall full of Marines headed for Kuwait for the big preinvasion buildup. The gunnery sergeant, a reservist, had a day job as an analyst of some caliber at one of the big Washington, DC, strategy think tanks like the RAND Corporation or the Brookings Institute. He had been pressed into uniform a few weeks before the invasion as part of the efforts to bolster forces sent overseas and fill in the ranks of some stateside services that had been stripped bare, like military police. In the hall, rows of chairs faced a large projector screen, and the seats were filled mainly with officers—a few lieutenants, but mostly captains, majors, and lieutenant colonels. The gunny was asked to speak on the cultural and religious structures of Iraq and the region at large.

The gunny used a PowerPoint slide deck—a tool quietly mocked as an intellectual death trap in military circles. He began his presentation with all the passion of a postal clerk. He opened with a brief overview of the demographics of Iraq, its religious and tribal divisions, then clicked through its long history as a Middle Eastern brass ring for occupiers—vied over by the British and Ottoman Empires during the First World War and then, as part of the Sykes–Picot Agreement, controlled by the British after the war. He explained how the Iraqi people had managed to win their independence from colonial rule in a bloody revolt in the 1930s and how they had existed as an independent monarchy until the Second World War, at which point their government brutishly aligned itself with the Nazi powers, leading to the reoccupation of Iraq by British forces. He carried us sleepily through the reestablishment of the Iraqi monarchy and its downfall after the Iraqi army staged a coup d'état—one of the many overthrows that rippled across the Arab world at that time. Then came the Iraqi Republic, short lived in the realm of history, he said. The leaders of this new government ousted themselves nearly a decade later when the Iraqi branch of the Arab Socialist Ba'ath Party—a political party that blended Arab nationalism, pan-Arabism, and notably, anti-imperialism ideas into an ideological force—took control of the country, led by an army officer and political leader, Ahmed Hassan al-Bakr, and two leading Ba'ath Party members: Salah Omar al-Ali and Saddam Hussein.

Only at the end of his briefing did the gunny come to life. When the British occupied Iraq, he said, their soldiers were met with violence from the Iraqis almost as a pastime. British soldiers patrolled the streets in armored cars and relied on firepower and technology as their chief means of controlling a population they cared little to understand. The Iraqis would not tolerate a prolonged occupation, he warned, and an insurgency was sure to erupt if they perceived America as an occupying force. The gunny's message was clear: we had a longer road ahead of us than we realized.

His stark assessment flew right in the face of every rattling saber and croaking jingo / freedom fries nonsense that had drooled out of the White House, Congress, and some of the national media. But there was nothing anyone in the hall could do: Marines do not form American foreign policy. The gunny might as well have been speaking to a room full of cats.

As a coda, the gunny showed us *The Battle of Algiers*, the 1966 French film showcasing the determination and resolve of rebellion against the ignorance and violent folly of a Western occupier. At one point, I glanced around the room. The audience looked bored. Those were fifty-year-old French colonial problems, not the problems of the American democracy. History could not repeat itself. Surely, we would do it right. I spied an aging colonel a few rows behind me. He was asleep.

It was mid-March, just beginning to warm outside. The Marines and soldiers overseas were lined up on the Iraqi border, ready to pounce across the Line of Departure. As I sat in my rickety office chair waiting for news of Someone Else's War, I could almost see them all out there huddling in their fighting holes as they sweated in their chemical protection suits, their black rifles between their knees, the Humvees and amphibious assault vehicles that would carry them over the berm idling nearby, dusty, lined with cases of rations and ammunition. But in the morning, I would get up before sunrise and deliver copies of *USA Today* to a few generals. Just doing my chores, the Needs of the Marine Corps.

The air campaign over Iraq was called "Shock and Awe," as if it were the catchphrase of some pay-per-view wrestling match or the tagline of some action-hero B-movie. A lieutenant and I and a few others watched it on cable news from her office on the evening it began. The anchors spoke ceaselessly over live color video of Iraqi antiaircraft fire glittering across the Baghdad sky as coalition bombs erupted in wide billowing fans of orange and white. Long gone were the days of those first-gen night-vision optics I had seen from the floor of Chris's living room. This was in full color and in stereo. Wolf Blitzer chattered like a sports announcer, regurgitating stats and plays: "As many as three thousand, *three thousand*, satellite-guided precision bombs, laser-guided bombs, would be dropped at various military targets not only in Baghdad and around Baghdad but else-where around the huge country of Iraq . . ."

It was a cheap presentation with more production value than substance, the clumsy sequel everyone watched but quietly knew no one needed. Though fighter and bomber pilots were executing the tasks asked of them professionally, its representation felt staged in a sense, as if we needed to see it here just as much as we wanted the bombs to fall there, all for our vengeance. The empty calories of a fast-food war. Somewhere out there, somewhere far beyond the sounds of people being killed, men and women were in bars and chain restaurants in TriBeCa and Topeka and Provo and Chandler and all points between, watching this display on the television. Maybe some of them weren't cheering, but more than a few certainly were.

A few days later, American and British troops crossed the border into Iraq in America's first preemptive war. They drove north across the old battlegrounds of the Persian Gulf War, through the oil fields in southern Iraq, and followed the Euphrates and Tigris Rivers into the southeastern end of the Fertile Crescent. Battles erupted in Basra and later in Nasiriyah, where Marines, some of the same Marines I had watched load onto helicopters and drive onto landing craft on Onslow Beach, were ambushed and now ceased to exist. When news came home that they were gone, those left behind felt it deep inside us. We felt it because we were Marines and they were Marines and they were dead. I also felt it because I was a Marine and they were Marines and I was not with them.

At night, I would return to my barracks room to drink beer and listen to music, and then I would sleep and awaken and read more news of Someone Else's War and lament my absence in it. Every city and town captured felt like notches on a cheap belt of history, but it was a history I wanted to possess.

After the statue of Saddam in Baghdad's Firdos Square was jerked to the earth by Iraqis and Marines, the lieutenant and I, along with a reporter from the local newspaper, were sent to the Bethesda Naval Hospital, just north of Washington DC. A general wanted to visit the wounded who had been evacuated. The lieutenant was sent to be the general's spokesperson for the media sure to be present and I was there to take photographs.

We left before sunrise in a cheap white Chevy van and pulled into the hospital complex just after morning rush hour. The general flew up from North Carolina with his aide in a private jet. For the rest of the morning into the afternoon, we walked the halls of the hospital as the general visited Marines who had been wounded in Iraq and sent home.

There was the captain who had been shot in the throat by an AK-47. The long wound where the doctors had opened him to repair the damage snaked up and around his neck like a cable. He couldn't speak, but he was awake and moving. He remained professional and calm in his silence. He even tried to stand up from his bed, but the general stopped him. I took a picture and the general smiled.

There was the lance corporal who had taken mortar shrapnel in his leg. Clothes and papers were scattered everywhere, a chaos any parent could understand, including his father, a nebbishy man with a beard who sat in a nearby chair. The lance corporal explained to the general he was going on leave to recover. The general asked if he had received his Purple Heart. The Marine said that he had. Some other general had already come by and given it to him. His father, beaming, displayed it like a trophy.

And there was the corporal who was walking but shouldn't have been. Just a day or two after the Marines invaded, he had been deep in sleep in a shallow sand ditch when a sixty-ton Abrams tank rolled over him in the night. The tank had pushed him into the soft Arabian sand but not before it splintered his pelvis into a blizzard of hairline fractures. The bone was fusing together nicely, he explained, though he had to be careful. He was given a Purple Heart, but the Marine Corps took it back a few years later. He hadn't been wounded by the enemy.

The general visited a sergeant who had been wounded in the fighting in Nasiriyah. When his fellow Marines had carried him to an amphibious assault vehicle to be evacuated, an American attack jet inadvertently strafed the column and nearly killed him. Friendly fire. His body had been emaciated by the desert and by his wounds. He had flatlined a number of times on the way home and had been in a coma. But he was awake now and his eyes were intense, even angry, defiant in the face of his own death. He already has his Purple Heart too.

There was the lance corporal who sat in a wheelchair with his leg protected by a metal frame. He explained he had been shot in the chest by an AK-47, but his armored vest had saved his life. Then a mortar round shredded his leg below the knee. He spoke about it flatly, as if his system had been shocked to static and he had not had time, or perhaps the nerve, to reboot himself. His eyes were glazed, and I wasn't certain if it was from painkillers or the images of seeing his own blood in the desert replaying somewhere behind his eyes.

When they all looked at me, it felt as if they were looking through me. They had Been There and I had not. I could read it in their eyes. Or maybe I simply perceived it to be true. Whatever the case, there were moments when I wanted to walk into a dark corner of the hospital and sob. But I also wanted to know everything about it, to absorb every detail. As we drove away that evening, back toward Camp Lejeune and lost in the sea of rush-hour traffic, I felt small.

The first veterans of the invasion came back from Iraq that summer in a storm of sand and desert camouflage, of Purple Heart Medals and Iraqi Campaign Medals and Combat Action Ribbons. The lines for the main gate swelled to their prewar length. The barber shops and pawn shops and dive bars and strip clubs burst at the seams, greased with new money. Car dealers hawked hot rods and fat-tire trucks to twenty-year-olds at 15, 20, and even 25 percent interest. Summer came in hot and the beaches were packed with Marines, some with their bodies scarred in places. But they were still young, and they drank beer and played in the surf and picked up women and fought in the bars and felt American.

Late spring was a time when the war felt over. America and its paltry "coalition of the willing" had beaten the Iraqi army, or at least chased it into the shadows, having toppled a dictator who had been compared to a modern-day Adolf Hitler or Mussolini. In May, George W. Bush landed on the deck of the carrier *Abraham Lincoln* like some kind of half-assed action hero and announced we had prevailed. It seemed America had lived up to the rose-colored ideas of its own legacy. But it was an absurdity dug up from the lie of its own bloated self-image, one that converted patriotism into a rhetorical blanket to hide the casualties of its hubris. When our dead came home, they arrived draped with the flag, the true cost of these deaths hidden from cameras.

The Second Marine Division held a memorial service on a bright Friday morning behind a large headquarters building along the New River—honoring the first of the nearly seven thousand US dead to come between all our various wars (. . . and counting). Marines and sailors stood in tight formations in the grassy amphitheater. The divisional band played the "Star Spangled Banner" and "The Marines' Hymn." A chaplain gave an invocation and we prayed with him or simply stared at the earth between our feet.

A general gave a short speech about sacrifice and America, and soon after, the memorial turned to honor the dead. A sergeant major stood with a list and boomed the names across the amphitheater as if running through a basic roll call. He called out a name and a marine somewhere in the mass called back, "Here, sergeant major!" The sergeant major called out another name, and another Marine responded. Then a third name:

"Lance Corporal Cline."

No answer.

"Lance Corporal Cline."

Nothing.

"Lance Corporal Donald John Cline Jr."

In the silence we knew the man was dead. The sergeant major did this for each casualty. By the end, there were tears on the faces of many of the Marines in the amphitheater. Some sobbed openly. A few broke from the ranks and moved quietly to the back to grieve on their own. They had lost friends, or maybe just acquaintances, but they had all been brothers nonetheless. Now they were gone and the survivors were crying.

When the service ended, I walked back to my car and tossed the camera onto the passenger's seat and lit a cigarette. Then I beat my fist into the steering wheel. I did it because they were dead. I did it because I had not been there.

Ken hung up his uniform. He wanted to go to the war, but he was sick of the bureaucratic sacred cows of military service. The military can be its own worst enemy, its rigid attitudes, spartan traditions, and demands for conformity getting in the way of reason. It has an inherent tendency to chew up its junior enlisted, NCOs, and junior officers with an overindulgence of dogma. Brand-new privates could get paid an extra monthly stipend to live off base, away from the grind of the barracks, as long as they were married, but sergeants who weren't had to stay in the barracks and have their rooms inspected once a week. I once worked for a staff sergeant who would get cranky whenever I went for my obligatory weekly haircut on Friday afternoons instead of waiting in the interminable Sunday lines. There was no rule or regulation as to when I was required to get a haircut, only that I keep my hair a certain length. But that I went two days earlier than some accepted norm meant I was apparently "on my own program." Little things like that were petty and said more about the insecurities of the individual than anything else. But rank still had to be obeyed if I didn't want to risk losing pay or privileges. These behaviors were easily accepted the first few years, but as time clicked by and more rank was pinned to the collar, they could be harder to swallow. Many leave the military because of this, more than any booster might like to admit.

When Ken left the Marines, he moved into an apartment in Crystal City, near the Pentagon, splitting rent with Big Joe, who had also left the service. I drove up on the weekends once or twice a month all through the fall after the invasion. During the day, we lounged around the apartment, drinking beer on the balcony, then at night showered and ironed our clothes and rode the Metro past the Pentagon and along the eastern edge of Arlington National Cemetery before coming up for air in Rosslyn. We walked north to the Potomac and crossed the Francis Scott Key Bridge into Georgetown, then proceeded to drink ourselves to a point just shy of oblivion in the bars along Prospect and M Streets.

In the early-morning quiet one night, Ken told me that a number of private companies had been hired to provide personal security for officials across the Coalition Provisional Authority and various other governmental and nongovernmental organizations. He said contractors were making huge sums of tax-free money, hundreds of thousands of government dollars, and all he had to do was find a way in.

In the months after the end of the invasion, Iraq had boiled over into a full-on counterinsurgency war. L. Paul Bremer, the administrator of the Coalition Provisional Authority (or "viceroy," as he was sometimes shamelessly called), disbanded the Iraqi army and turned tens, if not hundreds of thousands of Iraqi soldiers out onto the street, a brainless decision that managed to both effectively eliminate a ready-made security force capable of restoring public order and create the nucleus of the Iraqi insurgency in the same pen stroke. Instead of building a new army around this core of professional soldiers, the move fueled Arab sentiments that the American military would remain as an occupier and not the shining liberator it had professed itself to be to the world. Instead of offering the American

army a way out of the country, the former Iraqi soldiers now armed
themselves by raiding unguarded armories and ammunition dumps
and began to kill coalition troops. Al Qaeda began operations in Iraq
soon after.

Urban centers like Baghdad, Ramadi, Fallujah, and Najaf disin-
tegrated into near chaos. In Fallujah, the bodies of American security contractors were dragged through the streets and hung from
a bridge over the Euphrates. Angered, Marines launched a house-
to-house battle to crush the Iraqi insurgency entrenched inside
the city, only to be stopped by how the optics of their advance and
the breadth of civilian casualties might appear to the Iraqi people and the Arab world at large, never mind the American voters
ahead of an upcoming presidential election. Just as the campaign
was beginning, *60 Minutes II* released photos of US soldiers smiling
and hamming for the camera as they tortured and humiliated Iraqi
prisoners in Abu Ghraib—a clarion call for angry Muslims across
the region. Retired general Stanley McChrystal would later write,
"In my experience, we found that nearly every first-time jihadist
claimed Abu Ghraib had first jolted him into action." The Sunni
Triangle, a loose geographical boundary northwest of Baghdad, hit
the foreign policy lexicon as a beacon of antioccupation violence.
In 2004, the number of allied casualties doubled from the previous year and nearly twelve thousand civilians were killed. Though
the numbers were paltry compared to what would come, as Walter
Cronkite said of Vietnam during the Tet Offensive, it was a whole
new war.

Mercenaries have been a part of war since at least the campaigns
of Ramses II, but it was strange for me, perhaps a product of my
own naiveté, to imagine fighting an American war without a uniform or even the requirement of allegiance. And yet now we were
parceling out the fighting to private companies paid to blanket our
manpower deficiencies in a war undersold to the American people.
Still, I couldn't begrudge Ken this opportunity. Experiencing combat

was as much a goal for him as it was for me. If some organization was willing pay him a six-figure salary in tax-free US dollars to protect some "asset" around Baghdad, then who was he to object? It might have seemed unethical in a larger foreign policy sense, but it was also a reasonable opportunity for a twentysomething American military professional who had an interest in testing himself by being shot at. That the idea was possibly reckless only added to its attractiveness.

Ken eventually found his "in" in the spring of 2004. I was excited for him, but I was also jealous. I had this notion that his going to war would allow him to step across a boundary that would ultimately separate us. He was my best friend, and while I was concerned that he'd be gravely injured or worse, I was also worried he would return home to view me as an unrelatable neophyte because we wouldn't have shared similar experiences. He would be of "that world" once he came home, and I would not.

I traveled to Virginia one more time before Ken left to begin training for work overseas. He was in the process of shoving his everyday life into a corner to make room for the war that was about to take over his next six to eight months. In a quiet moment, he admitted he was nervous, both about measuring up to his superiors, who would undoubtedly be some of the former special-operations types who typically haunt those circles, and about the prospect of being wounded or killed.

We stood on his balcony and smoked cigarettes. The rush of the traffic of Highway 1 and the racket of Ronald Reagan Washington National Airport echoed between the buildings. I have always liked the noise and lights of big cities. There's something hopeful in them, a place of sparks. I was going to miss the fast burn I made on the weekends toward DC. The energy inside me always grew the closer I got, so much so that I typically risked a massive fine racing the last few miles up Interstate 395.

"I know you're probably pissed," he said. He was leaning against the railing, a cigarette dangling between the tips of fingers. In the living room, Big Joe clicked his way through *Grand Theft Auto: San Andreas.*

"I'm not pissed. I'm jealous," I said.

"That's what I mean."

He asked me to shave his head on the last day. Head shaving before going to war was not a ritual unknown to me. I had seen it before I steamed to the Med as a rifleman. Some of the Marines had made a party of it on one of our last nights in the barracks, getting blasted drunk, then shaving one another bald—a warrior molting of sorts, the shedding of burdensome things, the eschewing of petty and unnecessary weight. Ken pulled a chair into the bathroom. He produced a set of clippers and draped a towel around his neck.

Cutting, it felt as if I were shearing away the old identities of his world so he could better transition into one that awaited, and when I thought that, I wasn't sure if I meant into the world of combat or one of death. Perhaps one was the same as the other, the innocence of youth dying in the face of flying metal replaced by the tragedy of knowing too much about the rage of men, and of the self. Whatever the case, the idea of war was so daunting, so large, that it was easy for him to overcompensate, to prepare more than necessary, to make it bigger than what it is. Ken would later tell me that shaving his head did nothing but give him a nasty sunburn. But in that moment, we were children acting out the final rites we believed necessary to be whole as men.

When I finally left to make the drive back to North Carolina, where I felt I was rotting, I thought about how if Ken died, I would be sad beyond reason but that also through my grief I would find only a better justification to go to war and kill someone else for him. If I died and died well in terms of the metrics of what counts as heroic or dignified, then someone out there mining the gallows of American patriotism might read my name and want to go to war and kill and die too. This is the American way. Two months later, I was sent overseas.

HOTEL

War is like love; it always finds a way.

—Bertolt Brecht, *Mother Courage and Her Children*

A captain with black wraparound shades bursts onto the roof like a Ritalin tornado. A small fortune in aftermarket combat gear covers his squat body—overpriced drop pouches, map cases, and chest rigs, all bought on credit from the combat gear websites that have sprung up in the American wartime fanfare after 9/11. He carries pop-up flares and grenades, an assortment of multicolored pens and markers, various maps and protractors, a lensatic compass, an aftermarket GPS device, and a thick ring-bound cheat-sheet book with steps to handle everything from drafting an operations order to surviving nuclear blasts. A dozen magazines are full of polished bullets for the brand-new government-issued carbine dangling from his shoulder and clipped to his rig with a small D-ring. His pistol is tucked into a holster strapped to his thigh. His chief weapon, however, is the heavy radio that rests tightly against his back.

The captain is a fighter pilot who has been sent down from On High to help the poor dumb grunts handle airpower. He says nothing as he hustles to the wall. He seems like the kind of guy who can't be bothered with the troops. When he does speak, he does so with a patience that sounds like practiced charity. Swathed in all his combat gear, most of which he will never use, he cuts the sharp visage of the modern G.I. Joe he seems to want so desperately to be, but we love him because he is in command of American destruction.

With a map set atop the low wall, he presses the radio handset to his ear and prattles off a litany of instructions and gibberish into the mouthpiece.

Idling easily between ten thousand and fifteen thousand feet above, give or take a few, a Marine aviator sits tucked inside the scuffed industrial cockpit of his sophisticated fighter-bomber surrounded by a dazzling array of lights and dials and high-dollar monitors. After some back-and-forth with the captain below and some careful scrutiny of the black-and-white thermal image on one of his displays, he twitches the abductor pollicis brevis muscle group that lifts his gloved thumb over the required button on the control stick and waits while he watches a countdown tick on his shimmering green heads-up display.

"Stand by," the captain calls out. "'Bout to drop a jay-dam."

A jay-dam is a sample of military gibberish that is better known as a "smart bomb." The pilot, who in a few hours will be on Al Asad Air Base tossing around iron at the gym or just sitting in his trailer watching bootleg DVDs, presses the little red button and sends an electrical impulse to the bomb rack. The rack retracts its hooks from the jay-dam. Physics handles the rest.

The bomb reaches terminal velocity within seconds. The GPS and inertial guidance systems gather data from satellites and use them to chart the bomb's path and make small adjustments to its fall with the little fins on the tail. It has no idea what it is falling toward.

On the roof, a fair handful of Marines pull small digital cameras from their pockets and click them to life, lenses whirrrring out, shutters opening with cute flicks. The men line up like tourists along the eastern wall of the roof and hold their cameras at their chests. The pilot above relays a second countdown to the captain below—"Six, five, four, three"—but it isn't necessary. Once the countdown reaches "two," the bomb rips from the sky with a sound that can be described as the fabric of space-time being shredded apart—a sort of harsh warble that increases in volume and pitch until the bomb appears, for just a split second, like an olive-drab blur, and crashes into a building deep inside the urban morass.

A massive gray column of dust and hot smoke erupts into the sky. A broad, flat piece of concrete bursts to the top of the column, spinning up like Dorothy's Kansas house until gravity crashes the large slab into the earth. A geyser of dust and smoke spreads out from the blast. A few of the men hoot and whistle or bark "fuck yeah!" like grim spectators at a Fourth of July fireworks show.

Like thunder that follows lightning, the sound is out of sync with time. The sound wave passes over the roof—a deep crunch, lackluster compared to the raucous explosions packed into the sound design of high-end action flicks and television dramas. It is as if someone had simply struck a hammer against a wooden plank wrapped in a thin towel.

One or two Marines pass off their little Nikons and Sonys to their buddies—"Dude, get a picture of me with that shit behind me"—and flashes ignite their faces into the practiced masks of stone-cold killers with stiff upper lips as the expanding geyser of smoke spreads out above their shoulders like Old Faithful. When bits of rock and smashed plaster begin to tock and bip in ones and twos onto our roof and on the courtyard below, we breathe out nervous giggles and tuck our chins into our armored vests.

The geyser diminishes into a gray cloud of fine concrete dust. No one can see it from our roof, but in the center of that cloud remains the charred rubble of an Iraqi home. No one knows if the airstrike accomplished anything, but it doesn't matter. Satisfied, the captain leaves us to the morning without a word.

Later that night, after spending the day searching through Iraqi homes and fighting in the street, we fortify ourselves in a house and sit in the darkness with little cherries dancing at the end of our cigarettes. Someone cracks off a fart and we laugh the breathy chuckles of tired playground boys. Soft snores wheeze in the dark corners. The eyes and noses of a few are lit by the preview screens of their digital cameras as the men scroll through the pictures they took to remember this war and show to their children years later.

I sit next to Kemper on the long couch that smells like desert dust and pressed-in body odor. A drifting howl breathes through the blacked-out window of the room. It begins softly, or perhaps we hear it only in an ever-increasing volume until it finally registers and becomes recognizable as the sound of pure misery. It flows long and ghostly, deep and soulful, hurting, *clawing, trying to register a life with someone, anyone, who could provide a note of relief or understanding.*

"What the fuck is that?" someone asks.

"Sounds like a dying cat."

But it's not. Kemper tells us, "That's where we dropped that jay-dam."

The howling continues, but no one says anything. I know nothing about the man who lies beneath the stones of his shattered home. I do not know if he is a man with a Kalashnikov or a man with a shovel or a man with a family or a cat or a little shop somewhere, but I do know he is a man who wants to live and there is nothing I can do. Soon we are asleep. The howling stops long before sunrise. When I awaken, I drink chai from the abandoned cupboards and push through the streets like a Marine and forget the whole thing until now.

XIII

The sailor ruined the funeral and afterward sat in the van with his trumpet between his feet. We had berated him for being incompetent, a shitbird. But it was quiet now and I sat behind him and watched as his flat eyes remained fixed out the window. He had been invited along as an experiment, a risk for sure. He'd be a hero now if it had worked, but the experiment failed. Instead, he sat like a rumpled toad, the trumpet reduced to a tin kazoo.

Before I went overseas, I was assigned a temporary duty with an on-call funeral ceremonial team. The families of veterans who have served honorably may request a military honor guard to be present at the funeral and serve as pallbearers if needed; the twenty-one-gun salute, the folded flag, the playing of "Taps" are all part of the ritual. Our team was assigned this extra duty for a month; when we disbanded, another team took our place.

We were led by a studious gunnery sergeant named Anderson. She put me in charge of the rifle detail and put another sergeant, a country boy named Johns, in charge of the burial detail. We met in a warehouse a few times a week to practice with swords and rifles and a big casket draped with an American flag. My job was to give orders to seven Marines to load and fire the twenty-one-gun salute. Johns and his pallbearers were to carry the casket from the hearse to the gravesite and fold the flag draped across it. Anderson had the responsibility of handing the bereaved, the flesh-and-blood wife or daughter or husband or son, the American flag "on behalf of a grateful nation." No one envied their position.

We took the job seriously. We inspected our uniforms and cleaned our rifles. We rehearsed until the procedures were memorized, our timing perfect. Our problem was "Taps," the long, haunting notes that played at the end of a military workday and over the caskets of dead servicemembers. None of us could play the bugle or a trumpet. We were reduced to using a little speaker that played spurious notes while tucked inside the horn held to a "player's" lips.

Anderson wanted the real thing, not some fake bugle that played "Taps" through a speaker. It was a trivial detail, but it mattered to push for the real thing, to show our respect through authenticity. They were our dead, after all. Surely they deserved that much.

Finding a musician in the angry haystack of Camp Lejeune, and one willing to do some extra on-call duty, proved nearly impossible. She requested a member of the Marine ceremonial band, but they shut her out almost immediately, claiming to be too busy with concerts and related band business, something we all suspected was code for institutional malaise and general laziness. Apparently those Xboxes weren't going to play themselves. Anderson kept searching, asking around for hints and rumors of servicemembers who might be able to play "Taps" for us when we needed. She was well aware that we could be called at any time to perform our first ceremony. Finally, at the last moment, she turned up a young sailor at the naval hospital who was rumored to be able to play.

Our first funeral happened on a weekend, as would become the routine. We stopped by the naval hospital and picked up the sailor. He was tall and thin with wispy blond hair beneath his white Cracker Jack hat. He seemed somewhat put upon, as if forced into his role. The deceased was a naval officer of some caliber, though I never learned his name. We rarely learned anything about the dead.

Johns and the pallbearers stood ready to carry the casket from the hearse to the foot of the grave. The rifle squad, a cobbled mishmash of Marine truck drivers and computer technicians, all crowbarred into the job to fill a quota, stood by in a column next to me with their rifles at their shoulders. I pulled the noncommissioned officer's sword from the scabbard strapped to my waist and let it rest in its proper position against my right shoulder. The sailor walked to a knoll of headstones. He stood with his trumpet in his hands; his white uniform glowed against the spring sun.

I marched the squad to a position near the large tent where the family had gathered and quietly prepared them to fire the three blanks from their black rifles. Johns and the pallbearers, led by the gunny, marched toward the foot of the grave in front of the tent. Their faces were taut. They set the polished casket down on the pedestal above the grave and lifted the American flag from the top of the casket and stretched it flat. As Anderson watched, Johns and the pallbearers folded the flag into a trifold, which she then inspected. Once she was satisfied, she took the flag and cradled it against her chest.

Anderson handed the flag to the widow seated near the corner of the tent; she leaned forward and spoke a few quiet words to her. The woman nodded, her eyes shot with tears. Her husband had given decades of his life to a uniform and a flag and a country and now, long after all that had passed, he was dead, and though we knew nothing about him, we were here to honor that and what it represented. He could have been an abusive husband or deadbeat dad, a cheapskate, a member of the Klan. Or perhaps he was just an average American taxpayer, a good neighbor, a Regular Citizen. Everything he had been became secondary the moment he died as a veteran.

The gunny took a position nearby and faced me. I was up. I ordered the squad to turn and ready the first shot in their rifles. Seven rifles went click, then clack. On my order to take aim, all seven brought the rifles to their shoulders and pointed them to the sky. I commanded

them to fire and all seven rifles cracked with a single loud bang. A
few heads under canopy flinched. People always flinched. I ordered
the squad to cycle their rifles and aim and fire again. The second
time no one flinched. I ordered them to fire once more. The final
report weaved across the cemetery.

"Preee-sent, ARMS!"

The seven rifles lowered to waist height like vertical staffs. I lifted
the sword and issued a salute and waited.

Now it was the sailor's turn. Out among the headstones, he lifted
the trumpet to his lips. All eyes turned toward him.

His first notes blurted across the grass as a wretched throat clear.
At first, I thought the bugler was out of practice and just needed a
moment to get his head around the instrument, like the first wobbly
moments on roller skates. But it quickly became clear that he was
entirely incapable of playing "Taps" or anything else. He belched a
string of misshapen notes threaded together on the lines of crooked
chicken wire that served as a musical staff in his mind. I was morti-
fied, but a sardonic part of me howled inside. I felt like a character in
*M*A*S*H* watching Radar O'Reilly fall through a trap of his own ear-
nestness. From my position, I saw many under the canopy fix their
cold eyes on a would-be bugler, and I wondered briefly how much
time we would have to evacuate him before he was torn to pieces. At
least he wouldn't have far to travel if we couldn't save him.

He finished and lowered the trumpet to his side. No one said a
word. I dismissed the squad and they immediately fingered out the
three spent brass casings their rifles had ejected into the grass around
their feet. Then we quietly climbed into the vans and pulled away.

Once in the van, we erupted. Where the fuck did you learn to play
"Taps?" we asked. What were you thinking? Where did we find you?
He said nothing the entire trip home. He might have been a great
sailor, a stellar performer in every other military way, but in that
moment he was a travesty. Anderson had words with him once we
returned to the base; she was a stickler for protocol and respected

the importance of memory and honor. She also blamed herself. "How hard would it have been for the band to send someone?" she lamented, a rare break from her professionalism. Somewhere in the memory of the bereaved family live the ugly squawks of an abortive "Taps," as if etched into the headstone.

We never saw the bugler again. Pleas to the Marine band went unanswered and we cursed them for their laziness. For the rest of the season, Anderson used the fake bugle instead, manned by a lance corporal pulled from our own ranks. All the "player" had to do was push a button inside the horn and hold the apparatus to the lips. A battery-powered speaker did the rest. We pulled four or five more funerals that spring. The fake "Taps" played perfectly every time.

I met Jenn in a karaoke bar on New Year's Eve in 2003. We drank cheap beer, then kissed when the ball dropped in Times Square on the television above the bar. Then we ordered shots and by the end of the night we were making out in the alley like drunk twentysome-thing dummies.

She was a lab technician at an oncology clinic. She had recently split from someone she described as an aimless burnout. They had a child together, a young boy. She wanted to become a nurse, but her dreams were trapped in the flux of motherhood. She lived with a friend, another single mother of a young boy, and together they weathered their situation with the desperation of cynics. Jenn and I began dating.

Jenn was a voracious reader. She spent hours mining the shelves of bookstores, chewing over the merits of one book versus another in the center of the aisle, her eyes lost in the text. It was sweet to catch her in those moments, at least for the first hour. The amount of time she spent in a bookstore gnawing her lip became a running joke between us, one of those inside gags couples share in ways that are both endearing and eye-roll inducing.

As a pastime, we play-fought like a crotchety married couple in ways that made us double over in laughter and probably scared our friends and passersby.

"I swear to God I'm going to punch you in the throat," she joked to me one night in a bar.

"Yeah, I hope so," I groaned.

We made the drive between Georgia and North Carolina as often as possible. Our time felt like lightning compressed into a glass tube whenever we saw each other. We ignored the minutes and hours we spent in bed talking, smoking, entangled as we watched movies and read. There was a sense of permanence to it, at least to my young estimation of what permanence looked like. Our relationship built its own energy without effort. It was fast and easy, perhaps too fast. But we were young and it was allowed.

It would be natural to say the Marine Corps disrupted our lives by sending me overseas. It is true that in May I was told, practically in passing, that I was going. It happened on a Friday. There was no ceremony to it, no grand announcement. A Marine's tour in East Africa was nearly over and I was being sent to replace him. "You're going to Djibouti," one of my leaders told me. "For six months." It is also true that I wanted to go, regardless of what was there, or why. It is also true that now, years later, I cannot remember if I was sent without my consent, which was entirely within the Corps' rights, or if I had been given a choice. It didn't much matter. I needed to get away from the inanities of Camp Lejeune. I was going.

I had only a cursory knowledge of Djibouti or the American presence there. Later, I learned the American camp was named after General Émile René Lemonnier—a French colonial officer who was beheaded by the Japanese during World War II—and that we adopted the name from its previous French owners. Djibouti had been a French colony until 1977. The French maintained a garrison there, but after 9/11 the Djiboutian government leased the camp to the United States. What I did know, however, was that Somalia was "right there." As was Yemen. Both of them were considered harbors for terrorism training camps, and Islamic terrorist cells were believed to exist in nearby Kenya and elsewhere too. Keeping an eye on their efforts was important to the American war effort abroad. In stereotypical military language, one general described the Horn of Africa as the left flank of the American broader war in the Middle East, with Iraq as the center and Afghanistan as the right flank.

Jenn knew nothing about Djibouti or the necessity of protecting one's flanks, such as they were, and I didn't really expect her to learn. Her interests were simple—her son and her job and her life and me—but she was willing to be supportive. Our relationship was only a few months old, but Jenn wanted a role in my military life too, if only remotely. She decided she'd wait out my deployment, a gesture I had never experienced before. But I trusted it and it felt warm, a home of its own. We spent a few more weekends together and then I was gone. As for me, well, I *was* interested in Djibouti, but only as it related to my desire to go overseas, and if Iraq wasn't to be my place, then Djibouti would have to suffice. Once I came home, I would have about a year left and then I would leave the Marines. Maybe with Jenn, I thought, I could learn to live with missing the war.

I threw up in a helicopter somewhere near the border of Ethiopia and Djibouti. The pilot, who was also the general in charge of the small American task force on the edge of the War on Terror, had kept us low to the wasteland, where it was hot, rather than at a higher, cooler altitude. The inside of the open-air hold of the lumbering Marine transport was broiling and awash with hydraulic and exhaust fumes. Twenty minutes into the hour-long flight, I was clammy with airsickness and heaving into a trash bag.

We were on our way to a ceremony near Jijiga, near the Somali border. American engineers had spent the past few months renovating a school and it was finally opening. The general and some of the local leaders planned to cut a ribbon and say some big words on the occasion. I was going along to take pictures.

A sergeant major sat next to me. He was a big, red-faced man with his sleeves rolled tight around his biceps. We liked him for his toughness. He smiled and leaned in and yelled through the helicopter racket: "You puke on me and I'm gonna stab you with my fucking knife!" Then he put his fingers to the side of his neck and pantomimed the arterial spray of blood that would come from my jugular if I failed. I wanted to laugh but buried my face in the bag instead.

We had lifted off from Camp Lemonnier, just outside Djibouti City, a port city on the Bab al-Mandab Strait, the crossroads between the Red Sea and the Gulf of Aden. I had arrived from the United States on a commercial airliner at midday a few months before and was greeted with equatorial heat shimmering like a specter along the edge of the runway. The heat seemed like a physical presence born to crush the hubris of humanity into the earth. Helicopters baked in the sun while Marines who were stripped to their dusty green T-shirts repaired engines and rotor blades deep inside prefab hangars. A layer of dust had coated everything with a fine tan sheen.

In the evenings, in the desert south of the camp, the trash from Djibouti City was set on fire and putrescent smoke would drift over the camp. Once the sun went down, the camp cantina opened and servicemembers in T-shirts and shorts sat around plastic lawn tables and sipped their way through an enforced three-beer limit while Kid Rock and Toby Keith played over the speaker system. A breeze sometimes drifted in from the sea and in those moments the place was bearable. At night, we'd stagger back to our dusty tents and turn down the knobs of the big AC units as far as they could go before falling into bizarre dreams brought on by our antimalaria medicine, only to awaken confused the next morning when the units had frozen to a halt and the air in the tent cooked. Then we'd called Kellogg,

Brown & Root, the Halliburton subsidiary, and its crews would roll up in their golf carts and fix the AC for a few billion tax dollars per year.

To call our sliver of the War on Terror a "war" was farcical. I brought a rifle but never carried it. It sat in an armory coated in weapon oil until it was time to go home. We went to the markets and casinos and ate at the local restaurants. It was nothing to drive our SUVs through Ambouli or the nearby suburb of Balbala and, like tourists of postcolonial poverty, watch children and mothers draw water from puddles with green scum and trash floating on the surface. One afternoon during Ramadan, I escorted a photographer down a narrow alley that served as a market. The photographer, an American, had asked to see the "real thing." As we walked, he took photos of racks of beef dotted with flies. The Djiboutians tolerated us at first, but when he snapped a series of photos of a few female vendors without asking permission, a number of men began to close around us, yelling in Arabic and Swahili, until finally I managed to get the photographer back into the truck. As I drove away, a few Djiboutian police officers arrived and began beating people back with batons. We weren't sure whether to judge the police for their brutality or the people for their piety, both judgments that came from our sense as Americans with our size and scope and gravitas in the face of a perceived weaker culture, but a culture we knew little about. There were days when I felt as if I were chaperoning Western tourists through stops in an East African answer to *Heart of Darkness*.

I stumbled from the helicopter once it landed in Jijiga. I took off my helmet and ran my hand through my wet hair. The air was much cooler than it had been in Djibouti. Children in bright yellow shirts sang songs and waved small handmade American flags in front of their mothers and teachers and elders who seemed equally genuine with their pro-American sentiments. US State Department officials hung around the gallery in polo shirts and khaki pants, their heads domed with short frat-house haircuts.

The general, no doubt an honorable man, spoke to the audience about the bonds of friendship as the mortar that binds the bricks of common interests. I have no doubt he believed it. I believed it too. I am an American, and while we are flawed and somewhat self-serving in our desires to stamp out the fanaticism that can take root in poverty, I believed we were doing something real and important and meaningful in those moments. I wished only we were doing it for its own sake rather than weaving a blanket used to hide our fears of this world.

Then it was over. We boarded the helicopters to take us back to camp and felt humbled and equally proud, and we looked at the US flag as it's meant to be looked at, like a beacon.

I sat on the jump seat with a new trash bag at the ready. The helicopter spooled its rotors into a cacophony and wobbled aloft. I glanced at the sergeant major before I rested my head on my hands and closed my eyes in a long silent prayer to the gods of air travel. His eyes were invisible behind his sunglasses. He leaned his head back against the gray insulation on the bulkhead and put his fingers to his jugular. Imaginary blood sprayed across the deck.

The war was always in the background, casting a shadow over my experience, reminding me of my absence. Ken was in the Real War. He darted down roads in Mosul as a machine gunner on a counter-ambush team—a sort of fast-pedaling assault force wrapped in Humvee armor and Oakley sunglasses. He emailed me a few pictures not long after he arrived, the usual Western war-tourist snaps: in one, he was hamming it up in a red-checkered *kaffiyeh* and brandishing an AK-47; in another, he stood on the roof of some tall building with the dun urban vista arrayed behind him. Then he sent me pictures of an armored Chevy Suburban with its ballistic windows splintered by rifle fire. He wrote he had been in the SUV when it had come under fire and some of the bullets had come "that close."

After I had been in Africa a few months, I began talking with Ken over the phone. I had been given a cell phone tied to a local carrier to keep in contact with the US embassy and the local media. Ken had a cell phone on an Iraqi carrier. One afternoon on a cloudy day, I sat in a cheap gazebo outside the office and lit a cigarette. Workers swept the nearby street. I wasn't entirely sure the call would go through, but I entered the number he had given me and after a few scratchy seconds the phone began to ring.

"Hello," Ken said.

"Holy shit," I said, laughing, more to myself than to him. "It worked."

We spoke for ten or fifteen minutes. He was notably subdued about his time in combat and I assumed the silence stemmed from the slow-burn processing of his own events and also the river of experience that now divided us and that I had been afraid of back when we stood on the balcony of his Virginia apartment. I had long understood that combat could be described but never fully explained, not completely. The experience could come through only distilled into war-story tones, an emotional distance amplified by the imperfections of our vocabulary. I believed I could hear this separation, that there was some eternal secret in the experience that had to be earned.

I despaired when the Second Battle of Fallujah began. I watched it on the television in our office just like I had done with all the others. It was unbearable. I was missing it, missing every piece of it. Missing the goddamn war. I'm here. Take me. I'm willing to go. I'm asking. Take me. But the Great Scorer ignored me, instead leaving me in Africa in the faulty air-conditioning. My eyes were lost in the combat footage that I watched from my desk as my big Sony monitors blasted the AK and M-16 fire to the center of my desire. Then I went to the cantina and drank my three beers and walked back to my tent and slept in the dust.

Ken and I both came home in December and stood back on his balcony right after Christmas and smoked cigarettes and pounded beer like we had before. He told me a little bit about his time there, about how bullets had once ricocheted inside the metal armor of his Humvee turret and how the spalling had embedded itself in his neck in places. He said he was too shot full of adrenaline to feel it at the time, but later, once home, his girlfriend could sometimes squeeze the metal from his neck like popping zits. He laughed about it, but it was a dark laugh.

"I know you don't want to hear this," he said. "I wouldn't hear this either, but you shouldn't go. If I had my way, you'd stay home. But I know you'll go no matter what I say because there is nothing anyone can really say."

"If they ask, then I don't have a choice at all," I said.

He nodded. "Nope. Not one."

There is a cycle to the military. People come and work for a few years and then they leave to return to the Real World, or they reenlist for four more years and relocate elsewhere in the fantasy, moving their lives or leaving to pick up old ones. New people fill in the gaps and rewrite the professional and social structures and stresses of the platoons and battalions they join.

The leadership in my unit that existed before I left had given way to a new lineup. Before Africa, the unit had been a menagerie of petty conflicts, fueled by cheap leaders who used their stripes to press down on young Marines in ways that created a tangible divide between the haves and the have-nots of the unit. But somewhere in my time in Africa, the worst of the leaders had moved on to torment other circles of the military, and in their place came a pair of staff sergeants who would effectively become the proverbial "heart and soul" of the unit for the next two to three years. When I returned home in December, the mood among the troops was only beginning to lighten. These new leaders were also remarkably keen on sending Marines overseas, regardless of their position in the hierarchy. They wanted to see the desire rewarded, to the point of bending, if not breaking, rules. "Why the hell would I want to *stop* someone who *wants* to go overseas?" one of them said not long after I returned home. One evening, I ran into his counterpart at a bookstore in town. "Dude, if you want to go to Iraq," she said, "*we will get you to Iraq.*"

Jenn and I survived my deployment to Africa. After I came home, we fell into each other as we had before I left, only this time there was a sense of normalcy to it. The initial spark never lasts completely, but what remained seemed more than enough to sustain us. Nevertheless, we had been apart for nearly seven months, and while we had loved each other throughout it, my deployment had expended the energy we had built in those moments before I left. Then I began to talk of going to Iraq.

My cell phone rang at two in the morning on a Thursday. I answered, expecting an emergency. Jenn was frustrated with me. She had been talking with her roommate, and drinking, and she wanted answers. She wasn't mean or vindictive. She simply wanted more from me; she had been scared for me in Africa and she would be even more scared for me in Iraq. She was raising a child. She wanted me to complete the family for her, an ask that even then I knew was difficult for her but an ask that was also completely fair. She had given me her time, her support in the way of a spouse or a lover, and now she wanted more from me.

She was offering me a life or at least a different direction. But I was too stubborn, or perhaps simply too young and brash, to understand the selfishness of my leaving again. And even if I had been able to see it, nothing could have steered me away from Iraq once that opportunity began to slowly rise like a star on the horizon. And so, as it goes, by three in the morning, when we were both spent and Jenn was crying, I hung up the phone, having chosen the war over her, and somewhere outside my barracks room where I stood in the darkness, out past the flares dangling over the clatter of the live-fire ranges, the first morning bird chirped mindlessly.

It seemed unreal. But as spring rolled into summer, my orders were processed and signed, almost without my effort. I moved into the barracks. I checked out a new rifle from the armory and readied my combat gear. I was going to the war. Finally and officially. I was twenty-five years old, a quarter of a century, and I was going to war. It all made sudden sense, the completion of a story.

It felt, honestly, like breathing. I had been wrapped tight around the fear of missing the war, and now that I was finally going, I felt a sense of release. I knew even then that it was an absurd feeling. The fear of dying should have outweighed the notions of going, and it eventually would in ways that ripped torrents beneath my dumb wartime ideas of identity, but in those first moments, I felt light, unburdened of all this bile I had been carrying. I was really only trading one form of bile for another, but I could ignore that. That was tomorrow's problem. For now, I had the war.

I was assigned to an infantry battalion, the Sixth Marines, the same unit I had started with as a rifleman years ago. I could not help but see the irony; it seemed fitting that I end my time where I started. The summer then turned into a party, as summers tend to do. I was going to Iraq that August, and every barbecue and cheap night in the bars around Jacksonville carried an urgency, a charged tenor, a need to pack as much energy into the days as possible. I was twenty-five and single and filled with a blend of terror and uncut excitement and nothing held permanence. I was going to the war.

Erin wanted to go to the war too. Erin was young, in her early twenties. She was a sergeant who had pulled time as a Marine embassy guard before coming to Camp Lejeune. She was tough as a manner of style, tossing herself at the rougher elements of the Marine Corps as if attempting to disprove the tired notion that women were anything less than a full Marine. She went out to the field with combat units and spent her off time running through the Lejeune backwoods, maintaining an exaggerated spartan minimalism—the contents of her barracks room was packable at a moment's notice, ready to be tossed into storage along with her car. Her loyalties were divided between a punk-rock rebellion against the US government and a requisite respect for the Marine Corps. She knew the war was wrong, but it didn't matter in terms of her desire to be there. She pined for her own shot at going. It was a hypocrisy we both acknowledged with a dark wink as we drove to the beach in her Mazda or my janky blue Jeep, blasting mid-aughts rock into the air. We dated that summer, but it felt trivial and temporary, because it was.

Erin could be combative just for fun, always angling for a better position in a debate, which I usually met with equal fervor. We called out each other's inconsistencies, and I wonder now if I felt a quiet toxic animosity living under the surface, built from the efforts she put forward to be a good Marine only to have those efforts consigned to what she felt was a lesser rank. There was a desperation to her wartime desires that I understood but that also made me nervous. The cruelty baked into the masculine environment instantly shackled her wants to worn ideas of frontline privilege. She was always going to be forced to compete at levels far greater than the average man in order to get an equal share of its wartime opportunities.

My mind was too consumed with my own the future to realize how pernicious an issue this was between us. At night, I would go on long drives across the base, music blaring, picturing myself Over There. Although I am just as embarrassed now by my melodramatic predilections as I would have been then, I couldn't shake the feeling that I might be killed in Iraq. I had wanted to be in a war since I was a teenager and now that I was about to go, right at the end of my time in the Marine Corps, it seemed fitting, entirely appropriate even, that I would be killed as some kind of karmic lesson.

"What happens if you get wounded?" she asked me. "What are you gonna do?"

"I don't know. I don't have much control over it," I said. I told her I was nervous about losing a limb.

"Yeah," she said. "Statistics being what they are, though, you have a pretty good chance at coming home fine."

This feeling was amplified early one morning as I left Erin's barracks room to make the drive to the airport outside Raleigh. My dad had finally gotten his wish a few years before and was assigned to Denver by the FAA to finish out his career. I was on my way to catch a flight to see him. Not long after I climbed onto Interstate 40, the engine in my Jeep detonated, a shattered connecting rod blowing through the motor like a tank round. I pulled to the shoulder and popped the hood as flames began to lick around the edges. I called the local fire department, but it seemed I was on the border between two sleepy counties, and some dim-witted decisions needed to be ironed out over who would respond. It didn't matter one way or another. The Jeep was engulfed within minutes. As I watched nearby, the fatalist inside me couldn't help but see it as a foreshadowing of the roadside bomb and its hurricane of shrapnel that I believed was awaiting me in the pothole of some Iraqi highway.

I carried this notion with me the last few weeks before I left, but I never reacted or allowed it to tailor my behavior. If my mom or stepdad was nervous about me going to Iraq, they never showed it, nor did I expect them to. We were military; such is life in this world. I spent time in Maryland with Ken, who had moved in with his girlfriend outside Annapolis. "Remember, you can't miss fast enough," he said, passing along a snippet of wartime wisdom.

Back at Camp Lejeune, I spent the last few days packing and shoving my books and clothes into a storage unit in town. Gradually the fear of dying overseas began to feel stale, a tired melodrama built out of old war stories and lore. The world around me began to fade as if winnowed by the coming journey. Going overseas is a remarkably cold thing; I could almost feel my separation from the American world occurring and how indifferent it was to my departure. It was a transition that amplified how singular and small I was in the world. I felt stateless, no longer contributing to the thin tapestry of my own life but also not yet plugged into the socket of the landscape that waited for me a few thousand miles away. But even then, the war wasn't waiting for me. The war was entirely oblivious to me. It did not need me, and in between those two spaces, my life felt entirely meaningless.

Erin was not present during these last days. She was torn, I felt, by a triad of competing emotions—a mixture of fear and concern and probably jealousy. But I had no way of confirming this. She had pushed me beyond arm's length and would avoid the whole emotional mess of saying goodbye entirely. As I sat with a few hundred other Marines waiting for the buses that would take us to the airfield, surrounded by families and weeping girlfriends and mothers who had driven hours and countless miles, I was somewhat incensed that she couldn't drum up the emotional energy to see me off, but my mind was too lost in the sand ahead of me to be entirely upset. Instead, we talked by cell phone for a few stilted minutes. Then I turned it off for seven months.

I waited and watched as a flash summer storm came in over the New River and blasted the large parking lot. Families scurried into their cars while the thunderhead blew by. After a few minutes, the rain ended and then things began to coalesce. Seabags and combat gear were staged in rows for quick loading. The last of the family photos were taken and mothers with red faces climbed into their cars and trucks with plates from Ohio and Tennessee and Virginia and New York. Roll calls were made; rifles were drawn from the armory. Once the charter buses arrived, I climbed aboard and sat in the soft seat with my rifle between my knees. I put in my earphones and found a song that matched my own sense of action-movie melodrama. I pressed play as the bus began to move.

I wrapped a hand around the cold gray metal of my rifle barrel and leaned back against the headrest. I watched the highway pass in a wet blur from the windows. Mick Jagger and Merry Clayton screamed, "War, children, it's just a shot away."

INDIA

For war is nothing if not a return to childhood.

—John le Carré

Muscles move in the man who has been cut down in the Iraqi street. The machine gunner, a boyish kid with a mean grin, notices it from the turret of his Humvee. He calls out that the man he has shot might still be alive.

"So shoot him again!" the lieutenant tells him.

"What?"

"I said SHOOT HIM!"

The lieutenant's voice rages over the buildings and through the smoke and into the clouds above us. I light a cigarette while the machine gunner kills whatever life is left in the man.

What are we searching for in this war? Guns and money, drugs, the paraphernalia of fundamentalism? Wires and explosives and cell phones and propane tanks all gathered about in proximity to one another, roadside ingredients of rage and frustration and dishonor and flagging dignity, the incongruent devices of ideology against imperialism? The Islamic stone against the high-tech Western Goliath? Are we looking for the justification of our empire, the final answer that will end the fears of the world beyond our borders? And what am I searching for? G.I. Joe and his band of underdog heroes? The times that try men's souls? The stiff upper lip of middle America? The American Power and its Global Glory? Where is the monster I am seeking?

For days, we had pushed house to house like cops under the edict of some kind of high-powered search warrant. We beat stubborn dead bolts with sledgehammers, shattered hinges with slugs from shotgun barrels, and blasted doors with plastic explosives. I searched through kitchen cupboards and bathrooms and behind marital beds. I sifted through bags of USAID rice and closets full of old suits and slacks and loafers. I rifled through scattered clothes in children's rooms and tubes of toothpaste in bathrooms. We looked for bombs and guns and documents, anything that suggested fealty to the Other Side. Sometimes we found them. Far more often, we found the detritus of people who have fled in fear.

We had searched a primary school too. The lieutenant had ordered us to fire into the school on some fragment of intelligence that suggested the school was no longer a school but a terrorist stronghold instead. After his men and the tank peppered the building with lead and shrapnel, he ordered the first squad to charge across the street and into the school. I followed Kask, the tall leader of the next squad, as we dashed in pairs to the compound wall outside the school. I snapped photos of a pair of Marines waiting to rush into the building; one of the men in my frame would later tell me of his desire to work in the aviation industry. But he'll be killed instead, crushed when a Humvee rolls on top of him. I'll watch corpsmen load his body onto a helicopter and fly away. But in that moment, he waited patiently for the order, shotgun in his hands. When the signal came, he rushed into the building like all the others, stepping through the rubble of the gate.

I followed along with my rifle in my hands. The first squad that entered the building was given orders to shoot into the classrooms before physically clearing them, but after the first few rooms, the firing stopped. If anyone had been there, they were long gone. Shooting was pointless. Kask led us from room to room, past shattered beakers and textbooks written in Arabic. Posters on the wall showed the alphabet and math equations and the science flotsam of childhood—friendly pictures of bears and lions and dogs and insects and plants. A collection of tuning forks littered the floor of one room. Someone found a recorder, but no one tried to play.

We waited for orders to "push," and when they came, we stood and mashed out our cigarettes and moved out. Little thought was given to the failed intelligence that led us to put grenades and tank fire into an elementary school, but as we left, Kask mumbled, "We just shot up this school for nothing."

Kask is an off-the-boat Swede with a narrow waist and a pistol belt that gives him the gait of an Old West gunslinger. He is older than most of the men in his platoon, aside from his platoon sergeant, and had pulled mandatory service time in the Swedish armed forces before coming to the States. He enlisted around 9/11, along with the legions of others who saw the towers fall and said, "Fuck that!" He has just reenlisted for another four years. He leads his squad with an immutable will, a foundation of character and resolve and confidence that feels entirely organic and magnetic. When he praises his men, his praise feels like words from some duke of infantrymen. When he chastises them for errors and shortcomings, his ire feels like judgment levied against the heinousness of immaturity. But if anyone were to tell him this, he'd probably shrug and laugh and ask for a cigarette or just jam a hearty wad of Göteborgs Rapé tobacco behind his hairless upper lip, then fix them with a stare that suggests the impropriety of mentioning anything like that at all.

He leads us into the next house, an unfinished home molded completely out of concrete. We search the place quickly and then move on to the next while a group of Marines—the lieutenant, the platoon sergeant, and a cluster of corpsmen and radiomen—file into the large unfinished house behind us.

We find the next home abandoned, but the house after that is not. The squad that rushes it opens its compound gate and is ambushed by a handful of startled insurgents. No Marine is killed. The insurgents fired too early, caught off guard or perhaps from nerves of fear and excitement. The shorter the distance between us, the greater the fear for all, but in their fear, they killed only themselves.

A plucky Marine with a light machine gun immediately jumps onto an abandoned car outside the compound wall and sprays a burst into a man inside the compound while his compatriot retreats into the house. The second man reappears in the crossroads a few dozen meters farther into the city and is immediately cut down by a machine gun on the Humvee manned by the gunner with the mean grin. The man is left lying on the street.

After a pause, we continue our advance. The dead man lies in the center of the intersection. He is on his side, facing away from us. It seems he had tried to shield his face and chest from the bullets that struck him, as if he presumed, in a way we all might, that the back is somehow better armored than the chest. His right hip pivots away from us. His legs are splayed out in the middle of an interrupted stride and his sneakers are dark and bulbous on his feet. I am nervous as I approach him. Perhaps he's faking the whole thing, just waiting for the moment he'll trip some circuit and explode into a mist of flesh and shrapnel from a suicide vest. But I also recognize an innocence in how his body rests against the earth, as if he is a boy sleeping fully and deeply and peacefully with the knowledge of his future still before him. I know that he is not a boy anymore, he is a man, perhaps like me, but he is now dead, a lump of clammy skin and flesh and organs, an empty vessel for hopes and thoughts and dreams and even rages and prejudices and violence.

A few men drag his body into the next courtyard once we clear it. Some Marines from counterintelligence, along with an interpreter, search through his rumpled jacket and fatigue pants and find papers that link him to Syrian intelligence. At least that's what the Marine in charge tells us. I have no reason to disbelieve him. The Syrian border is a short walk to the west; we could be there in an hour. Syria has long been an access route for foreign fighters coming to Iraq.

A few around me prattle off American invectives and threats over backstabbings and invasions and treacheries while we stand in a loose circle over the body. It's all halfhearted and boring. We might feel like men, large and powerful with our firepower, but really we're small. We have killed this man and we have learned he is connected, if only by paperwork, to some faction outside our control, and now we act tough, but it is just an act. The truth is, we have little control over anything beyond the functions of our muscles. Our mythologies have formed our ideologies, our ideologies have led us to patriotism, and our learned violence as an expression of that *patriotism has led us to volunteer for this, and now we stand in a circle and look down at the dead man and judge him for doing exactly the same. Nothing is new. We have done this before and so has he. The only thing new in history is the difference in the results.*

After a moment, one of the intel Marines speaks with an eager voice. "We should totally get a picture of this."

XIV

War stories are the bookends of the American story. Every one might seem different, but they are fundamentally the same, built around similar characters and clichés and comparable origins: American boys and girls with patriotic lightning in their eyes, defending against those who would threaten American beliefs and foreign policy. The stories invariably make use of the same window dressing—the yellow ribbons tied to the posts of mailboxes, "The Star-Spangled Banner" blasting from tinny speakers on the Fourth of July, the roar of fighter jets and the clap of rifles. Uniforms and promises of honor and the chance at heroism are all things that can be traded for beer and cheap sex and fireside stories to tell later. The lost, the dead and the destroyed, the fucked—all these are woven into the American war story too. It is a very old story.

I joined the Marines and came to Iraq riding a wave of these stories, but throughout my time in the Corps, something was changing inside me—the stories that once fueled my military love and admiration were slowly stirring up emotions more nebulous and confused. *Disillusionment* feels like the right word, if not overused. Reflecting now, I think the disillusionment had been there all along, under the surface, as if it were a place I was meant to end up, a natural terminus of the American wartime experience, a finish line I quietly expected. If all the other war stories, those expounding old Homeric ideals of heroism and sacrifice and brotherhood, had any truth to them, then it seemed natural that disillusionment would wait for me in the American war story as well. I felt its culmination in the day ahead as a mixture of rage and terror. I also felt futility.

After we broke our circle around dead insurgents on the street, we moved on to the next house and the house after that. I don't remember much about that night. No doubt Kask posted rotating guards on the roof while the rest of us ate MREs and smoked cigarettes on sleeping mats that we'd pilfered from the last house we'd searched. Kask led a squad of good Marines by anyone's metric. We might have never met in the American world, fractured as it is by class and race and geography, but here we were together, a blizzard of identities and attitudes and heritages, all in service to sanctioned American ideals and American myths to execute the final ugly half mile of American foreign policy. Finally, we turned off the lights affixed to the ends of our rifles and we slept. I have little doubt we slept well.

I awoke beneath my poncho liner in the morning. I stood and stretched and threaded my arms into my body armor, its weight wrapping around me as I closed the Velcro flap. I slung my rifle across my chest, then sat my helmet on my head and buckled the chin strap. Within a few minutes, Kask led us out of the house.

There were still houses to search, but we were nearing the end of the operation. Another two days, maybe three, and we would reach the end of the city, and the entire valley from the Syrian border stretching forty miles east would, presumably, be free to determine its own fate, even if only by Western political standards. A referendum for a new constitution and government elections would follow. So would more American money. This was the story we told ourselves, one that was proven true, if only for a while.

The day was a blur of shattered locks and hinges and the ransacking of cupboards and closets while we searched for insurgent contraband and, our primary purpose, the monsters under the bed.

There was a sense of calm over the city that morning. Engagement with the enemy had fallen nearly to nothing. It was as if we had broken through some barrier over the previous few days. The home-grown insurgency fled south into the desert or blended into the Iraqi civilians who had stayed behind. All that remained were the threats of roadside bombs.

There was a Marine in Kask's squad named Smith. Smith was in his late twenties, a grandfather by infantrymen standards. He was a short man from some Appalachian hollow. He had the look of someone who had spent his life at the bottom of some barrel and was using the Marine Corps as a way out.

Smith had been lugging around a light antitank weapon since the beginning of the operation, which hung from his back like a totem of burden. Now Kask spied something move in the carport of a house a few blocks away. A van was parked in the carport. Kask called Smith forward and after some back and forth Smith was given the chance to shoot his rocket from the wall surrounding the roof of our latest house.

"Don't miss," Kask warned.

The squad waited inside the house. I stood on a nearby roof with the lieutenant and watched. There was a pause while Smith extended the rocket tube and placed his hands in the correct spots. There was another, far more pensive delay while Smith placed the rocket on his shoulder. I could feel his tension. He did not want to miss and disappoint Kask and so he aimed carefully.

Smith was enveloped in a cloud of dust and smoke when he fired the rocket. The projectile snapped between the wall and the van in a millisecond and erupted with a hard crack inside the cab. Smith was cheered. It was sunny and warm. We filed down the stairs and out onto the street and approached the house with the van we had just destroyed.

One way an insurgent could trigger an improvised explosive device was to wire the charge with one cell phone and call it with another. Insurgents routinely destroyed allied vehicles with their Nokias as they watched from rooftops. So standing on a roof with a cell phone against the ear was a surefire way to get riddled by your average American twentysomething standing in the turret of a passing Humvee. We could generally rationalize enemy fire. We could react to it in the moment with our own levels of violence. But there was nothing we could do about an IED but bottle our anger and rage inside of us and hate them, hate them dearly, hate them for killing us so unfairly, so one-dimensionally, so finally, so casually. The IED conflicted with our sense of honor and fair play. Sometimes it made us into monsters.

I shot at only a handful of human beings in my months in this war. I suppose in saying that I must be trying to assuage some inner guilt, as if qualifying with "only" or "just a few" somehow ennobles me. It does not.

There was the sniper Cory and I and the others shot at from our roof along the wadi when the bulldozer was carving out another base for Americans. He was too far away for us to actually see *him*—we could make out just the shadowy windows of his presumed location. But there were others I fired at. Men I did see. The first happened as the city was crackling with rifle fire on a cloudy afternoon. A man with an AK-47 burst from around the corner and began sprinting across the narrow street. I saw him and immediately let out a string of profane invectives as a warning to the others on the roof. Then I leaned over the roof and fired five or six times. The others on the roof fired, too, and in the milliseconds he had available to cross the street, his feet and legs were peppered with bits of exploding concrete and debris and he ran with his legs dancing about, as if trying to cross a bed of hot coals.

He reached the other side and vanished around another corner. I have no doubt he was wounded, as evidenced by his jerking dance.

Once he was gone, I felt immediately embarrassed by all the hot emotions that had flooded me when I first saw this armed man running. I felt ugly, sheepish. It was all incredibly futile: my anger was meaningless and nothing I did in that moment had any value outside the slim satisfaction of making tangible our conflicting ideologies and policies. I did not know him and he did not know me, but in that moment I was shooting a rifle at him and he would, presumably, have shot his rifle at me if given the chance, and while we both were bound to our loyalties, it all felt remarkably useless and wasteful and hollow.

This sense of futility gripped me again when another man emerging from another corner fired a rocket-propelled grenade toward our roof. The rocket streaked about ten meters and landed against a building, far short of its intended target. The man disappeared behind a wall before anyone could react and then reemerged a few moments later as he ran down a street about a hundred meters away. A few of us opened fire on him as he ran. He looked back with a cross of wide-eyed terror and what I could only perceive with my own prejudices as an expression of wanton guilt.

What are we doing this for, why are we here, what the fuck is the point of this, really? I knew that if I voiced this, well, the odds would be better than average that I'd be looked at as a wayward apostate. These people were fighting us and we were obligated to fight back. This was war and we were Americans and they were not and this is what we do when those two immovable and immutable objects collide.

But my reservations about our hollow efforts only increased over time. "SHOOT HIM!" the lieutenant had ordered, and as I listened, the Marine with the machine gun strafed the man lying in the street as the smoke of a burning house billowed overhead. I was a participant in this world, a volunteer, like the machine gunner and the platoon leader and all the others. But as I rested against the wall and listened, it felt as if the clothes on me had become alien and uncomfortable, my boots awkward and spongy, my helmet irritating my scalp. I looked down and hid my face and wiped my eyes. A sadness flowed through me until it broke and was replaced with a quiet dial tone of numbness, a psychic shield against the realities of eradicating human life with metal.

From that moment on, the sounds of grenades did not seem as loud, and the distinction between rifles—the controlled pops of the American M-16s and the high-pitched rattle-can clatter of the insurgent AKs—became so crystallized that I registered the former only as part of the backdrop, whereas the latter raised the hair on the back of my neck and tightened my blood vessels with adrenaline. The Pavlovian response to a need for survival.

We reached the house with the van we'd destroyed by rocket. The lead fire team broke through the iron compound gate and found the van still ablaze under the metal awning of the carport. We moved carefully. Smith fired the rocket because Kask had seen movement of some kind, or one of his Marines had. The van or even the house could be wired to blow. The house could contain a last-ditch nest of insurgents waiting to kill us all.

I was scared as I passed the van. I had been scared every day in some way, a fear now locked away beneath the surface of this new numbness like a roaring subterranean river. It was deep and broad, and I felt anger toward its presence and my need to be exposed to it whenever it frothed up from between the cracks in my ego. This was the fear I had read about, the common subtext in all the books I had devoured, but its breadth was something I could not have predicted. It was an everyday fear, both noxious and relentless, the kind that makes the daily fears of the average Westerner seem petty in comparison.

I was afraid of closed doors, of abandoned cars, of odd spots on the road. I was afraid of men between the age of puberty and the onset of Alzheimer's. I was afraid of women and the weapons they might have hidden beneath the robes of their piousness. I was afraid of orange-and-white taxis that took a little too long to slow down when approaching our patrols. I was terrified of being captured and having my head sawn off like in all the terrorists' videos aired to frighten and outrage us. I was afraid the men around me would be hurt or killed. I was less afraid we would hurt someone else. The things I was afraid of directed the traffic of my emotions, motivators for frustration and resentment and anger and even rage. I was afraid my fears would come out as real fear—shaking and stuttering and baying with indignity—and not as bravado.

The door to the house was on the far end of the carport, beyond the burning van. The lead fire team reached the door and prepared to breach the lock, but before they could, the door was opened by a haggard man with a short beard. The Marines on point ordered him back at gunpoint and moved into the house.

I followed Kask as he stepped into a small living room with doors leading to other parts of the house. The room was dark and smelled like the smoke of the burning van—rubber and bitter upholstery.

A mother in purple robes huddled on mats in the back corner of the room. I could see by her eyes she was terrified, but she did her best to act calm for the sake of her child, a boy of four or five who was dressed in dusty pajamas. His hair was dark and his face was smooth. His arms and legs were wrapped around his mother. He clawed against her. The pitch and tenor of his voice warbled into a panicked wail whenever a Marine walked by on his way to search one room or the next.

It would be easy to say I saw myself in the boy in that moment. It would also be a rotten lie. I can acknowledge only in retrospect that I was roughly the same age as the boy when I saw the Fighting Falcons lift from the flight line in Utah. But at no point can I claim anything in common with having armed men blasting the family van with high explosives and storming into my house. I had lived inside the apparatus of American security, and its ideas and the weapons that enforced them had always been pointed outward, toward some televised devil living in opposition to the shifty notions of the American Dream.

The man who had opened the door had been placed on his knees next to a younger man, away from the mother and the boy. They were both MAMs—military-aged males, men or boys who were old enough by coalition standards to load a rifle and kill Americans. The older man looked to be in his forties, paunchy and balding slightly, his large jaw covered by a short, thick beard flecked with gray. The younger man seemed like a late teenage son to the man beside him, or perhaps a younger brother. His hair was short and black. The hair on his face was thin and patchy and his mustache looked like the kind of mustache teenage boys grow to feel older. Both wore gray robes and sandals.

They stared straight ahead with a practiced passivity that was understandable in the face of all the guns they were surrounded by but also maddening. It was the kind of blankness, a seemingly cattle-like acceptance of fate, an indifference, that made us ask why we were doing any of this for a people who, to us, raised on bloated mythologies of self-determination, seemed unmoved to help themselves. It was a blankness designed as a survival mechanism.

The teenager's hands were on his head, but the older man had his hands buried in the pockets of his robe. As the little boy continued to sob behind us, my mind flashed on a blizzard of terrors: the bombs we couldn't see and the cell phones that detonated them, powered by someone with dreams of martyrdom. What if, at any moment, this MAM's cloaked hands pressed a few buttons and killed us all with shrapnel and fire? I was afraid of being blown to bits, of having my skin charred away. I was afraid, but because I was supposed to be strong and unafraid, and because I was frustrated by the crying boy, I became angry.

I lifted my rifle and aimed at the man's chest.

"Put your hands on your head," I said. I patted my head with a free hand.

The man blinked, but otherwise he did not move. His hands remained in his pockets. He did not exude defiance in any way; it may be that he simply did not understand my gesture. Perhaps he was mentally challenged or too scared to think. It was unreasonable to expect him to understand English. Why should he? I was in his country, in his home. But I was the American, the patriot, the Marine, one of the many, or perhaps just the few, who felt worthy enough, righteous enough, to travel thousands of miles to someone else's country with the presumptuousness of pressing our freedoms onto them all for the sake of maintaining our own precious security. Who was he compared to the gift America was trying to give him?

The fire in the van outside continued to crackle. The boy continued baying. My anger became rage, but both were grown from fear in absence of fact. Nevertheless, his life was not worth more than mine in that moment. I again ordered him to place his hands on his head, but still he did not move.

I clicked off the safety of my rifle.

The 5.56-millimeter bullet from the barrel of the average M-16A4 service rifle, the rifle I now aimed at the chest of the man on his knees, travels at about 3,110 feet per second. It is a speed that is conceivable only as a data point for ballistic experts and fodder for gun nuts. I wasn't thinking about the speed of the bullet and the snap it makes when it breaks the sound barrier as I looked over the sights and the round gunmetal barrel. I wasn't considering how the velocity of the bullet and the kinetic energy it would generate would penetrate the man's body and how the dissipation of that energy as it traveled through his body would shatter his bones and rupture his organs. Bodies do not fly about when struck by bullets. The average bullet does not have the mass to effect a change in velocity or direction.

The human body merely flumps to the ground at whatever grotesque angle its bones allow for or continues to travel in the direction it was moving until something in the body sends an error message to the affected appendage or organ or just goes dark entirely. This is what I learned in combat.

I wasn't thinking about how all that energy might end his life or, worse, leave him in the limbo between whole and destroyed, that place where he would have to rely on the charity of his family and friends, a burden, a shattered reminder of how impotent he was in the face of the warring factions that demanded his fealty. I did not think about the younger man at his side, the speed at which his resentment would grow once the bullet damaged or destroyed the life of the man next to him. Whether he would become another man dead in the street with a squad of Marines staring down at him was entirely irrelevant, too far removed from the fear and anger and frustration that clouded my vision past the barrel of my rifle, the two MAMs in front of me, and the wailing of the young boy in the corner. When I was ten, I sat in a living room and watched America bomb Iraq for the Stone Age stupidity of its dictator and army. Now I was twenty-five and I was standing in the child's house with a gun pointed at his family. The end of one war had only been the genesis of the next.

An Iraqi *jundi* stepped between us, dressed in his Gulf War–era camouflage, waving his hands in front of me. He must have sensed the ugly energy coming from my pores. My barrel was inches from his chest. I was incensed. I was scared and I wanted to kill the man.

"He okay, he okay," he said.

One of the fire team leaders walked by on the way to search another room. I stopped him.

"Put your barrel in the back of that man's head. Get his hands up," I said.

Without a word the lance corporal turned and placed his muzzle squarely on the crown of the man's head. The man immediately took his hands out of his pockets and interlaced his fingers on the top of his head. The lance corporal silently turned and moved on.

I stepped away from the *jundi* and immediately walked out of the house, past the burning van and into the courtyard. I felt foolish. I had managed the problem with the old man, if there even was one, but I felt little pride in it. I had wanted to kill him, and now I felt small.

I knew some Marines would undoubtedly call me a "pussy" or a "bitch" for feeling this way, but I did not care. They also might say, "Stop bitching. You signed up for this," and they would be right. I did. I volunteered for this, and because I volunteered, I had no right to shift blame or bemoan my station. I almost killed a man in his home for making me afraid, for making me frustrated over his practiced passivity and indifference. I wanted to be in this place. I was not drafted or conscripted, threatened with prison if I refused. The legacy of American war might have pointed me in this direction, but it was also my choice.

And yet even now, many years later, I know there is a part of me that would make the same choice. I could not alter my desire to go to war. There could be no other way. Such is the nature of war.

When I go back home, young men will sometimes ask me if I killed anyone in this war. They don't realize it, but this is a trick question. To say no implies I didn't do enough. To say yes makes me a monster. The best I can say is, "I don't know." But if I had killed the man on his knees, there is a better than fair chance I would have been pardoned for my crime, if I were charged at all, and likely politicized into a hero at the inevitable expense of my soul. That is the nature of American war too. I hope that man is still alive.

After a few more minutes, the squad left the house and we kept searching. After we cleared the bulk of the city, Rebel Six ordered me to the battalion headquarters to take photos of Iraqi detainees being released. I remember they came off the truck with haggard faces and their robes dusty from whatever holding cell they had been placed in. They had surely been questioned by military police or an intelligence team. Their faces did not have the same impassivity I had seen in the man I had wanted to kill, or in so many others. They did not make eye contact with us as they came off the truck. Instead, they found their families, if they were there to greet them at all, and just walked away. They were angry and scared—the chief emotional states of war. I wondered how long their anger would persist. Afterward, I drove around with Rebel Six and his immediate superior, a lanky Marine colonel, as they toured the old battlefields. At one point, we stopped and the various officers in the entourage gathered around a map laid out on the hood of a Humvee while they plotted their next moves. Someone handed Rebel Six a big chrome sword that was confiscated from somewhere in the city. I took photos while he used it to point to the map like a crusader. His eyes were sparked with ambition behind the orange tint of his sunglasses.

The operation wrapped up a few days later. I met up with Cory at a youth center that had been bombed and nailed with a tank shell a few days earlier. We smoked cigarettes outside just after sunset and talked about going home, the ceaseless pivot point of wartime conversation. We traded stories of our pieces of the fighting, the things we had seen and heard. I didn't tell him about the man in the house with the burning van and the crying boy.

Over the Humvee radios, an explosive ordnance disposal team announced its intentions to detonate a bomb that had failed to explode after it was dropped in the courtyard of some house buried in the city. A lieutenant burst out of the youth center.

"Hear about the controlled det, gents?" he asked. His broad face was flush with excitement, like a kid winded after a playground sprint. We said we had.

He pointed out and away from us. "Well, it's gonna be over there if anyone wants to get a picture. They're counting down now."

I could hear the countdown on the radio—"six, five, four, three . . ." The lieutenant turned on the small camera in his hands and aimed the little box. The bomb exploded in the usual way, with a big cloud of dust and smoke and detritus, the delayed boom. Cory and I sighed cigarette smoke. The lieutenant gawked before the blast, his big ham hands snapping the shutter of his little camera.

"That's motivating, gents," the lieutenant said. "*Ooo-friggin-rah!*"

JULIET

You fight the war with guns, you fight the peace with stories.

—Omar El Akkad, *American War*

Burger King messed up Michael's order. He had ordered a Double Whopper, but they gave him a regular. That's one patty instead of two. It was late in the evening, sometime near ten. "I gotta get them to unfuck this before they close," Michael said to me before he trotted across the gravel to the outdoor food court with his brown paper bag in his hand and his rifle across his back. Michael is one of Cory's friends.

I wait for both of them outside Green Beans, a coffee shop cut from the same basic cloth as the standard Starbucks. The coffee shop is closed, but the benches outside are nice. It's quiet.

We are going home soon. Just a matter of days. We left the Syrian border for the confines of this massive air base in the middle of the Iraqi desert. We've come here to decompress. That's what we've been told. The base has the coffee shop and a Subway, a Pizza Hut and a movie theater. There is a big PX here, too, and a recreation center where kids can play foosball and check their email. I'm told there is dancing on Wednesdays. Salsa Night. There's also the Burger King that will mess up an order. Just like home. It all feels like training.

The large recreation center is still open. Cory is inside, printing off his divorce papers. All he has to do is get them signed. Should be done within the week.

I received an email from Erin a few days earlier. She wants to get back together once I'm home. I got a great place out near the back gate of the base, she wrote. It's quiet. You can come stay. You know . . . if you want.

I just want to go home. Anything after that is extra.

The day after we arrived here, Rebel Six gathered the entire battalion in a dusty lot near the transient tents. A thousand Marines stood around him with their rifles across their bodies, their uniforms beaten and torn and faded by sweat and weather. Each man seemed fully alive in the eyes. We had stood tall, the toughest men on the planet. We believe that.

Rebel Six thanked us for being good Marines and good men. He was proud of us, prouder than anything. At one point his voice broke, but he held back. He is a professional. He told the battalion they would have a month off once home and Marines erupted in a mass of oorahs and growls of affection. Get your uniforms squared away, he said. Take the time to get acclimated, he said.

We are going back to the Real World now.

You know . . . if you want.

Erin's offer hangs in the sky above the benches outside the coffee shop. I'll probably take it. It's something to come back to and it beats moving into the barracks. She is beautiful and tall with long hair, and the promise of carnal things matter in this moment. She also understands the uniform. I'll take her offer. I just want someone to grab and hold on to me. For just a minute. If I deserve it.

I look out toward an army cantonment down the hill from the main base. The night is clear and black and marked with stars. Two points of light rise from the horizon past the perimeter. I see them, but I don't. Or at least I don't think I do. But they are there, truly, climbing into the sky.

The sound makes them real. When the stars reach their peak in the sky and turn toward the earth, the sound of their rockets makes my heart rate climb. My muscles vibrate with untapped energy. Light enters my eyes; sight crystallizes with intensity and clarity. My brain stem wants me to run for cover, but I don't. I remain still. There is no bravery in this. I am simply not the target and it is already over.

The insurgent rockets lance into the ground and erupt with dense arrays of sparks far and wide above the cluster of tents and prefab buildings where they've landed. Their sound comes a moment later, out of sync, a hearty phrumpphrump that signals itself unnecessarily, like fate stating the obvious.

The base turns into pandemonium. Soldiers and a few Marines sprint past with their faces drained of color. A few lonely sirens cry out in other parts of the base and crackle with warnings of incoming. Most of the grunts laugh.

Cory comes from the recreation center. He bums a smoke. "Dumb motherfuckers were in there diving under pool tables with their rifles ready to git some," he says. He doesn't say anything about the divorce papers.

Michael comes back from Burger King with his two patties, not one. We wait for the shuttle that will take us back to the transient tents. It's a little after ten now. In less than two hours, it will be my twenty-sixth birthday. Someone on the shuttle tells me a couple of soldiers were killed in the rocket attack, but he has no way of knowing for sure. I never find out one way or another.

XV

HOME! The end of dirt, the end of the color brown saturating our skin, stiffening our uniforms and body armor and helmets, coating our rifles and weathering the brown suede of our boots. We pined for home, hallucinated about it in the ghostly spaces between sleep and the endless rush of being awake in That Place, in those bunkers, those dugouts, the forward operating bases and combat outposts and battle positions, those Iraqi homes we'd commandeered, inside the chest-beating fear, inside the lonely ache of being trapped in war's parentheses, as the poet David Jones referred to it, while the rest of the world ticked forward unfazed. Home took on an eerie, almost ethereal, quality, talked about like some farther shore the way evangelicals talk about heaven.

Home was the settling of scores. Of righting wrongs. Of divorces and reconciliations and coups counted. It was about fast cars and motorcycles and vacation. Of drinking and sex. If home was the dream, then the dream, in part, was a quiet pornographic fantasy. But there were also wide-open roads that weren't mined and laced with roadside bombs, there were moms and dads and sisters and uncles. Home was cell phones and wireless internet and television. Home was instant access. Everything NOW and FAST! Home was lawn care and barbecues, Christmas and New Year's. Home was the soft lounge chair we pass out on after Thanksgiving dinner, our socked feet hanging off the footrest. Home was the final off button. Home was everything the war wasn't, the things we hoped would fill the cavity drilled out by war. Home was love.

As the days clicked by and we neared the date when our replacements—the follow-on battalion that would take over where we had left off in the cycle of deployments—were due to land, we peered out toward the long helicopter pad and *waited, waited, waited*, like waiting for rain, waiting like sailors on the prow of a ship looking for new land. Maybe tomorrow would be the day, maybe the day after, until finally—*BAM!*—the big gray helicopters landed on the pad in a roar of blinding dust and wind and disgorged troops in clean lines of fresh fatigues and black rifles, their faces untanned and unlined, eager and well slept save for the jet lag glazing their eyes. For a solid week, they clogged up our berthing space and the mess hall, and shadowed the veterans in the headquarters building, supply warehouse, and the battalion motor pool, until at last they were shuttled out to the battle positions across the entire valley in a Mean Marine Diaspora with magazine pouches full of ammunition and heads full of speeches about hearts and minds. We had done our work. The valley belonged to them now. For all it was worth.

The Chateau began to deconstruct. We trashed everything. I tossed old socks, leftover stripper clips for bullets, empty bandoliers I had saved for no reason. Pressure bandages still, thankfully, tucked in their unopened wrappers. MRE flotsam. Old government-issued reporters' notebooks filled with gibberish about troop movements and cheerleader Marine Corps quotes. I shoved books and uniforms and extra boots, all my maps and movies, an old alarm clock that played the Islamic call to prayer, into a dusty black footlocker, locked it, and mailed it home. Early in the tour, I had bought a guitar from an army sergeant from psychological operations. He sold it on the condition that I sell it to someone in the next rotation, the next generation. And so I sold it to a Marine from my DC days who appeared in the Chateau just days before I left, and I made sure to tell him to sell it to the man who came after. I found the old photo of the Iraqi with the AK-47, the anger on his face accusing me. I held it in my hand a long moment before balling it up and tossing it into the trash with everything else. I was sick of anger.

Coming home felt like a slow molting. What might come after was beyond comprehension. I had survived a war; I had survived the Marine Corps. I felt this overriding notion that I was nearing some new form. A veteran but also a regular person in the sea of American humanity complete with the house and family, college, the job with benefits, everything that's supposed to define the fantasy of the American Dream. I could feel it out there, almost *see* it through the haze, as I stuffed my field pack and seabags and lugged them to the waiting trucks that carted Cory and Kask and many others with the same vision to the airstrip. I knew as I felt my boot lift from the tarmac onto the steel deck of the cargo plane that I wanted to remember every breath, every single sigh and pleasant groan and laughter of release in each moment of this transition from war to home. I felt it again as I stepped onto the stairs of the airliner that removed me from the Middle East.

I wanted to feel the changing time zones—the hours slipping closer to the East Coast of America as we unraveled the war and pressed the play button on our lives, landing back into the slipstream of pedestrian American affairs. When Cory and I sat down at a table with two fellow sergeants at the air terminal near Frankfurt, our first stop on the leg home—*can this be real?*—I wanted to savor the first burning swallow of vodka we sipped straight from the duty-free bottle while we waited for the plane to refuel. I wanted to grab the sun and the sky in each place and examine all the ways it was different from the sun and the sky over Mesopotamia. I wanted to run my hand over the grass that bordered the airstrip and shove a patch of it, dirt and all, into my pocket and pull it out somewhere over the Atlantic and let it rest in my hand, still damp and lush, filled with moisture. We crossed Western Europe, where the Allied powers marched from the French beaches at Normandy to the final end of Nazi rule and the apex of the American war story. We passed through the final corridor, between the towering glows of Paris and London, green smears of the countryside between, and the blue-green slot of the English Channel.

The first fuel stop in the States was Bangor, Maine, just before sunset. We were ushered from the plane into the terminal. As we entered the wide hall leading into the spacious waiting area, men and women in USA T-shirts waving American flags on tiny plastic sticks barraged us with a litany of soft cheers and wheezy "atta-boys" and "welcome homes." Some handed out candy and prepaid calling cards. None of them appeared younger than sixty. A few sported ball caps with VIETNAM WAR VETERAN or KOREAN WAR VETERAN lettered in yellow. The caps had military ribbons stitched to the front and were dotted with pins representing unit patches and rank insignia. These vets were here to welcome us, perhaps in the way they hadn't been welcomed when their airliners deposited them in America decades ago.

I used the calling card handed to me by one of these patriots to call home. My mom answered and we spoke quickly. I explained I was home, or at least in America, and that I'd visit them soon. Maybe a few weeks, maybe a month. I wasn't sure.

"How was it?" she asked.

"I'm tired," I said.

The final flight was at night and the cabin took on an eerie, almost stony darkness as we cruised far above the urban web from New York to DC and beyond. Cory slept in the seat next to me, his stout frame and cherubic face tucked under a stiff airplane blanket. I watched the expanse of pinpoint light glitter by the airline window. It's not enough to travel at thirty thousand feet to understand how immense America really is. One has to leave it for a period of time longer than a honeymoon to recognize its true size, how indomitable its reach, and how much it can mean to see it like a dream come to life when one has been separated from it. But something about that separation felt terminal as I looked down on the highways and interstates that cut through the land like veins and arteries. I couldn't reason through it, at least not yet, but it was there, right under the skin, a sort of barrier permanently estranging me from ease of life for the basic American citizen. I had left the country for one of its wars, and because of that, there could be no true reunion regardless of the number of flag-waving octogenarians greeting me or SUPPORT THE TROOPS bumper stickers slapped on the back hatches of SUVs.

There is a lot of back-page talk in modern circles about the "civil-military divide," the growing separation between the military and its veterans, and the population it serves. This divide has grown from the elective experience of professional military service that has, by virtue of its volunteerism, created a class largely removed from the greater American culture, becoming a kingdom all its own. In a few months, I would step outside those castle walls into a world that would amplify that separation, and for a long time I would feel trapped between the kingdom I had left and the world I was attempting to be absorbed by, even desperately. But it was impossible. There are so few of us—about 7 percent of the population—and our stories so unusual compared to the relative safety of the American landscape that the terrors and virtues of military service will always set us apart. We become veterans: the avatars of patriotism, psychic wounds, presumptions of action-movie heroism, and sometimes even unspoken pity, all acknowledged with the guilty platitude "Thank you for your service."

But at this moment, as the plane landed and we boarded buses for Camp Lejeune, this divide was lost on me and it wouldn't surface for a good while. For now, I sat watching the black countryside slip by for an hour as we neared the Marine base. If I and the rest of my fellow Marines hadn't been knotted by fatigue and jet lag, we might have howled once the buses hissed to a stop outside the battalion armory where nearby our loved ones were waiting. We quickly unloaded and were ushered into lines leading to the custodial windows of the battalion armory. I pulled the black sling from my rifle and the tan magazine pouch I had Velcroed to the buttstock. When my turn came, I locked the bolt to the rear, took a quick look into the chamber, and without a word handed the rifle I had carried every day for seven months, that I had used to shoot at humans, into the waiting hands of the armory custodians and watched it disappear. When I turned and walked away, I felt exposed, as if a limb had been removed. I would never see the rifle again, until I began to see many like them everywhere, owned by Americans as over-the-counter totems of patriotism and dubious political vitriol.

A staff sergeant who had come home a few weeks earlier had managed to pry Cory's Chevy truck from his estranged wife; it waited for him once we had turned in our rifles and gathered our seabags and field packs. After some quick talk about taking it easy on the alcohol, which was taken as a line of fly-blown gibberish, the powers over us cut us loose for four days to spend with our families or just generally unplug from the daily military grind. I lugged my bags to the truck and waited as Cory fumbled with the keys. Inside the cabin was everything Cory had left at home before leaving for the war—uniforms and books, old clothes and award citations, family photos and movie DVDs. All his possessions had been gathered and tossed into the truck like the garbage remains of an estate sale. When he opened the door, the detritus fluttered to the pavement and he cursed savagely. For a brief moment, I thought he might drift into a fugue and disembowel some drifting lance corporal, or even me, for sport. Aside from his life's remnants that had been carelessly dumped into the back of his truck, the interior of the vehicle was a mess of stains and cigarette ash. Spilled cola had dried to a sticky patina in the bottom of his cup holders, and the crushed remains of fast-food containers and plastic energy drink bottles had been ground into the carpet.

His wife seemed to have treated his truck much like their marriage and now he was fuming in an eruption of estranged rage on his first night home as he struggled to clean it up.

We loaded our bags into the bed of the truck and sped off in a torrent of diesel fumes and tire smoke. Whatever fury had gripped him was now soothed by the power of the motor in his hands as they gripped the steering wheel. He would have to see his wife tomorrow for the final signatures on his divorce papers. But for right now, he was free and home. After we stopped at the Lejeune convenience store for cigarettes, cheap hot dogs, and a case of beer, we blasted hard and fast toward the main gate of the base. Somewhere on that dark, broad stretch of road, Cory suddenly burst forth with a jubilant howl, "Fuck, dude, we're *back*! We fucking made it, man!" I jutted a fist into the cool night air and rapped it against the top of the cab, bellowing into the ether, "*We're home, you motherfuckers!*"

"Hey!" Cory said, suddenly serious. "Stop beating on my truck."

"Sorry, dog."

We were home.

Erin was away at a military photography school in Maryland when I returned to Camp Lejeune. I agreed to her offer almost blindly after a pair of nights alone in a Jacksonville hotel. She had arranged to have keys given to me by a mutual friend. I lugged my gear with a cheap rental car to the small place she had found in a community east of the base. It was quiet and peaceful. I was happily alone the week between coming home and going on leave for a month. I'd spend a little time at the battalion headquarters but would then abscond back to her small house where I'd read for hours or just nap. Aside from some basic administrative need to show my face around the battalion for brief periods, the days were mine and I spent them tooling around, eating at restaurants, shopping for new clothes, and otherwise lounging in a state of safe disconnection.

There was just one unexpected problem: Erin's neighborhood was right by the shattered fields the artillery batteries pummeled on a regular basis. Like tank battles, artillery had become something of an anachronism in the block-by-block / war fighter–turned–policeman / hearts-and-minds counterinsurgency mode the Iraq War had settled into. But the gunners were out there nonetheless, always training for the Next Big War, snapping their lanyards and sending high-explosive shells arcing through the air with their fluttering warble before they crashed into the charred, beaten earth. Their rending concussions would zap me awake and send my pulse skyrocketing into an electrified arrhythmia and briefly tighten my muscles into tortured knots. My reaction was purely physiological. I just wanted a quiet space away from the chest beating and destruction that had dominated my past seven months—and it was quiet, until more artillery rounds jerked me awake, the jolts clawing up the ladder of my ribs. Sometimes it made me laugh. Sometimes it didn't.

When I look back at my Amazon purchase orders from March and April of that year, the Vietnam War leaps at me like a ghoul that won't let go. *Death Valley: The Summer Offensive, I Corps, 1969* by Keith William Nolan, *Red Thunder, Tropic Lightning: The World of a Combat Division in Vietnam* by Eric M. Bergerud, *A Patch of Ground: Khe Sanh Remembered* by Michael Archer, and *Valley of Decision: The Siege of Khe Sanh* by John Prados and Ray W. Stubbe were all piled in the mailbox along the road, as were documentaries like *In the Year of the Pig* and *Dear America: Letters Home from Vietnam*, the latter of which I'd watched incessantly in the dark living room of my dad's California duplex. It was as if I had come home from one war and immediately dove headlong into another. Perhaps it was a security blanket, a safe way to begin processing one war by filtering it through the lens of another.

I lugged all these with me across the country, to see my dad in Denver. I bought his Jeep, the same Jeep he had bought when I lived with him in California. We drove it together through New Mexico and on to the vast gaps of hollowed towns in the southern corner of Oklahoma, where my grandfather had left my dad and his brothers. From Oklahoma, I headed to Alabama and spent a week with Cory's family, a raucous, patriotic bunch—lots of barbecues, God bless the troops, yellow ribbons, and atta-boy glad-handing. We climbed into our Marine Dress Blues and took pictures with his nieces and nephews and his shuffling grandparents, then cadged free drinks in bars along Mobile Bay. I then drove east to Atlanta, where for an entire weekend my friends and I blasted ourselves stupid with a parade of shots and cheap beer in midtown clubs and patio bars. Then I cruised to see my mom and Alan.

On a Georgia spring night, cool with patchy clouds glowing with moonlight, Alan and I stood in the driveway with beers. He listened well as I plied him with my anecdotes and snippets: the Black Hawk helicopter that clattered dust all across the Chateau at night when it hauled away the wounded and the dead, the house we had bombed, the little snaps and whizzes of bullets, the desert and the dogs and the rage—all the scenes that I was attempting to parse and understand and untangle.

He told me a few stories from his own experiences in the Middle East—about the Fighting Falcons blasting to and from the airfield on their way to drop bombs, of working all night and sleeping during the day in sweltering tents under a baking sun, little details that I took in as his own unique experiences, worthy of being held up on their own merits and respected. We had never truly talked about his time overseas. Not for fear of tapping into trauma; rather, it had just seemed buried by his humility. He spoke about it gently, as if delicately pulling a silk cloth to reveal a gem he was reluctant to display.

I dropped a cigarette into an empty beer bottle at my feet. I was happy to talk to him like this: it felt as if we were on some equal footing, men of standing and worth. We had both been Over There. Combat is the least common denominator of military experience; our similarities existed in the experience of war in general terms—the loneliness and isolation, the feeling of being placed on pause in the larger trajectory of our lives while equally tethered to world events that have no substitute in the human experience. Finally, near the end of the conversation:

"In a weird way I guess you and I were in the same war," I said.

He squinted. "What do you mean?"

"If your war doesn't happen, neither does mine."

Alan considered the idea for a moment, then nodded and said, "Yeah, I guess so."

There was a strange sadness in that. We seek to end wars for our children, not provide the instruments of their succession. That is the story we tell ourselves, but in that moment under the stars, that story showed itself as a lie. Maybe it always had been. I finished my beer and picked up the scattered bottles at my feet and dumped the dead soldiers in the trash.

I packed up the Jeep and sped north, back to the house in North Carolina for a reunion with Erin. We spent the weekend between the bedroom and kitchen. Our time was sweet to the point of pain and yet traced by a hollowness in a weekend that moved too fast to define. Once Erin went back to school, I decided to spend the final few days of leave with Ken. We sat in a dark Annapolis bar trading war stories in muted tones while a pair of arrogant naval midshipmen in their dark dress uniforms, like background actors from some remake of *An Officer and a Gentleman*, chatted up polished debutantes. But that wasn't for us anymore. We were on the Other Side. We briefly talked to one of the midshipmen at the bar, but we didn't share a language. He was cocky and his ego was filled with flags and the religious graft of battles. He was looking forward to the future, with all its mythical fantasies of being a man in an American war. Ken and I were looking at the war from the other end, through the sensory realities of death on an Iraqi street. The war was the haze between us, and through it we saw the twinkling frenetic energies of who we were. I had no faith the midshipman could see through it and recognize us—the fatigue, the shiftiness, the bewilderment over what we were now and what it would mean for our own futures. I'm not sure he would have acknowledged it if he had.

I returned to Erin's house in North Carolina once the weekend was over. I worked on my Jeep. I read more about Vietnam. I let the artillery tighten my muscles and play with my heart rate as I smoked on the front steps and watched squirrels flit around the trees. It was May. I had two months left on my enlistment. Ken offered me the spare bedroom in the condo he shared with his girlfriend once I was free from the service, but my future felt hidden behind a fog I was struggling to see through. The military had been in my life since birth and I was leaving it, stumbling from it almost blindly. Everything beyond was a fantasy to me—college applications and class schedules and tuition, bland office jobs and health plans—ideas I was happy to embrace but that still felt remarkably foreign to me. I didn't even know what questions to ask. I read a book on résumés and attended the perfunctory military transition classes on job interviews and VA claims, but it was as if they were talking about some mirage divorced from anything I had ever known.

It was simply too hard to see past the moment. A week past the day I would leave the Marines felt like light-years. A month was inconceivable. The military had been a psychic safety net. The net was beginning to unravel, but I did not mind. Such was the state of my disconnection that I didn't even consider its impact on my relationship with Erin. I could remain in Jacksonville, drifting around the edges of the military like some kind of camp follower, but it was such a middling idea—one foot in the military, one foot out, and never sure where I would land as a person. My identity would be torn between progressing into some new life and locked by the ankle into the old one, and on terms not my own. I knew that when I left, I would have to leave all the way. But where did that leave Erin?

In the end, it didn't matter. She came home in late May and by the end of June we were through. I wasn't able to muster the requirements of a partner. I was an emotional cripple, drained, unable to churn the energy to be present. I had buried my head in books and in my computer, clacking away at the keyboard, ignoring all the signs and symptoms of a mired relationship. We went to the beach, but I refused to see the sun. We watched comedies, but I laughed little. We listened to music, but I remained unmoved. She tried to fight with me, almost as a prod to make me acknowledge where we were, but I refused to engage. Finally, after a night of drinking with Cory, I returned home to a note demanding that I leave. She was in bed, but I woke her up and finally we had the fight she had been seeking, and it was terminal. By the early morning, my life was packed into my Jeep, much like Cory's had been stuffed into his truck when we first returned home. I took refuge in the same Jacksonville hotel I had crashed in my first nights home. I climbed into the stiff, vaguely familiar bed and watched television, rebooting and nursing my wounds.

What was all this for? Where do I go from here? I enlisted in the US military, fought in one of its wars. And for what? Lying on a Days Inn bed, just weeks away from leaving all the uniforms behind, these questions seemed largely unanswerable. I could have said Country, or maybe Patriotism, Liberty, Freedom, and all the rest, but I knew that was trite and absurd. Short of just propping up their symbolism in American culture, I was not convinced my service in Iraq truly defended those ideas or that they had ever been threatened, for that matter, in ways I could hope to prevent with a rifle. Our guns, much like our bombs, had caused as many problems as they solved. I had to admit, even if it pained me, that the efforts of American soldiers had been largely spent on an aimless and arguably self-serving foreign policy, despite the dubious American vocabulary used to justify them. I knew that much then and still believe so now.

But I believe that war is also an inherent article of violence hard coded into our DNA. Author and Vietnam veteran Karl Marlantes explains, "We're not the top species on the planet because we're nice. We're a very aggressive species. It is in us. People talk a lot about how well the military turns kids into killing machines. I always argue that it's just finishing school." It is important to understand this, to analyze and dissect it, to look at its face and recognize that all war is truly us. For every kid sitting in his bedroom pining for some kind of punk-rock fantasy or the flash of *The Rap Game*, there are teenagers no different than I was, who lie in their rooms at night and play video games and read books and imagine they are in an American foxhole with a rifle and a helmet, their dreams suspended on the weight of American history, if not the history of humanity. It is an unavoidable dream for them just as it was for me. No amount of eviscerating human destruction represented in the arts and in history can steer some young men and women away from the strange atavism of war. A warped love of country, a simple desire to serve, a fear of missing out on some piece of world history, or the support of some subjectively righteous cause are all certainly motivators. But not once in the history of the world has a statesman, ruler, or despot thrown a war where no one willingly showed up to fight in it. The military understands this, knows it lives inside of us, even if subconsciously, and while there are those in America who might call it brainwashing, rest fully assured that it is not. I wanted to experience this, directly or indirectly, and because of this, I will always be somewhat embarrassed by any genuine gratitude from well-wishing Americans. Not just out of humility but because of an underlying question I'm not sure I can fully answer: Did I enlist to serve America, or did I enlist to serve the military and myself? I knew I was going to enlist the moment I saw fighter jets roar through the cool Utah air and watched their munitions fall on television, and certainly when I stood in the Humvee turret at twelve years old and fired machine-gun blanks into the air. It was up to the world and the hubris of old men to provide the war. They do not fail. As Brecht said about love, war finds a way.

War has entrenched itself into the larger American landscape, something I have come to see in the decades after 9/11 as a default position, an assumed state entirely normalized in the American narrative, its components distilled into the culture as a fashion trend, both literally and figuratively. Politicians use the service of its volunteers as props. Dewy-eyed stanchions in uniforms sell auto insurance on television. Tactical backpacks are used as book bags by schoolchildren. Retired US Navy SEALs are hired as motivational speakers to deliver pick-me-up speeches to sales teams; they're placed arm in arm with celebrities and in some cases are championed like sports heroes for their body counts. War criminals have become politicians and consultants for cable news. Armored vehicles built for mechanized warfare roll through American streets, helmed by police who have come to equate their roles with those of soldiers fighting in Kabul. Hard-right paramilitaries and armchair patriots have adopted the cheap poster image of the soldier as a vehicle to intimidate or express superiority over those exercising their freedom of speech through protest, and worse, they've used dubious nativism against those America should help. The war is everywhere.

Over the years ahead, I would watch the conflict continue to kill military men and women in a trickle largely imperceptible to most civilian Americans. Sometimes we die on the battlefield; more often, we die years after those battles, by suicide or some other collapse of our wounds. These casualties are hidden enough to allow most people to ignore the basic fact that if we truly "support the troops," we would avoid wars, not blind ourselves to our failures to end them. I must confess there are times when I am filled with rage over the hypocrisy and stone moral cowardice of it: How can America continue to kill us? How can we continue to kill? Children are now fighting the wars of their parents. If the point of going to war is to prevent it for future generations, we have failed.

But because there are always volunteers, other Americans do not have to take responsibility, much less make sacrifices. Since the end of the draft in 1973, our national leaders have made little demand of the populace for the wars our soldiers have been systemically committed to, aside from tax dollars and shallow cultural gratitude. Most politics is local; as long as the human cost of American wars remains hidden in the folds of its daily domestic grievances, the national will for unending low-intensity conflicts in the Middle East, or perhaps anywhere, can largely be sustained through ignorance. And for that, we are still killing people in the desert, fighting enemies we've partially created with hubris and crumbling imperial filigree. For all it's worth, we are killing them for you.

But I was done.

I packed my things into the U-Haul and on a hot July Wednesday I put on my uniform for the last time. I dressed slowly that morning, checking off the steps, conscious of the efforts I had so often made blindly—sliding into the camouflage trousers with my name stitched onto a fabric strip sewn above the pocket and pulling on the big tan boots with my dog tag suspended in the laces, tucked there for sake of legacy and in case my upper body was destroyed beyond recognition. I felt the canvas tighten when I jerked the laces and wrapped my ankles with elastic bands just as my dad, mom, and stepdad had done, blousing my trouser legs around them so that when I stood the trousers pulled tight. I picked up my camouflage blouse from the bed and slid my arms into the sleeves, rolled just tightly enough to grab my biceps. I buttoned it and pulled it down against me by the bottom, the pockets straightening, the US MARINES and ALEXANDER name tapes bringing the final notes of this identity into stereo.

I went through the final motions that last afternoon: auditing my service record, signing my discharge papers, performing the final handshakes and see yas. I had already partied the previous weekend, drinking myself dull with Cory and a few others. When it was all over, my papers signed, I returned to the barracks and undressed with the same deliberate intent, folding each article, feeling the fabric and the stiff canvas, the final iterations of the American generations. I knew that I loved it in the way that I had as a kid playing war in the woods. It was deep, but I would no longer be guided by it. In the years ahead, I would sometimes wrap my wartime experiences in nostalgia, a warm rosy light of seductive righteousness and pride and brotherhood. This is part of being a veteran: the pride of service, of being a part of a cause, flawed or otherwise. Other times, I would look back and not recognize myself in my own story, instead seeing something angry and ugly. There are times when I wish I had been more patient, more thoughtful. Certainly there were times when I could have been a better Marine. But my feelings will always be split. In my memories, sometimes I hate the Marine Corps, sometimes I love it. Sometimes it feels like looking back at something old and tired, a love clinging to a memory. I have put the uniforms away. They are no longer my life.

I remember I climbed into my Jeep and cruised down along the river, one eye out for cops. I stopped near the Sixth Marines' barracks and climbed out with an extra pair of boots tied together by the laces. I walked to a set of power lines near the river and tossed the boots high so they dangled from the black cable—another barracks-room tradition, some final rite of passage, apropos of nothing.

The Jeep drove easily along the broad main boulevard toward the front gate. The afternoon rush hadn't begun yet; the roads were clear. I could see the gate ahead, bright in the heat haze. Military police waved through cars in the opposite lanes. I rolled down the window. Marine helicopters clattered in the air. I could not see them, but I could hear them, a clarion call I would recognize forever. The sound crawled up my spine like the rocky promises of Calypso.

But no, enough. I'm done with all that. The light before the gate was green. I toed the accelerator. Energy built its own momentum.

The Jeep flashed past the gatehouse and suddenly I was outside the castle walls for the final time, in the Real World, another hope in the desperate census of the American Dream. I looked into the rearview mirror and shot a pair of fingers into the sky—a V for Victory, a peace sign. I'm still not sure which.

Maybe both.

ACKNOWLEDGMENTS

It would an understatement of immeasurable proportions to suggest this book took a long time to write. While I began the first major iterations of this work in late summer of 2015, bits and pieces of prose and ideas lingered from old manuscripts going as far back as 2007, a year after I left the US Marines. It took me eight years of effort, more unconscious than conscious, to unravel the experience, then another six to dial the words into something meaningful. To this day, I'm not certain if that was due to the peculiar demands of memory and war, the need for emotional distance, or just figuring out how to get out of my own way. Probably a mixture of all three.

Whatever the requirements, I have been blessed to have people in my life over these past years who have been key, even necessary, to helping me along, whether it was with a good drink, a well-timed ear, or just a kick where it counted. In many ways both large and small, these incredible folks deserve my thanks: Scott and Naomi Eaton, Ryan Freeze, David Z. Sharpe, Nicholas and Amy Tecosky, Parker Davidson and Gina Richiche, Stephanie Farley, Lauren Vogelbaum, Jed Drummond, Rob Mosca, Katie O'Neill, David Bruckner, Adam Lowe and Ellaree Yeagley, Kelley Brooke McLaughlin, Zoë Simone De Fino, Dana Haugaard, Meredith Blankinship and Jordan Samet, David Pierce Ervin, Seth Lombardy, Charlie Kondor, Derek Schujahn, Elizabeth Cantrell, Denise Rosenhaft, and my brother, Kenny Young.

I also owe an endless debt of gratitude to Robert S. Boynton and his team at the literary reportage graduate program of New York University's Arthur L. Carter Journalism Institute; equally so for the craft and editorial acumen of Daniel Buckman, Brian Mockenhaupt, Amira Pierce, Terry McDonell, and David Grann; and for the NYU Veteran's Writing Workshop at the Lillian Vernon Creative Writer's House, specifically Dan Murphy, Drew Pham, Ryan J. Ouimet, Leigh Sugar, Leo Farley, and many others I met in that extraordinary program.

Lastly, I need to give significant thanks to two individuals, and their respective teams, who I have been absolutely honored to know. First, my agent, Elias Altman of Massie & McQuilkin, who has been a steady hand in guiding me through the arduous process of publication. Elias, I owe you immeasurable thanks. Next, to my editor at Algonquin Books, Betsy Gleick, who throughout this process has offered experience, patience, and goodwill. Betsy, you have been an absolute dream, a tough-minded but open soul who pushed me to places in my work I would have otherwise considered unreachable. I cannot thank both of you enough, though I will certainly try.

Finally, I'd like to list a few works that were inspirational in the development of this one, for a litany of reasons:

A Rumor of War by Philip Caputo
The Last True Story I'll Ever Tell: An Accidental Soldier's Account of the War in Iraq by John Crawford
The Short-Timers by Gustav Hasford
War Is a Force That Gives Us Meaning by Chris Hedges
Dispatches by Michael Herr
Goodbye, Darkness: A Memoir of the Pacific War by William Manchester
The Return: Fathers, Sons and the Land in Between by Hisham Matar
The Color of Water: A Black Man's Tribute to His White Mother by James McBride

ACKNOWLEDGMENTS

If I Die in a Combat Zone, Box Me Up and Ship Me Home by Tim O'Brien

M by John Sack

Jarhead: A Marine's Chronicle of the Gulf War and Other Battles by
     Anthony Swofford

Hell's Angels: A Strange and Terrible Saga by Hunter S. Thompson

This Boy's Life and *In Pharaoh's Army* by Tobias Wolff

Questions for Discussion

1. Much of this book describes the author's experiences as a child growing up on military bases. What are some of the things that he loved about this experience? Do you think his depictions are accurate? Surprising?

2. How was Jerad Alexander's desire to join the military influenced by representations of war in American culture? At any point in your life, did you consider joining the military? If so, what motivated you to do so? If not, what factors pushed you in other directions?

3. When you think of the word *patriotism*, what is the first image that comes to mind?

4. Do you believe patriotism is a required trait for a person to serve in the military? Discuss ways a person could demonstrate patriotism without serving in the armed forces.

5. When the author's stepdad leaves the base to serve in the Persian Gulf War, young Jerad recounts watching the war unfold on television. Reflect on his observations and reenactments of these images. What effect do you think televised representation of war has on children? Do you believe children should be taught lessons about war? If so, what do you think they should be taught?

6. Do you believe war is ever necessary? If so, when is it necessary? When is it not?

7. How has the military been commodified in American culture?

8. The author includes many descriptions of guns and other weaponry, both toys and real weapons, from his childhood. Discuss the ways firearms are used as representations of manhood. Do you

believe Americans think gun ownership or simply the use of guns represents the ideal image of a man in American culture?

9. Did you support (or refuse to support) the decision to enter the Iraq War? How much of that decision was based on your emotions or political beliefs, and how much was based on the information you ingested?

10. Do you believe the population of a country should be required to make sacrifices for the wars its country fights? How much sacrifice is enough, and how much is too much?

11. How does the United States demonstrate how much it values the efforts of the members currently serving in the armed forces?

12. Why do you think this book is called *Volunteers*? What is the author trying to say about the experience of those who choose to enlist in the U.S. military?

13. Did any member of your family serve in the armed forces? If so, talk about what they did and what you remember of that experience. How is their experience different from the experience of the author's family?

14. What other books or films about military service and war would you recommend, and what did you find most compelling about these works?

Jerad W. Alexander holds an MFA from New York University, and his writing has appeared in *Esquire*, *Rolling Stone*, the *Nation*, *Narratively*, and other publications. From 1998 to 2006, he served as a U.S. Marine infantryman and combat correspondent with deployments to the Mediterranean, East Africa, and Iraq. He currently lives in New York City. His website is www.jeradalexander.com.